THE FINAL VOW

This was his last chance to get rid of his assault on her. That evidence was his wife of ten-plus years, Tara.

Steve squeezed and squeezed, four minutes, according to a later medical estimate, the time it takes to choke the life out of someone.

"I think, at one point, she realized I wasn't stopping," Steve said. "But it was too late. She finally grabbed my hand, but then it was too late and I couldn't stop then. I knew I was going to prison. I panicked."

At one point, not too far into the process, after she had vainly clawed at his hand, she looked at him.

"I covered her face up . . . with a pair—with gray underwear or a gray T-shirt," he said.

"And that was it, she stopped moving."

A SLAYING IN THE SUBURBS

THE TARA GRANT MURDER

STEVE MILLER AND ANDREA BILLUPS

BERKLEY BOOKS, NEW YORK

THE BERKLEY PUBLISHING GROUP
Published by the Penguin Group
Penguin Group (USA) Inc.
375 Hudson Street, New York, New York 10014, USA
Penguin Group (Canada), 90 Eglinton Avenue East, Suite 700, Toronto, Ontario M4P 2Y3, Canada
(a division of Pearson Penguin Canada Inc.)
Penguin Books Ltd., 80 Strand, London WC2R 0RL, England
Penguin Group Ireland, 25 St. Stephen's Green, Dublin 2, Ireland (a division of Penguin Books
Ltd.)
Penguin Group (Australia), 250 Camberwell Road, Camberwell, Victoria 3124, Australia
(a division of Pearson Australia Group Pty. Ltd.)
Penguin Books India Pvt. Ltd., 11 Community Centre, Panchsheel Park, New Delhi—110 017,
India
Penguin Group (NZ), 67 Apollo Drive, Rosedale, North Shore 0632, New Zealand
(a division of Pearson New Zealand Ltd.)
Penguin Books (South Africa) (Pty.) Ltd., 24 Sturdee Avenue, Rosebank, Johannesburg 2196,
South Africa

Penguin Books Ltd., Registered Offices: 80 Strand, London WC2R 0RL, England

The publisher does not have any control over and does not assume any responsibility for author or
third-party websites or their content.

A SLAYING IN THE SUBURBS

A Berkley Book / published by arrangement with the authors

PRINTING HISTORY
Berkley mass-market edition / January 2009

Copyright © 2009 by Andrea Billups and Steve Miller
Cover design by MN Studios
Cover photo by Veer
Book design by Laura K. Corless

ISBN: 978-0-425-22548-6

BERKLEY®
Berkley Books are published by The Berkley Publishing Group,
a division of Penguin Group (USA) Inc.,
375 Hudson Street, New York, New York 10014.
BERKLEY is a registered trademark of Penguin Group (USA) Inc.
The "B" design is a trademark belonging to Penguin Group (USA) Inc.

PRINTED IN THE UNITED STATES OF AMERICA

10 9 8 7 6 5 4 3 2 1

FOREWORD

The taking of a life prematurely is a painful and final gesture with widespread effects.

And yet people continue to commit murders, including the case of a suburban husband with no criminal history who, one cold winter night, strangled his attractive wife, chopping her body into fourteen pieces and burying it haphazardly in a snowy forest in a macabre act of deception.

The murder of Tara Grant drew some of the most intense public interest in Michigan history, and the case will not soon be forgotten. Having reported on it initially for *People* magazine, we were instantly drawn into this dark tale and its painful legacy. In this book, we dig deeper, beyond the intense news coverage, into the lives of Tara and Steve Grant and set these against what led up to that fateful night, when their family was destroyed forever.

The Grant story is a gripping tale of loss and one in which there are no winners. That it occurred in an upscale town, in a nice home, in a seemingly loving family—the truth of what went on behind closed doors we will never know—shakes observers to the core. The Grants were an attractive, upwardly mobile couple, and to outsiders, at least, positively normal. And that changed in an instant of horror and an act of rage that defies logic.

And the victims continue to accumulate: Tara's family and friends, who lost her love, support, and companionship; Steve's relatives, who must bear the shame of a son and brother who will forever be known as one of the state's most brutal killers. His father, Al Grant, committed suicide less than six months after his son's conviction. Steve's friends, shocked that their pal could suffer such a bizarre break from reality, were affected as well. Most heartbreaking, two children have lost both parents, one to murder and one to prison, and must grow up with the knowledge that their father killed their mother, an act that will be difficult for family to explain and for them to ever understand.

In researching the book, we reached out to as many sources as possible—those who knew the victim as well as the killer throughout their lives. No one is born either all good or all bad, and our aim has been to uncover the story of what happened between Tara and Stephen Grant in as thorough a manner as possible. To that end, we conducted dozens of interviews,* including with the incarcerated Grant, as well as compiling information from court documents, police reports, newspaper accounts, and other sources.

We were aware that anything Steve Grant told us

---

*All present-tense quotes come from interviews we personally conducted; past-tense quotes are from secondary sources.

would be suspect. This is, after all, a man who managed to lie his way to freedom for three weeks and engage in an act of deceit so thorough that even his mother, sister, and paramour believed his twisted tale. His fabricated tears, his bizarre willingness to help comb the site where he had disposed of the body, and the fibs he told to the world were pathetic.

Still, to fully understand this sad story was to sit with him and allow him to have his say. We all have the right to tell our own story, and those who listen have the right to believe or disbelieve what they hear.

Much effort was made to encourage the family of Tara Grant to respond for this book, opening the door for their reflections on their beloved relative whose horrific death thrust them into the national spotlight. They declined to participate, however, and we respect their choice.

What follows is a frank and heartbreaking portrayal of murder in the suburbs.

CHAPTER 1

Stephen Grant was trapped. Near the corner of 28 Mile Road and Van Dyke Avenue, a little over a mile from his suburban Detroit home, three Macomb County Sheriff's vehicles blocked his Jeep Commander. He was ordered out of the truck by Deputy Tony Szalkowski, patted down, and instructed to have a seat in the back of one of the squad cars.

It was shortly after 4 P.M., with snow falling steadily from the darkening Michigan sky. Sheriff's cars blocked access points to the Carriage Hills subdivision, where Steve and his family—his wife, Tara, their two kids, an au pair, and a dog—lived. A news helicopter chattered incessantly overhead, and a news camera poked its light into the back of the squad car where Grant sat, adding more drama to the winter Friday afternoon.

It was like an episode of the TV show *Cops*; although no one had put handcuffs on Steve, he was nonetheless a captive, breathlessly struggling to maintain his composure as the officer matter-of-factly explained what was going on. A local judge had signed a search warrant for Grant's home, and police were about to execute it. Steve was not sure how the warrant had been obtained. But there it was. His wife had been missing for three weeks now, since February 9, 2007.

"What we want from you, Steve, is for you to let us in the door," the deputy told Grant, who was having trouble focusing. His cheeks were flushed. "We're going to let you do that, to drive yourself over there. You aren't under arrest, but you do need to comply," Szalkowski told him coldly. "Where are the kids? They don't need to be there for this."

"They're still at Kelly's, it's no problem," Steve said, referring to his sister, Kelly Utykanski. Verena Dierkes, the au pair, had recently returned to Germany, and the Grant children, Lindsey, six, and Ian, four, had been staying at his sister's since the night before, when the power at the Grant home had gone out during a winter storm.

Steve got out of the squad car and hopped back into his Jeep. He wheeled onto Westridge with a squad car trailing him and parked in front of his house, which was already being prepared for the search, officers draping the perimeter with yellow crime-scene tape.

There was a law enforcement party in his front yard. Cruisers and an unmarked car surrounded the two-story brown brick ranch home, which still had two green Christmas wreaths up on each side of the front door. Media satellite trucks perched on the lip of his front yard, jousting with the cops for position.

Grant walked up to the service door next to the garage and turned to Captain Tony Wickersham, who was following him.

Steve looked at the deputies, their breath streaming in

wintry clouds outside the garage, as he slipped the chrome key into the lock and turned.

"Before I do anything, I need to call my lawyer," he stated.

Wickersham obliged. Grant was not under arrest, just detained. The captain followed Grant inside, and the two walked into the kitchen. Stephen's fingers jittered as he punched in the familiar number for David Griem, a slight, bespectacled defense lawyer who worked at a top Detroit firm and was well liked in the Michigan legal community. Known for practicality rather than courtroom bombast, Griem's benign appearance, with his mane of wild white-and-gray hair, veiled a tough guy, a man who defended accused terrorists, murderers, and rogue cops. His interactions with the Macomb Sheriff's Department had so far been testy.

"Neanderthals" is how Griem described the lead investigators, Detective Sergeant Brian Kozlowski, and his superior, Detective Sergeant Pam McLean. Both had dogged Stephen Grant almost from the beginning, convinced he was somehow connected to his wife's disappearance. It wasn't so much this assumption that irked Griem, it was the arrogant, harassing swagger he felt the detectives affected.

"I liked Wickersham a lot and was glad to speak with him," Griem recalls. "Stephen told me that he was under arrest and that they were going to search his house. I had him hand the phone to Wickersham."

"Is Stephen Grant under arrest?" Griem asked the officer.

"No, not at all. We are executing a warrant on his house, though," Wickersham said, leaning against the kitchen counter. The officers still waited outside.

"Well, make sure you lock it up when you finish," Griem said. He paused. "Is Stephen free to leave?"

Wickersham eyed Grant, who was watching him intently.

"Yes. Yes, he is free to leave."

Wickersham would later say that Grant was "very calm" as the search started. "There was nothing unusual about his demeanor. Our conversation was civil. Very normal, very calm . . . [I] didn't notice anything unusual about him. I explained that he could leave and he asked if we were going to tear his house apart searching for evidence. He was concerned that we were going to rip out the ceiling tiles.

"I offered him a ride, but he was making arrangements to meet up with his sister. He declined and said he had his own transportation. He took the dog and walked out the garage door and down the drive."

Along the street, neighbors peered through shrouded living-room windows. They were mostly irritated by the media blitz that had struck their residential enclave, and some had posted handmade signs on their doors, letting nosy reporters know that they were not interested in participating in the feeding frenzy. The action around the Grant home had been keeping the whole neighborhood abuzz for weeks. A little over two weeks before, on February 14, Stephen Grant had walked into the sheriff's office and reported his wife, Tara, missing. Within days, notice of her disappearance was appearing in crawls at the bottom of televisions screens around the United States, with many recalling the fates of Laci Peterson and Natalee Holloway, both, like Tara, youthful and attractive.

Neighbors knew that Tara Grant was an international business executive for Washington Group International, an Idaho-based engineering firm. Stephen, with the help of the au pair, acted as full-time parent while his busy wife was away on frequent business trips. Neighborhood moms often saw him at the local Meijer, a Midwest-based supermart chain that outperforms Wal-Mart in the region.

They watched him play with his kids, ferrying them about during the week and sometimes waiting in the morning for the school bus with the other moms. He was pleasant enough, if a bit nervous and high-strung, some said. Yes, he was a live wire, always seeming to know something about everything.

Still, the Grants appeared to be a normal suburban family, and a happy one at that. The family went on vacations, including an annual trek to remote parts of northern Michigan. They took the kids to the local Chuck E. Cheese for birthdays, and in the summers grilled out on their small deck. Steve was six two, 190 pounds, and had a runner's lean body. His chestnut hair, worn close-cropped, was naturally curly. Tara, at five six and 120 pounds, was blessed with natural beauty, and had a cascade of brown curls framing her delicately featured face. It was, on the surface, a blandly pleasant life they were living, and neighbors admired their relationship.

Until this turn of events.

———

Grant's account of Tara's departure went something like this: On Friday, February 9, Tara Grant took an evening flight home for the weekend from the office she managed in San Juan, Puerto Rico, during the week. Her flight stopped in Newark for a plane change, and she arrived at Detroit Metro Airport a little after 9 P.M., collected her bags, and hopped into her white 2002 Isuzu Trooper for the hour-long journey to her home, about thirty miles northeast of the city. Records would later show that she placed a minute-long call after landing at 9:10 P.M. to Steve. A 9:44 call from Steve to Tara lasted one minute. A call from Steve's cell phone to Tara's at 9:47 lasted eighteen minutes, almost until she reached their home. It was the last activity recorded by Tara on her company-issued cell phone.

Her return home for the weekend got off to an emotional start, Grant told police. The couple argued. After initially agreeing to try to reduce her travel schedule, Steve said, Tara told her husband that she would have to return to Puerto Rico on Sunday, rather than the usual Monday. He was not happy to hear that she was leaving so soon, and he told her that her career was interfering with their family life. After angry words were exchanged, Steve told police he heard Tara speak to someone, presumably on her cell phone. Then she walked out with her luggage to a black car-service sedan and did not return. The entire exchange, Grant said, lasted twenty minutes from the time she arrived home to the time she left again.

For five days, Steve said, Tara did not call to check on him or their children. Worried, Steve called his mother-in-law, his sister-in-law, and even Tara's coworkers to ask whether they had heard from her. He confessed to their fight, of course. And they told him she was probably cooling off. But as the days wore on, Grant grew increasingly disturbed.

He left messages on her cell phone on February tenth and eleventh, some frantic, some angry.

Typical of these messages was a brief afternoon call, twenty-five seconds in duration, in which Grant threatened, "Tara, next time I call you, you better pick up your phone. Do not hit ignore. It is absolute bullshit you don't call me or the kids. It's bullshit. Call me or the kids. I know you're mad. I'm mad. You travel too much. It's not right. Just call me."

On February 12, Steve called his wife's supervisor, Lou Troendle, a fatherly gentleman who had mentored Tara in her rise through the ranks at Washington Group.

Troendle was nervous about Tara's absence, and he told Grant it was time to go to the police.

"Do you want me to come up and do this with you?" Troendle asked.

"No," Steve said. "I know it's something I have to do."

So on February 14, he walked into the sheriff's office to file a missing-persons report. It was Valentine's Day, and while most married couples were celebrating their love, Stephen was calling in the cops to find his missing wife. If he was aware of the irony, he did not note it in his conversation with the officers.

The department initially treated the matter as a normal missing-persons case. But as the investigation broadened and records were checked and alibis verified, foul play rose to the top of the list of possibilities. There was no activity on Tara's cell phone for the past five days, and the last transaction on her American Express card had been payment for airport parking at 9:32 P.M. on February 9. The couple's joint credit card with Chase Bank showed no changes since February 8, and their joint accounts at LaSalle Bank also showed no unusual recent activity.

Tara was considered an endangered missing person because she had been gone for five days, there had been no family contact, and her accounts were unused. Twelve detectives were assigned to the case, and many other officers found themselves on nothing but "Tara duty" for days at a time.

Fearing that authorities considered him a suspect in his wife's disappearance, the day after he reported Tara missing, Steve wrote a check for $10,000 to retain David Griem as his attorney. He had been moved to hire counsel after being stopped by police earlier that day, and taken into the station for failure to pay outstanding traffic tickets. He'd been held for several hours. Griem called it a "pretext arrest."

"My client has been very cooperative and helpful with police," Griem said to a reporter. "But sometimes an investigation is done by gathering all the available facts and then seeing if a theory of the crime fits all the evidence. And sometimes, certain investigators will have a theory first and try to find some evidence to fit it."

"We are not calling him a suspect," Wickersham told reporters at one point. But, he added, "At this point, there's no one cooperating with us."

Indeed, Grant was not talking to the police. His family, including his sister and parents, had also clammed up. But he had plenty to say to the media, which had begun to stake him out.

At still another time, Macomb County sheriff Mark Hackel told reporters that "we would think if this is a person who is intent upon finding his wife, which is what we want to do, then he would be by our side talking to investigators, knocking down our door and hounding us, just to see if we're doing enough."

Very quickly, word spread in the neighborhood that Tara Grant was gone. Neighbors, many curious and most sympathetic, came by to offer their support. Some felt sorry for Steve, who carried on as a single parent. The German au pair's agency had sent her home. As the days passed, Grant continued his role of primary caretaker, taking his kids to medical appointments, feeding them, making sure they were not worried about their mother. He told them she was working—like she always did.

A search was conducted at nearby Stony Creek Metropark, a 4,500-acre, county-owned playground that the Grant family frequented for family picnics, walks, and bike rides. A Web site, www.taralynngrant.com, was launched, and family members, including Steve, made public pleas for help.

But three weeks passed, and there was nothing. No news. No calls. No record of credit-card use. Nothing. Tara Grant had seemingly disappeared into the winter night, without a trace, leaving behind what seemed to many a picture-perfect modern-day existence—a nice house in an affluent area, a big, playful dog, two gorgeous children, live-in help, and a husband she'd married right after college. Their life was the realization of the traditional American dream.

For the past two weeks, Grant had made emotional public pleas, asking the public for help via the ever-ready TV cameras. The weeks since Tara's disappearance had taken a toll on him; his eyes were rimmed red and his work schedule was scrambled as he tended to media calls, his counsel's questions, and the chores that were part of running a household. Grant's mother, Sue, had come to Michigan from her home in Arizona for a few days to help take care of the kids, but then left on a previously planned vacation to Hawaii. Grant, meanwhile, continued to vocally puzzle over Tara's absence.

At first, it was in hysterical interviews on the local news. As the days passed, he calmed down during his media appearances.

"I think about 'what if something happened' and I just can't get further with that thought," he told a bevy of reporters on February 23, two weeks into the Tara search.

The press now kept the Grant residence on deathwatch. "Yeah, it's been explained to me that as time goes on what happens to the chance that she's going to come back or call, but I just don't want to think that."

———

On March 2, as Grant stood in the kitchen, police began the routine of searching his house. They fanned out, moving from room to room, shifting furniture, opening dressers, shuffling papers, and closing cabinets.

The search warrant covered "latent fingerprints, blood samples, hair samples, animal hair, stained clothing, fibers and other trace evidence which corroborate the crime. Any and all electronic devices, including but not limited to, computers, media storage, answering machines, cell phones and digital recorders."

Free to leave, but with his vehicles impounded, Grant moved onto the front porch, freezing in the twelve-degree temperature, and dialed Mike Zanlungo. Tara and Steve were good friends with Mike and his wife, Leanne, who lived a couple miles away in another subdivision.

Mike, a stout, square-jawed thirty-five-year-old, was an employee at Chrysler. He and Grant had bonded over a love of soccer and their kids. The two had met in the fall of 2005 when Steve was head coach of a team in the local American Youth Soccer Organization league. Both of them had children on the team, and Grant had been looking for some coaching help.

"At the time I was working an off shift and I volunteered to help coach," Zanlungo said. "Steve and I had things in common, [for example] we both liked to coach soccer . . . at first we only saw each other at the games, then we kept running into each other around town, the ice cream parlor, at the mall."

Soon, their wives also bonded, he said, and Steve and Mike became "the best of buddies."

Now, on this blustery March evening, as officers began to search Grant's home, Steve needed a bit more than some of the easy camaraderie Mike so readily provided. He needed to get away from the house. It was all too much . . . the cops, the warrant.

"He asked me to pick him up at a crossroad in his subdivision, which I didn't understand," Zanlungo said. It was dark, with an east wind that was bringing in some snow. But once Mike agreed to pick him up, Grant grabbed a leash, took the family dog, a shepherd/retriever mix named Bentley, and headed out on foot to meet him.

"It was one house west of his house. He was very nervous. I turned to the east and he told me to stop, he didn't want to go by the news crews. We turned around, he was sweating, looking over his shoulder and as we drive out of the subdivision, we hit Mound and went to 28 Mile and turned left—he saw a Taurus behind us and asked me if we were being followed."

Grant's behavior bothered Zanlungo, who asked, "What's going on? You're not acting like an innocent person."

Steve told Mike he had something to confess. It was eating at him and he was fully ready now to tell the truth to someone.

"He sighed, and we had a long silence. Then he told me that they took his computer."

On that computer, Grant said, were e-mailed communications, flirtatious ones, between him and Verena Dierkes, the au pair.

"And they are going to find out I was with Verena," Grant told his pal.

It was not a stretch to imagine that a man like Grant, left alone with two children to care for during the week, could grow interested in someone like Verena.

At nineteen, Verena was a bright girl on the cusp of womanhood, blond and exotically beautiful. She was taking Spanish lessons at a local college, had become friends with some other au pairs in the area, and was committed to the Grant family.

In June 2006, she had graduated from Gymnasium St. Xaver, a state-run Catholic high school for advanced students in Bad Driburg, Germany. Her father was a medical attendant and her mother a trained nurse.

Verena had wanted to do something different, something to go beyond her small-town upbringing in a village of less than a thousand people. After she learned to speak English, "coming to the U.S. was a dream," Verena would later say. She signed on with Au Pair in America, a London-based company that matches American families with young women from different countries. Verena began her work at the Grant home on August 21, 2006, at a rate of $285 a week, plus board and a vehicle. Not long after that, Tara began her weekly commute to San Juan.

So while the news shook Zanlungo a bit, there was also a shred of understanding. It was Friday evening and Mike had planned a night out with his wife while their kids were going to stay at his mom's. But his distressed friend needed him, so the date would have to wait. Zanlungo drove over 28 Mile Road and pulled into his own subdivision, but instead of heading to his home, he drove around a bit "to give Steve a chance to talk some more."

Zanlungo acknowledged that a dalliance with a teenager would not cast Stephen in a good light—neither with the media nor with the cops.

· "Steve, it's not going to look good for you. You're not the first man to commit adultery, but you didn't kill your wife," Zanlungo assured his friend.

When they finally pulled up to Mike's house, Steve declared that he wanted to go see his kids, over at his sister's. Although aware of Steve's poor driving record—which was peppered with reckless-driving charges, parking citations, and numerous speeding tickets—Mike, ever the good friend, handed over the keys to his wife's Dodge Dakota extended-cab truck.

The two stood for a minute in the driveway, Grant's dog, Bentley, at his side, and then Steve opened the door to the vehicle.

"Oh, Mike, you have a leather interior in this, you don't want my dog in there." It was a curious comment given the circumstances. Zanlungo waved him off. He had three dogs of his own. He would see Grant a little later, he thought. After all, Steve was his friend.

Grant called Kelly's cell phone to let her know he was coming by, and she told him that she and her husband, Chris, dedicated Catholics, were at St. Malachy Church with his kids for a Friday fish fry.

Grant headed over to the church. It was dark now, and the chill was getting to him, even in the heated truck cab. He wore no heavy coat. The highways were still crowded with evening commuters making their way out of Detroit and into northern communities like Clarkston, Mt. Clemens, or Washington Township.

Kelly greeted Steve in the church hallway and immediately noticed that her little brother was in panic mode. She had seen it before, but it was still unsettling. He talked to his kids briefly, then asked to borrow his sister's house key so he could drop Bentley off at the house. The dog, he said, would only get in the way at the house on Westridge.

Then, he confided to Kelly, "I'm going to get arrested. Deputy Szalkowski told me that if they find one drop of blood in the house, I'll go to prison."

Kelly stared without a word. It had never occurred to her that her little brother could be a murderer. For all of his ham-handed antics—the arrests for driving with a suspended driver's license, a concealed-weapons bust, the childhood shenanigans—Kelly had never thought of Steve, a fun-loving kid with a sense of humor a mile wide, as a killer.

"I'm going to go for a drive," Grant told her, interrupting her train of thought, which had turned rather bizarre. "I'll give you a call soon."

He drove to Kelly's house with a plan. Suicide. Grant looked around for the .38-caliber handgun he knew they had, but could not find it. The medicine cabinet yielded something else, though; a fairly new bottle of Vicodin, a powerful painkiller. Steve pocketed the pills and left.

———

After leaving Kelly's, Stephen Grant began a travel odyssey to end all travel odysseys. He hit Interstate 75 North, then met Interstate 69 South, heading toward Lansing. Grant had gone to college at Michigan State University in East Lansing, about eighty-five miles away. It was familiar territory, and he even had an ex-girlfriend there. More importantly, he had a good friend, Tom Munley, who was a corporate lawyer in Lansing.

"I went to Tom's house and wanted to turn myself in," Steve says. "I knocked on the door and he wasn't home. I couldn't get him on the phone. So now I had to think of how to kill myself."

But though he was considering suicide, there were no available means that appealed to him.

"I thought I would step in front of a truck out on the highway, but then worried that the truck would try to miss me and hit someone else and kill them. And then I thought that if he did hit me, he'd have to live with that the rest of his life. Then I thought about jumping off a bridge, but there were no bridges that high in the area."

Steve considered all this as he drove through the streets of Lansing, drinking whiskey and occasionally taking a Vicodin from the bottle he had taken from Kelly's house. He was getting wrecked and his mind was racing.

"At one point, a cop pulled up behind me as I was driving down a side street in East Lansing," Steve says. "He followed me for a little while, but then turned off."

He stopped at a Meijer on Lake Lansing Road in East Lansing. Then he went to another in the suburb of Okemos.

He bought an odd array of items: some razor blades, a bottle of Tylenol PM, a notepad, calling cards, a temporary-use cell phone, a black Magic Marker, and a small, plastic cap gun. He had an idea.

"I had heard of suicide by cop," Steve says. "So I took the pen and blacked out the red end of the toy gun. I figured that if I got pulled over, I could point the gun at the cops and they'd shoot me."

Grant jumped back in the truck and drove north again, taking back roads and lonesome highways as the night wore on. He stopped at an ATM and withdrew five hundred dollars. At a convenience store, he bought more Jack Daniel's and a quart of Baileys Irish Cream. He drank from each bottle without bothering to mix them properly. At some point, he also called his sister to check on the kids. And he also made two calls to Verena in Germany.

"Jumping from a bridge would be the best, and that's how I began to head north, to the Mackinac Bridge," Steve says. "But on the way up there, I remembered Wilderness State Park."

———

Back in the neighborhood in Washington Township, a handful of evidence technicians were combing through the house but finding little. There were tiny drops of dried blood on the floor in the family room, by the fireplace, and a bloodstain in the basement wine cellar. But nothing raised a red flag—a little bit of blood is common in most households, the result of everyday cuts and scrapes. The house was basically immaculate. Steve had had plenty of time to keep the place up; he was home most nights by six, and often in bed and asleep by nine-thirty.

Officers gathered an impressive array of electronics, including a Compaq computer tower, several thumb drives, a digital camera, a webcam, an HP laptop, and a loaded 9mm Ruger pistol. As they searched, another crew of officers and detectives bided their time in the garage, stomping their feet to stay warm and waiting their turns for a crack at the house. Tara's Isuzu Trooper was in there, so one officer searched the vehicle while others looked around the perimeter, hardly expecting to find much.

There were work notebooks in the Trooper's backseat and a used coffee cup in the console, but nothing seemed amiss. The officers scanned the neatly arranged garage and found some dark stains on the concrete that didn't look like mud or oil. They took samples to scan in their lab. There was a workbench, a toolbox, a snowblower. Then their attention turned to a green plastic container marked KIDS CLOTHES. They figured Tara had stored her children's outgrown togs in the container, so they moved around in other areas to see what else they could find in the garage.

———

When Steve met Tara through friends at Michigan State University, he had been instantly attracted to her. She was a young, pretty farm girl from Michigan's Upper Peninsula. She was innocent, smart, organized, and determined, many qualities he did not share. While Tara graduated with honors and a degree in business, Steve dropped out before completing his degree to work in the Lansing office of state senator Jack Faxon, a Democrat from Farmington Hills.

Tara wasn't interested in Steve at first, but he was persistent and eventually won her over—and though things might have started off slowly, once they actually began a courtship, it moved quickly. Steve proposed not long after Tara graduated from MSU in 1994. By the fall of that year, she had a job at Washington Group International's Troy office in the Detroit suburbs. The two lived together in an apartment in nearby Auburn Hills in 1995, and in September 1996, they were married.

Grant, however, could not jump-start his stalled career. There were few opportunities in Michigan to earn a living in politics. Facing uncertainty, Steve joined his father at USG Babbitt, a tiny tool-and-die company located in a whitewashed concrete block of a building on a dead-end industrial street about a mile from downtown Mt. Clemens, the Macomb county seat. Incorporated in 1997, USG Babbitt was one more blue-collar shop launched by his father, William "Al" Grant, a hard-drinking Canadian who had made a living as an entrepreneur, and who had started several businesses that supplied the auto industry. Al made a fair success of his businesses, too—when Steve was growing up, there were usually new cars in the driveway, Pontiacs and Chevrolets and Volkswagens, and the family always had a nice home.

For Steve, who had some years of college behind him, his working life was decent but hardly glamorous.

But Tara appeared fulfilled. Considered a "high-potential employee," she found her niche at Washington Group and quickly became a rising star. Although she soon gave birth to two children, she increasingly devoted more time to work and less to motherhood.

Steve enjoyed Tara's success. The money was good—she was soon earning a six-figure salary—and the hours were tolerable at first. But soon the travel left Grant at home alone. It became a source of heartache and sometimes anger. Steve spent days making lunches and playing with their toddlers while Tara flew to England, Spain, Germany, all over the world. As her path widened, his narrowed—and he started to resent it.

The tension spilled over into their sexual relationship. The less supportive he became, the more she pulled away. Steve grew suspicious of some of Tara's relationships with coworkers, especially a friendship with a male colleague in the Cleveland office, with whom she frequently text-messaged. Grant felt like an outsider, fueling his anger at being left alone to raise two small children.

"I really did take care of the kids all the time, and it wasn't a bad thing, really," Steve says. "I love them and wanted to make life the best for them. But I also wanted some help from my wife to help make it feel like we really were a family.

"She was gone all the time. If the kids needed someone to take them to swimming, to parties or soccer practice, I took them."

But Tara never stopped working, pushing to get ahead. And starting in the summer of 2006, she was away from home even more frequently. She was assigned to the Washington Group's office in San Juan as office operations manager, staying five days a week and returning to their home on weekends, where she barely had time for the children, let alone a husband whose self-esteem was rapidly eroding.

———

Detective Mark Grammatico was standing in the garage with several other detectives as the evidence techs did their thing in the house. He had been there along with most everyone else since around 5 P.M.

Now, ninety minutes later, he and the other officers were freezing and wanted to get things going.

But their attention suddenly focused on the other side of the room, where Detective Sergeant Brian Kozlowski had been quietly poking around.

"I was on one side of the garage, when on the other, I heard Sergeant Kozlowski say, in a voice of disbelief, 'What the fuck!' It kind of surprised us all," Grammatico said.

Kozlowski had spotted a container he hadn't seen during his previous visits to the Grant home. When the detective had surveyed the garage during his visit on the night Tara had been reported missing and he and Sergeant Pam McLean had been at the Grant house, he had noticed some plastic storage containers. But this one hadn't been there. It sat under a black mesh tarp—green, with a blue snap-on top and red handles. He pulled the tarp away and unsnapped the handles to find a mass of black plastic bags stacked one on top of the other.

"There was a spot in the garage with a container in it that I was confident was not there before," Kozlowski said. "It was new to me. The toys appeared to have been moved. It was not in the same picture that I had observed it being on February 14. I immediately saw a black garbage bag. The bag was dusty. It was soft. It gave to my pressure." He said he almost closed it up and dismissed it as another bag of salt like the one sitting nearby. But something in his gut, call it instinct or experience, told him to focus and look further. And so, slowly at first and then more quickly, he began to tear the black bags away.

As the veteran sergeant tugged and tore deeper into the bags, he came across one that was clear and smeared with what looked, in the dim light, like blood.

He used his flashlight to get a better look, jerking it out quickly, his warm breath steaming in the bitter cold as he peered in to examine the bag.

"I saw red. I pressed [the bag] again. It was soft and moist. I thought it was a deer carcass. I saw clothing, and then what I recognized as a woman's bra."

In that moment, the mystery of Tara Grant's whereabouts was resolved. She'd been found, all right. At least, a large grisly piece of her was found, nearly frozen solid in the corner of her suburban garage.

Instantly, Kozlowski was filled with rage. After weeks of searching, questioning, hundreds of phone calls, poring over tips, the case had come to a horrifying climax.

"I've been shocked a lot but not like that," Kozlowski said.

Tara Grant's headless torso lay on its back in the container. What was left of her bottom half was still clad in the black, pin-striped Isaac Mizrahi slacks (now severed at the top of her thighs) that Steve had described her as wearing when she'd supposedly left. Her top half was clad in the same gray Ann Taylor blouse Grant had also described, now torn open.

The discovery prompted a gut-churning reaction that even seasoned forensics experts never get used to. The lawmen gathered around the container, then choked down dry heaves simultaneously. Quickly, Kozlowski pushed the human remains back into the bag and into the tub. It was dusted for prints and then moved into a van for the long ride to the county's medical examiner.

And then, in the dim light of the garage, the officers all looked at one another and asked the million-dollar question: Where was Grant?

Their only suspect had quietly left his house. And no one had followed. He had not been under arrest, but still . . . where had he gone? And where was he now? The APB went out immediately, to the state police, to other jurisdictions. Stephen Grant was missing and wanted in connection with the murder of Tara Grant, his wife of ten years. He had apparently killed his wife, cut her into pieces, tried to hide her body in his garage. Mister Mom had flipped out.

———

Grant was buzzed, and could probably have registered a legally intoxicated reading on the old drunk meter if he'd been pulled over. He yanked the Dakota into a convenience-store parking lot and pulled out the prepaid Motorola cell phone he had bought in Lansing. He sat there, mulling over his options.

He dialed his attorney. It was 1:30 A.M.

David Griem struggled to see the phone number as his cell, left on his nightstand, buzzed him awake. He had left repeated messages for Steve earlier in the evening, to no avail. Finally he was getting the call he'd hoped for.

"Stephen, where are you?" Griem queried angrily.

There was silence and then he could hear weeping. "Stephen. It's okay. Let's talk about this."

Steve spoke of suicide. The water so close. He had a gun, he said.

"Stephen, this is not worth killing yourself over. I will defend you. I will work with you. We can work this through in court," Griem argued, trying to talk some sense to his distraught client, but knowing deep down that Stephen was on the edge. "I CARE about you . . ."

Silence . . . breathing . . . a long pause.

"How did it get this far?" asked Grant, swapping from hurt to ferocity, the anger roiling in his voice. "She treated us like shit . . ." he told Griem. "It's HER fault this happened. Everyone hates me, but it's HER fault. She cheated on me . . . She left us alone. We meant nothing to her."

Griem searched his heart for the right thing to say. Steve had switched from fear to anger and back to sadness. He was at once belligerent and childlike. Seething and repentant. Griem had noticed before that when things weren't going well, when police pushed the right buttons with his client, Grant got flustered and pissed off, and those emotions were tinged with a childlike need to be taken care of.

"Where are you?" Griem demanded. "I will meet with you. Just tell me where you are. I will come to you. I will get in my car . . . just tell me . . ."

"Too far gone," said Steve, now starting to cry again. "Tell my kids that I love them. I tried to be a good dad. I did. I loved them—so damned much."

And with that, he hung up.

Griem sat up in bed and stared into space, his heart racing. Over and over, he frantically redialed the number of the cell Steve had purchased three hours earlier. The calls did not go through. He lay back in bed looking at the ceiling. He worried that his client meant business and would kill himself. He prayed, *please, Stephen, don't do this.*

Griem drifted uneasily back to sleep. He had actually decided the previous day to drop Grant as a client—it was the discovery, which he'd made on his own, that Grant had been involved in some semiromantic shenanigans with the teenage au pair, Verena, that had made him want to drop the case. But now, with Steve on the run, was no time to let him down.

Two hours passed. The phone rang again. This time things were different. Grant was on the edge; drunker, angrier, sadder. The nonstop rant coming from Steve's end was full of non sequiturs, rambling, jittery riffs that started in one spot and ended miles away, talking about driving, snow, Tara, dogs, children—and in the middle, a moment of clarity: "It was an accident."

The statement stopped Griem in his tracks: *What* was an accident?

Then, before he could finish that thought, Steve was back to the rambling.

"We can work this out, Stephen. Where are you? Come home. Let's go to the police together and talk about this," Griem told him, using a muted voice in an attempt to assure Steve that someone cared. He reminded Grant of his family and how much Steve meant to them, no matter what, especially his two children, who needed him now more than ever.

Steve just ignored him and continued his verbal

stream-of-consciousness with nonsensical exclamations that started with one thought and ended with another. Finally he stopped. He was resolute. He was going to kill himself, somehow.

"I have never been more convinced of something than I was at that time that Stephen was going to kill himself," Griem says. "And I couldn't do anything to stop him."

He turned on his bedside light and wondered whether he would ever speak with Stephen again. He didn't know what to say, whom to tell, where to go. He'd had difficult clients before, but a suicide? Those kids' mother was gone, and now their father was going to end it all. They would be orphans. *Oh God . . . what would happen to the Grant children?* Griem's heart broke at the thought. And then his mind moved to duty. He would have to call the police. He had no choice.

———

Steve fiddled with the radio as he drove a zigzag route around Michigan's Lower Peninsula. From Lansing, he drove east to Flint on Interstate 69, then back again to Lansing, then north on U.S. 127, then cut across dirt roads that ran between dead cornfields and through the forests that make Michigan's countryside so gorgeous. After weeks of talking to the press, of giving interview after interview about his missing wife, he had nothing more to say to anyone, not even to those who wanted to help.

At around 4 A.M., he stopped in Mt. Pleasant, home of Central Michigan University and the Soaring Eagle, a fairly high-ranking casino, and little else. He walked into the casino, a mile off State Highway 127, and wandered through the crowded banks of pinging slot machines to the hotel desk. Country duo Montgomery Gentry had played the night before and the hotel was sold out. A convention had the neighboring motels filled. No room at the inns. Steve moved on, heading north, past towns like Harrison and Clare, then jutting east at Lake Houghton.

He drove in the darkness, wondering what his accusers were finding back at his home, and sipping occasionally from the bottle of whiskey. The radio was on, but he couldn't get 950 AM, the all-news station in Detroit that would surely report any findings about Tara.

He pulled into Honker's Travel Center, a truck stop outside West Branch at around five-thirty, and parked the Dakota around back where a line of semis idled as their operators slept. Steve dozed fitfully, awakened by daylight around 8 A.M.

"I went into the store there and saw the *Detroit News* and there was my picture on the front," Steve says. It was an early edition, and the headline COPS SEARCH GRANT HOME did not tell of the macabre finding at the house, although Grant knew what the cops had discovered. Grabbing a copy of the paper, Steve folded it over so the clerk wouldn't see the photo as he made the purchase.

Grant got back on the road, pushed the truck northward, honing in haphazardly on a place called Wilderness State Park, 8,300 acres of undeveloped wooded territory in the most northwestern portion of Michigan's Lower Peninsula, fronting Lake Michigan and Sturgeon Bay. He had spent many happy weeks there with Tara and the children during summers. It was located about four and a half hours northwest of his home. But it had taken him more than six hours to get there, crisscrossing the state, finally driving down State Highway 36, which ran around Camp Grayling. He took side roads near the 147,000-acre military and law enforcement training center that should have gotten him stopped. At one point he approached a sign where the road abruptly ended. It read: DO NOT PROCEED: UNEXPLODED ORDNANCE.

Grant finally found the place he'd been looking for, a spot reminiscent of good days with Tara. Outside the resort town of Harbor Springs was State Highway 119, better known as "The Tunnel of Trees," a two-lane road shrouded by thick groves of maples, beech, and birch trees that wind northward into the serene woodland of Wilderness State Park. To his left was Lake Michigan.

"Tara and I, we'd driven that road lots of times, it's a beautiful road," Grant said later. "That was the first place we'd ever went, our first trip ever. It's a good place to end it."

He stopped nineteen miles later in Cross Village, population 294, an Indian settlement in the late 1700s and now a beer stop, consisting of not much more than a small market. It was around 2:30 P.M. on Saturday, March 3.

"I was going to stop at the store and get something more to drink, but I was afraid that my picture was everywhere by now and they'd call the police, so I kept going," Steve says.

As he drove around the area, looking for a place to ditch the truck, he passed Dennis Fay, a local who was out on his cross-country skis.

Fay saw Steve twice as he drove near Cross Village and noted the yellow truck and Grant's confused appearance.

"He looked lost, and he turned around after he passed me, and he waved as he went by," Fay says. "Then I saw him a little later, and he waved again."

At one point, Steve stopped to call Verena. The conversation was brief, but Verena later told police that Steve told her he and Tara had argued and she struck him. In response, he'd pushed her and she'd fallen, and died. He apologized for his lies.

"So I don't know where he was but it was like a good-bye," said Verena, who added that Steve was crying as he spoke to her. He asked that she pass along a message to his children: "Tell them they [have] to be strong, tell them they [have] to be good and live and tell them I'm sorry for everything that I did."

Shortly after speaking with Verena, Steve pulled the truck to the shoulder of the road near the south entrance of Wilderness and called his sister, Kelly. He told her to let the kids know that he loved them. He told her where he was, outside Wilderness State Park. He said he was going to kill himself. Then he moved on into the park.

Kelly promptly walked to the officers parked outside her home, who were keeping watch in case Steve returned to his sister's place.

"Steve just called me, he's in Wilderness State Park and he says he is going to kill himself," Kelly told them. "Please help him."

Wilderness Park is jammed with campers during the summers, but in early March it is virtually abandoned and quiet, usually under more than two feet of snow. Steve turned off the radio and sat quietly in the truck, occasionally hitting the bottle of whiskey.

"I tried to write a note to the kids," Grant says. "But I couldn't focus on the page as I wrote. Now I thought I would just start walking in the snow and eventually I'd just fall asleep and freeze to death. I'd drank all I could and taken those pills and I still wasn't out. So I was sure this would do it."

But he did finish the note to his children, attempting to portray his suicide in a noble light.

"Lindsey and Ian—I know that you two don't under-stand yet what has happened to mom and I. When you get a little older, Aunt Kelly can explain better. For now, though, just know that I love you both more than anything in the world. Because I don't want to put anyone through MORE suffering, I have decided to end my life . . ."

It was ten frigid degrees, with a slashing wind. The cold enveloped him when he opened the door of the truck.

Stephen grabbed his bottle, cap gun, and a notepad and started his trek into the forest. He walked off into the darkness, the ice-crusted snow crunching beneath his feet as he trudged into the dense woods, walking more than a mile. His breathing slowed as the freezing tem-perature started to numb his feet and hands. The world was getting darker and colder. He began to hallucinate, seeing his sister-in-law Alicia and her husband, Erik, among the trees, pointing their fingers at him and chas-tising him, accusing him. He could feel reality slipping away. It would be easy this way. He would drift off and things would be quiet. He was resolved that this was how it should be.

———

The FBI had been peripherally involved on the missing-persons case since it began, but now took its own steps independent of the Macomb County Sheriff's Of-fice. As often happens in big cases, law enforcement agencies get territorial, and oftentimes the smaller agen-cies are unwilling to give up the glory to their counter-parts. The FBI office in Macomb County also covers two neighboring counties, Sanilac and St. Clair. The small operation has just nine agents, but when Stephen Grant fled, the office did several things that were being over-

looked by the local law enforcement agencies. The first
was to send an officer to the area where Steve was suspected of heading, based on the intermittent tracking of
his cell-phone calls. The FBI contacted authorities at the
Mackinac Bridge, which opens onto a vast area where
anyone could easily get lost or hide out and lay low in for
some time.

The agency also dispatched an FBI agent from the
Macomb office who arrived in the Wilderness area by 5
P.M., at least twelve hours before any of the Macomb
County sheriff's deputies arrived.

But while the FBI agent was an extra hand on deck, it
was the local sheriff's department in Emmet County
that handled the nuts and bolts of the case. Sergeant
Timothy Rodwell took a call at the sheriff's office from
Lieutenant Elizabeth Darga at the Macomb County
Sheriff's Office around 4:30 P.M. She informed Rodwell
that a murder suspect was in the area and he "may be at
a cabin at Wilderness State Park and is supposed to be
suicidal." According to police records, "Sub possibly
took narcotics."

Steve was indeed moving toward one of four cabins on
the north end of the park that looked onto Lake Michigan, a place called Waugoshance Cabin, where he and
Tara had spent beautiful, warm summer nights. It was
nearly two miles from where he had ditched the truck.

The entire north portion of Wilderness State Park was
inaccessible by car and difficult to negotiate on foot. The
local sheriff's office mobilized a team of snowmobiles. It
was tough going out there, and a guy *would* have to be
suicidal to be navigating the area without the proper
gear.

Even the dogs that were brought in were unable to get

a scent because of the strong winds and heavy snow coming off the lake.

———

U.S. Coast Guard Lieutenant Robert Kornexl got a call about 8:45 P.M. at home. A former helicopter pilot in the Marines, Kornexl now flew mostly rescue missions out of Traverse City, Michigan, a resort town about eighty miles southwest of Wilderness State Park.

"It was the shift commander in Emmet County," Kornexl says. "He said there was a murder suspect on the run at Wilderness and asked if we could get a crew up there to help with the search. They had already mobilized forty people to get out there." The weather was tough— "pretty crappy," as Kornexl puts it—with snow squalls and thirty-five-mile-an-hour winds from the northwest. He and his three-man crew lifted off around 10 P.M. "By the time we got in, the weather had leveled off and we had cloudy skies, a big moon, and a 2,500-foot ceiling."

Steve had been walking into the darkness for about an hour when he heard a distant whirring noise, sounding like fluttering. Although he was losing consciousness in the cold, he realized quickly that the sound was a helicopter, moving closer, its searchlights casting a beacon on the white snow. His pursuers picked up his tracks along a tree line, following them as he then moved to the shoreline, then back to the woods, where searchers found items that Grant was shedding. The cap gun, a notebook with a page or two torn out of it, and a pint of whiskey that was a quarter full.

Kornexl says, "The ground team was finding spots in the snow, around fallen trees, where he was stopping to hide when we would fly over, to keep out of our spotlight. They knew he was stopping because the snow was partially melted. He was being smart, and really seemed to know how to hide from us."

Steve, startled out of his cold-induced lethargy, crawled under the branches of a thick pine tree. They were looking for him . . . or chasing him . . . and he did not want to get caught. He lay still in the snow, wet, shivering, trying to control his breathing so he wouldn't be noticed. He could now hear voices muffled in the distance. He continued to lie still. By the time they caught up with him, the winter weather would have taken its toll. They would not find him alive if he had his way.

CHAPTER 2

Stephen Grant was trapped. Only this time, he was thirteen years old, a rambunctious, skinny, fun-loving kid with mischief in his brown eyes and a bent for trouble.

It was the kind of spring day that made the dehumanizing Michigan winters bearable, a sunny Saturday afternoon in March with temperatures cresting forty degrees, a welcome, albeit relative warmth. A perfect day for Steve and a few of his pals to wander over to Clinton River Park North.

The city-run park was a quick hundred yards from their homes on Riverland Drive, a cut-through street that connected two main arteries of suburban Sterling Heights, where Steve lived with his dad, William (whom most called Al), his mom, Susan, and his older sister, Kelly.

It was the time of year when the ice breaks on the Clinton River, a twisting inlet that winds its way through Macomb County, and Steve and his friends were getting into the fun of jumping on passing floes and riding them ten or twenty yards before jumping off.

Steve, his friend Ken McCauley, and a couple other neighborhood kids were always trying to build floats to ride on downriver, usually poorly executed jobs with empty beer kegs lashed to a few boards. But on this day, the ice floes were serving that purpose and the kids were riding, pretending to surf, then jumping off, once in a while accidentally dipping a sneakered foot in the icy drink. It hurt until it went numb, then it was back to business. On a thawing day like this, the floes came fast.

It was a Midwestern version of Tom Sawyer, without the politics. They were just goofing and had all been at it an hour or so just by an overpass at the mouth of the park's entrance, which cuts beneath Riverland Drive and lets the river flow into the park proper. The kids were oblivious to the other patrons scattered around the area, tossing Frisbees, walking dogs, taking advantage of a break in the season.

Ken and Steve had become friends when the McCauleys moved to Riverland Drive in 1977, three doors down from the Grant family.

The Grant house was a 1,500-square-foot, four-bedroom job, with a two car garage that Al Grant loved to work in, fussing with cars and tinkering with his inventions. The neighborhood was solid working-class, composed of sturdy nuclear families the fathers of which were mostly employed by the auto industry. The McCauleys had four kids and Ken's oldest sister soon began babysitting for the Grant kids. The first time Ken and Steve met, though, was a few days after the McCauleys settled in, when Steve came knocking on the door. He had heard there was a new kid on the block, and Steve was never shy about making friends. His nonstop chattering nature and his relentless curiosity would not permit him to overlook a new playmate.

Every day, the two would pair up for some kind of adventure, scouring the local apartment Dumpsters for treasures, maybe a little shoplifting from the local dime stores, shooting off some fireworks, or just tossing dirt clods at each other.

As well as trying to sail down that river. But this day's effort didn't go so well.

Steve, Ken, and a couple others jumped off the shore and onto a passing piece of ice, riding it surfboard style for a few yards before they jumped off. All except Steve. He narrowed his legs to a slight squat to keep his balance and get a little longer ride. But as he did, the floe moved to the center of the river, about twenty feet offshore. That was where it snagged on some branches that were trying to float to the surface, encouraged by the warm air. The small iceberg came to a halt. Steve froze, panicked. He looked at his friends on the bank.

"C'mon, Steve, that one's done," Ken yelled to him. "The water's not very deep, you can walk back here."

Steve shook his head. No way. It *was* deep. The river got to be seven feet at some points, he had heard.

"I—I—I can't make it," Grant said. "I n-need help."

It was a mild stutter that Steve had, a condition that ebbed as he got older, though it reemerged in tight situations. Like this one.

"Let's go, get off there, Grant," another friend urged. "There's bigger ones coming anyway."

Steve started to cry. His pals kept urging him to make a jump for it, and he kept crying. And their early adolescent pleadings started to draw a crowd to watch the scared boy standing on an iceberg in the middle of the river. Someone ran down the two hundred yards to a pay phone at Riverland Plaza, a small strip shopping center, and called the police to report that a boy was stranded in the middle of a raging, ice-choked river. The crowd tried to calm Steve, but he only cried more.

"Help is on the way," someone offered. But he just blubbered as he heard the sirens, police, fire trucks, the whole bit, coming to the park to save him.

Back at the Grant home, Al and Susan Grant were in the middle of painting the living room. The doors were open to ventilate the room as they painted and let in the fine spring air.

As the sirens headed down Riverland, past the Grant house and into the park, Al Grant—a man who knew his son's proclivity for finding trouble—said, "I hope that's not about your brother."

Kelly, who was sitting in the dining room reading, crinkled her nose and went back to her book. Al and Sue kept painting.

Meanwhile, the firemen quickly assessed the situation and unrolled a fire hose, dragging it the fifteen yards or so across the open parkland to the shoreline, where police officers were telling Steve to hold on, help was here.

"I can't g-g-get out of here, h-help me," Steve sobbed.

"Take this line and wrap it around your waist," an officer instructed him. Through a steady stream of fearful tears, Steve did as he was told, but as he edged off the floe, he slipped into the water.

It was only two feet deep, about up to his calves, the water soaking his Wranglers.

The stranded boy, still standing in the water, unwrapped the hose and looked at the small, narrow shore, jammed with a dozen people. Above them on the overpass, lights blazing, were two fire trucks and a police car.

Steve waded to the shore, ignoring the outstretched hands of his rescuers, and bolted. He ran across the open park, onto the road leading to Riverland, out of the park and down to his home, water trailing him the whole way.

The cops stared, incredulous, as he kept running. The park patrons began to move off, show over.

"That was the Grant kid, right?" an officer asked McCauley.

"Yeah," Ken replied, sheepish again about his best friend's conduct. Sometimes, Grant just vanished. He was good at it, but it was a little vexing, this habit he had of taking off when things got tough.

Steve walked into the house, soaking wet from the thighs down. He went straight up the stairs to his room without a word. No one asked. The cops arrived ten minutes later. They explained what had happened to Al and Sue. It was just another day with Steve.

———

Stephen Grant always told his friends that he remembered January 18, 1970. It was the day he was born to Al and Sue, the former Susan Payne. Married in 1966, the two were hard-living, solidly blue collar, both enjoying a hearty cigarette habit and, incongruously, a rousing game of tennis. But through their hard work and love for each other, the years had been kind to them. Their daughter was born in June 1967, and their son came along three years later. Their family was a traditional homespun fairy tale: two kids, Kelly and Steve, two dogs, a black Lab named Princess and a poodle named BJ (short for Black Jack), and Al Grant's sturdy work ethic.

The family lived on Al's successful entrepreneurial endeavors as a supplier of tools and bearings to the auto industry. Hailing from Wawa, Ontario, four hundred miles north of Detroit, on the northeast edge of Lake

Superior, Al was an amateur hockey player of some talent, but his real skill lay in working with his hands. And he soon discovered that the U.S. auto industry, then booming, was a treasure trove that would reward his considerable engineering skills. Al gravitated to the Detroit area and began his march to prosperity.

Usually working with some well-connected partners, he opened and closed a series of small, profitable shops every seven years or so. They went by unremarkable names like U.S. Grant Manufacturing, A.G. Manufacturing, and USG Babbitt. His places of business were small, dingy, utilitarian shops where hard work was done, small profits were counted, and the whole Grant family pitched in to help. Susan would sometimes do the paperwork, and Steve loved to poke around the shops, collecting ball bearings for later use in slingshots.

A quiet, solidly built man, Al was possessed of some considerable business knowledge that complemented his engineering prowess, and he became a minor player in the sizable supplier business in the days when Ford, General Motors, and Chrysler were really the Big Three.

Al Grant was a prolific man when it came to ideas.

There was the GameTracker, which tracked a deer that had been shot with an arrow via a cable, and the Trunkit, a bungee-cord device with two cords coming off of one in order to tie down stubborn car trunks. He kept boxes of the products in the garage and in the basement, and when he received an order, it was right at hand.

But life on Riverland was not always happy, and for Steve, it was pointedly marred by Al Grant's drinking habit. Al was a heavy drinker who would often stay at area bars until last call.

"I remember my mom coming in and waking me up and getting Kelly up and we would ride in the car with her to some bar where the bartender had called her to pick my dad up," Steve says now. "It really hurt me. I didn't understand for years what was going on."

The family had moved to Riverland in 1971, and seven years later, in 1978, Susan Grant left Al after twelve years of marriage. It was a sunless, seventy-four-degree June day when she filed a complaint for divorce, citing a simple "breakdown in the marriage relationship."

The family assets included the home, a 1976 Pontiac Sunbird, a 1977 Chevy Blazer, and checking and savings accounts at the National Bank of Detroit. Al's net earnings the previous year had been $30,000, a decent figure for the time.

Al moved to an apartment not far from the home, but after a brief separation, the couple reconciled, and he moved back to Riverland, life continuing much as before.

Steve was turning into a spirited boy who undoubtedly today would be harnessed by a Ritalin prescription and after-school detentions. But in the seventies, he was simply seen as energetic, curious, and fun-loving. In other words, he was a kid, albeit a somewhat impish one who didn't mind risking his or someone else's well-being for a good time.

And even before he got his driver's license, Steve would "borrow" his mom's car when she wasn't around. He truly never met a rule that he liked to obey.

The Grant home was filled with a preadolescent's delights. Al, an avid hunter and a bow-and-arrow enthusiast, liked to make his own shotgun shells, compacting the gunpowder and BBs into a combustible vessel in his beloved garage.

For Steve, his father's predilection for homemade shells was an invitation to make his own fireworks, devices that were every bit as cool as the M-80s the family brought across the border when they went to visit their Canadian relatives.

Steve took his access to the weaponry as far as he could. One May afternoon in 1984, he made a device that was too radical to explode just anywhere, a long copper tube, packed tight with gunpowder and buckshot, and capped, with a fuse coming out one end. He went over to Ken's and told him about it, showing him the bomb with pride. They were elated over the device, but it also presented a problem: Where could such a thing be detonated?

So Steve took it to the safest place he could think of: his own backyard.

It blew a hole in the lawn, eight inches in diameter and six inches deep, and scattered shrapnel in every direction. When Al Grant discovered the hole the next day, he called the police to report a bombing in his yard. Steve denied everything, telling police that he had been home alone when it happened and had seen two individuals lurking around the backyard.

But when police ended up hauling Ken in for questioning, he told them straight out that Steve had come by his house with a bomb and asked him to help set it off.

A police report concludes that "Stephen's only explanation for not telling his father immediately and waiting until his father discovered the hole in the backyard was he was frightened of any discipline coming from his parents . . . due to the fact that he has been to numerous hunter safety courses and is very careful with firearms when hunting with his father."

"It was a case where all he would have had to do is apologize and tell the truth," Ken says. "But that's how Steve worked. Fiction was always better."

One summer afternoon several of the gang, now in

their early teens, were walking through Circus World, a national toy-store chain based in nearby Taylor. The store was one of the first big-box toy stores and offered everything from infant distractions to hobby items. On this day, Steve eyed a remote-control airplane. It was a beauty, with a thirty-six-inch wingspan when assembled. The price tag, though, was prohibitive at seventy-five dollars. Who had that kind of cash, especially as the local economy groaned under an unemployment rate in the double digits?

Nonetheless, Steve resolved to get the plane and bragged to his friends that he would have it the next day.

This, he promised, was better than his usual retail trick, stealing merchandise, then returning it claiming to have lost his receipt. No, this model plane was too big to lift in the traditional way.

Circus World was situated in a strip mall about a ten-minute drive from Riverland. It was built with its rear to an open muddy lot that extended a hundred yards, which gave way to a thick grove of trees, then a small forest in which kids often played. As the ground dipped a bit, the lot was almost always damp with runoff, creating a thick muck. But it was generally navigable if you were careful with your steps.

"I'm going to grab the plane and run out the door," Steve told his friends as they walked home. "The alarm is gonna go off, but once I get to the woods, they'll never be able to get me. I'll have that plane tomorrow and we can play with it in the park."

The guys were duly impressed. This was ballsy. This was why they liked to hang around Steve Grant.

The next day, Steve borrowed his mom's Fiero and drove to Circus World, going around the back first to inspect the emergency door that opened onto the lot. He parked the car and walked briskly into the store. A few minutes later, Grant hit the back door in a burst, the alarm crying loudly, the airplane under his arm. He had a good jump on the Circus World staffers, who never expected such a brazen shoplifter to come in such a small package. And he was fast, too, as he headed for the woods. He had a thirty-second jump on them, but as he hit more and more mud, his Sperry Top-Siders, a dock shoe that Grant favored, began to gather mud. One young assistant manager gained on him as Steve's feet began to drag, but he still had a good lead. Until one of the shoes was sucked off of his foot into the mud. How would he go home without a shoe? What would he tell his mom?

So he stopped and tried to dislodge the shoe. And of course he was caught. No airplane. Just another bit of juvenile trouble.

Shoplifting was, in fact, a favorite pastime of Steve's. He liked walking into Dart Drugs at Riverland Plaza and waltzing out with a fifth of apple schnapps under his coat. He didn't care so much about drinking it; he just wanted to get away with something. More often than not, he would hand it over to his pals. Booze didn't do much for him. Just like occasionally taking the Pontiac out for a little drive, just like sneaking into his parents' bedroom, opening his Christmas gifts, playing with them, then putting them back into their packages. And just like stealing a gun or two from his maternal grandfather's collection.

"Steve would take things one step further than anyone else," Ken McCauley says. "We might think of doing something, and Steve would do it."

"They would think up things to do but be too afraid to do them," Steve says. "But I wasn't afraid."

Steve also had a curious habit of burying things to

hide them, then digging them back up. Ken noticed it
when Steve took a small machine gun, a Mac-10, from
his grandfather. He frequently visited his grandfather's
home in Shelby Township, not far from Riverland, where
he was always amazed by the military weaponry.

Steve took the gun, a lightweight military-issue machine gun that looked like an Uzi, stuck it in a suitcase,
then went about hiding it.

Borrowing his mom's car once again, he drove up Van
Dyke Road and cut west to a relatively remote area at the
corner of 22 Mile Road and Shelby Road. There, he fur-
tively buried it amid a grove of tree falls, leaves, and
overgrown weeds near a city public-works plant.

"Then he went back to school, told everyone about
what he did, and then freaked out, thinking the kids would
go out there and find it," McCauley recalls. "So he went
back there after school, dug up the machine gun, and took
it home to hide it."

Grant did like his guns. Some nights, when the sun
had set, Steve and Ken would walk over to Clinton River
Park and shoot at the park signs with a little .32 pistol
that Steve liked to carry around with him. Other times,
they would take some of their homemade fireworks,
small shells jammed with pellets and gunpowder and a
fuse. Mailboxes, signs, trees—none were safe from the
little bombs.

There was one strict rule with Steve and his weapons,
though, and no one can ever recall it being breached. No
harming of animals. For all his insouciance, his irrever-
ence, and his ham-handed handling of things that blew
up or caught fire, Steve was adamant that outside of hunting game, animals should not be hurt.

But everything else was fair game.

"Hanging out with Steve, I was always two seconds

away from being a statistic, losing a limb or having an eye put out," McCauley says. "I could pinpoint unsolved crimes as he was on the brink of adulthood that it seemed could be attributable to him, from breaking in to blowing up."

In 1984, Al and Susan split for good, and this time there would be no reconciliation. It ended eighteen discord-full years of marriage, and the end was not pretty. Steve later said that his parents' loud arguments upset him beyond measure. In the divorce filing, Susan stated that she lacked the financial resources to care for her children and asked for child support, which the court granted.

The assets were split, and the kids and Susan remained in the home, although the two parents had joint custody.

Al was ordered to pay $103 a week in child support. He quickly fell behind, racking up $5,648 in arrears. Records show that the couple and their lawyers tussled numerous times in court over the debt.

———

While his out-of-school life was full of unpleasant domestic drama and juvenile high jinks, Grant's school life was decidedly quiet. There, he was shy and subdued. He went to Dresden Elementary School, then Sterling Junior High, then Utica Ford High School.

He and his older sister, Kelly, often walked the mile each weekday to the high school, home of the Falcons. The suburban school is on a sprawling campus with eighteen brick buildings, including an aquatic center and a theater and performing-arts complex. It is ensconced inside a circular drive and surrounded by parking lots. Today, it boasts nearly two thousand students in grades nine through twelve who live in the area, which has slowly become an upscale Detroit suburb, not far from prized areas like Troy, where many professional athletes keep expensive homes and condos.

Grant's former classmates recall him in a number of ways, all of them noting that he was largely unremarkable. He was "nerdy," "goofy," or "uncool," hardly the stuff of legend. At the same time, given his above-average intelligence, he was known to hang around with kids who were "scary smart," another classmate says.

"He just kind of went under the radar," recalls Dawn Furlow, who was a tormentor of Grant's in her youth. He would walk by her childhood home on the way to junior high in the early eighties.

"My sister and I were brats, and we'd shout his name and call him 'Grunt,' " she says.

"He was quiet and kept to himself," recalls Dean Stramer, who was also in Steve's class of 1988. "He was gangly and bug-eyed, and he was very unsure of himself. He was no extrovert."

Grant was also no jock, at least not going for the organized sports. He wasn't into joining anything, actually, but instead hung out with a group of kids like himself. He still liked his guns, and hunting and outdoor activities, but he was a solitary soul in many ways, despite his often-garrulous nature.

Steve was somewhat cowed by the large class he was in, around five hundred students. His boisterousness was tempered by the fast pace, and he was quickly assimilated into a crowd that his classmates described as "brainy." Some of his closer pals ended up as lawyers and doctors.

He is pictured just twice in his senior yearbook. His senior picture shows a boy who seems to be determined to be innocuous, his thick, curly brown hair and bold brown eyes simply *there*. The only other mention of Grant in the book is in a photo where he is sitting down and donating blood during a student blood drive. The class colors were maroon and gold and the senior song was "Best of Times" by Styx. The festive colors and class song certainly didn't apply to Stephen Grant. He was doing his best just to get through school and into adulthood.

But he was also given to moments of fun. Near the end of his senior year, Steve was in the mood to show off. He realized that his high school time had been tame, although news of some of his extracurricular activities, mostly his engagements with the police, had gotten around.

On this day, assured that he would graduate and with strong grades to bolster his confidence, he made his own final statement.

"We were standing in the hallway, and there was an air horn, like they use for fire emergencies to clear the school," says Paul Buss, who lost track of Grant after high school but later reconnected with him. "And he just says, 'Watch this,' and sets it off. We were freaking out, people are hitting the doors, and we don't know what to do."

Steve did. He stood there as an assistant principal approached, ready to deal.

"And he talked his way out of it," Buss says, still with some incredulity. Paul met Steve his freshman year at Utica Ford High School in 1985, and Buss felt that Steve, although quiet in the presence of larger groups, was always a good conversationalist.

"He was a great talker. He could talk himself out of trouble. And when you had a conversation with him, there was never a dull moment, never an awkward pause. He would make sure to fill them all up."

But Buss, like a few others who got close to Grant, also found him on occasion to be an annoying know-it-all.

"It got to be enough that I just kind of started avoiding him," Buss says. "He was putting up this facade that he was knowledgeable about everything, and I just couldn't take it after a while. But at the same time, he was very intelligent."

Given the size of his senior class, graduation ceremonies were held at the nearby Pontiac Silverdome, a monstrous covered stadium that could hold 76,000. It was better known as the home of the NFL's Detroit Lions for a spell in the seventies and eighties. A week before graduation, Grant left another odd impression.

"We had an all-night senior party at the school, where they closed the doors and we could run around in the school anywhere we wanted," says Kerri Madden, one of Steve's classmates. "They had activities for us, it was fun. And we had a hypnotist there, picking people out of the crowd. And Stephen went up on the stage and volunteered to be hypnotized. All I remember is that he was hypnotized and started crying. It was very weird."

———

By the time he graduated, Steve had lived for a short time with his mother and her new husband in Warren, a few miles away from Utica Ford. Every morning, he would get up and drive to school. Shortly after he graduated, Steve moved out and bunked in with his father on Groesbeck Highway, nine miles from Riverland.

Postgraduation, Steve was intent on going to college, and enrolled for classes at Macomb Community College, then a two-year institution, with its main campus not far from Steve and Al's place.

Attending full-time from the fall of 1988 through the spring of 1991, Grant took a smattering of classes, yet never declared a major and, therefore, never completed a degree. He had odd jobs and lived a fairly monastic life in those years, although he was never far from trouble.

In 1989, Steve was stopped in Clinton Township for driving seventy in a forty-five-mile-an-hour speed limit zone about five miles from the house. It was routine business for Steve, whose driving record was always poor. A lead foot combined with his hyperactive need to get everywhere in a hurry made him prone to tailgating and fast lane changes, and he was a cop magnet.

During the stop, an officer with Clinton Township Police, Mike Friese, noted a pouch at Grant's feet near the brake pedal. In it was a small Colt pistol, unloaded, and Steve had no permit for it. Grant was arrested and charged with failure to possess a weapons permit. He was later fined $500.

Steve soon figured out what he wanted to be when he grew up: a teacher. It was an intellectual pursuit and he was beginning to crave knowledge. Also, his love of the outdoors, running, fine food, and sports cars was beginning to motivate him toward a professional career, something where the money was good and his colleagues might be interested in similar things.

So in fall of 1991, Steve entered Michigan State University as a sophomore, with history as his major. He applied to the school of education, but was turned down, yet soon set his sights a little higher, possibly even law school, he thought. Grant lived with mostly freshmen in Snyder Hall, one of the older dorms on the east side of Michigan State's campus in East Lansing.

But Grant's academic career failed to take off. He matriculated for four semesters, moved around the college town, and finally found himself working a couple of jobs, one at a local bike shop across from campus and another in the kitchen at a nearby Olive Garden, and dabbled in beer and girls.

"I saw him on the street in East Lansing one day, and he looked great, he had grown up," says Martha Anaud,* a former high school classmate and neighbor of Steve's who was finishing her undergrad degree at Michigan State. "He was on a racing bike and he had his bike-racing gear on. He [told me he] was running, too, half marathons."

But Grant was still able to find trouble. Landing a job at Denny's Schwinn, a bike shop that was an institution in the college town, was a nice coup for Steve, who loved bikes and the culture around them. He made a couple of friends quickly at the shop, and sometimes the crew would go on bike outings, tackling the country roads that stretched for miles.

"Steve was a good guy, he was always talking about his car, he had a Mazda RX7, and he told us he raced them," recalls Don Hewitt,* who worked with Steve at Denny's.

Steve claimed that he was from money, thus the sports car, and the somewhat lofty air, Hewitt says. But he was also likable and friendly, and his mild stutter gave him a certain charm.

"Steve was a good worker, too," Hewitt says.

Until one evening about two months into his new job, when Steve was closing the place. He was running the vacuum cleaner in front of the counter, between the door and the cash register. Leaving the vacuum running, Steve jogged around the counter, hit the cash button on the reg-

---

* Denotes pseudonym.

ister, and lifted a twenty-dollar bill out of the till and slipped it into his pocket. Bad move. The manager saw him through a surveillance window and fired him on the spot.

When he first started at Michigan State, Steve dated Deena Hardy, another old friend from the neighborhood on Riverland. She had lived around the corner from him from the time they were seven years old, and they had often chatted easily throughout their childhoods. The two started seeing each other the summer before Steve entered MSU.

"I was in the library at Macomb Community College, and she came in," Steve says. "I hadn't seen her for some time, and we started talking and rekindling our friendship. And it moved on from there."

Deena was a little fireball, skinny and feisty, with rather plain looks and shoulder-length brown hair. And, like Steve, she always had something to say. Between the two of them, there was not a moment of silence. She had spent a year traveling the country, Steve says, which attracted him. She attended some classes, then moved on to follow the Grateful Dead for several months. Now she was back on her home turf, sharing a house with friends, and Steve joined her for the remainder of the summer there. She joined him in East Lansing the next year.

Grant's family was happy to see the two together.

"She was always welcome at our family gatherings, and Steve brought her to everything," Steve's sister, Kelly, says. "My dad liked her, we all did. It was good and we thought maybe they were going to get married."

But the couple, both in their early twenties, broke up in 1993. "We got along great, we were good friends, but we just couldn't live together," Steve admits.

Meanwhile, Steve was finding a new calling shortly: politics.

He came to the office of state Senator Jack Faxon as an intern, securing the position through Michigan State, where he was still a part-time student. His friendly, helpful nature and gift of gab served him well, and by the spring of 1994, Steve was a legislative aide answering the phone at Faxon's office across from the state capitol.

"Steve came to the office with no political connections at all, just a guy looking around," Faxon says. "But someone in the office thought he was all right."

Faxon was in his last term, having started his political career in 1964 as a state senator from Farmington Hills, outside of Detroit. He was one of the more colorful characters at the statehouse, and with his wide, showbiz grin and a flair for theatrics, he was also something of a Renaissance man. Faxon had sung at one point with the Michigan Opera Theater, garnering national attention for his appearance in the acclaimed theater's production of *Die Fledermaus*. He also took a turn in the Detroit Symphony Orchestra's production of *The Nutcracker* for several years beginning in 1979.

Steve was known to everyone as the "young guy who was always hustling," says Pam Mechachonis, who was on staff with Steve as a secretarial aide. Grant loved to talk and it worked well in the small office, which was staffed by four, mostly young idealists.

"He had a very youthful face, he was boyish, kind of happy-go-lucky. Senator Faxon trusted him enough to have him go meet constituents when he was in session. He was entrusted to do the right thing, and I'm sure he did."

As reliable and as voluble as Steve was, his political career ended with Faxon's, and he found himself without work at the end of 1994.

"I couldn't find another political job," Grant says. "That was right after . . . the year the Democrats lost their shirts, and there were a lot of out-of-work Democrats."

Like the rest of the nation, the state's traditional Democratic rule was being taken apart by a Republican revolution, and Faxon retired.

But Steve didn't forget his work mates. About a year after Faxon stepped down, he called Pam at home one night, just checking in.

"It seemed that he thought we were all tighter than we really were," she says. "He had left the office after me, and I almost had to say, 'Who are you again?' The whole experience had kind of moved to the background in my life, but to him, it really must have meant something."

In the summer of 1994, Steve had met a new girl, the successor to Deena. She came in a small package with big, heavy-metal eighties hair. She wasn't from downstate, though, so current fashion was a little lost on her. Her name was Tara Destrampe.

CHAPTER 3

The web of roads that move north from the town of Escanaba, Michigan, toward Tara Grant's childhood hometown of Perkins merge the beautiful with the backward. The landscape, with tall pines, sturdy maples, and rolling hills dotted with farms and homesteads, provides a bucolic backdrop for visitors. Tourists bask in the serenity and remoteness that drives Michiganders past the Mackinac Bridge and into the Upper Peninsula, and every year over four million cars transit the span.

Michigan has two distinctive parts separated by the five-mile-long Mackinac Bridge, which stretches across Lake Michigan. The differences between the cultures of the two are dramatic and pronounced. The Lower Peninsula holds the state's big cities, with their perennial traffic problems, a crime rate that ranks in the top twenty in the United States, and a sense of increasing crowdedness that can be unsettling. The Upper Peninsula is the yin to that yang, both heavily forested and with wide-open spaces, a low crime rate, and small communities. Its slower pace provides respite to visitors and tranquillity to natives.

It is at once lovely, untainted, and unsophisticated, and the "UP", as it is known, is a thing of natural beauty for many. For Tara's driving ambition, life there also became a woodland cage, a place where pickup trucks were ubiquitous, money was scarce, and the small towns that dotted the forested landscape were closed off from a fast-moving world that seemed, to her at least, light-years away. But she knew that world was out there, teeming with possibilities, and she was driven to discover it.

Tara was born on June 28, 1972, the first child of Mary and Gerald (known to everyone as Dusty) Destrampe. The family lived in Escanaba when Tara was born but moved north to Perkins when she was twenty-one months old. Three years later, her younger sister, Alicia, was born.

Rural, unincorporated Perkins, twenty miles north of Escanaba, lies in an area where chickens roam front yards and trailer dwellers, with their dogs chained to fences, drink beer in the afternoons. It is crude in some spots, a rugged blot of humanity, and in others, a comforting place where churchgoing people know your name—as well as your business.

What passes for the town, a little south of the farm that the Destrampes settled on, has a blinking traffic light, a general store, a couple of churches, and a bar. It is surrounded by back roads that lead to more back roads, with potato farms and evergreens that are taller than telephone poles.

Family members in this area are closely knit and are typically born, reared, and eventually die all in the same spot. According to friends who could see there was a brighter fortune brewing behind her curious green eyes, Tara was determined that this would not be her fate.

Whatever her friends hoped and dreamed—get married, have some kids, settle down close by—Tara had other interests as she grew older, and those increasingly did not align with those of most of her peers.

It was not always that way. As she was growing up, the Destrampe clan provided a close family unit from which Tara and Alicia could draw strength and independence. But the household was not always harmonious, as one letter from Tara to her parents noted. The missive, penned in 2006, addressed her father: "Dad, I have not fully forgiven you for how you treated Mom throughout my entire childhood . . . Mom, I have not fully forgiven you for being passive and not standing up for yourself."

Mary Destrampe was a sturdy, doggedly religious type, who kept a spotless home and had great reverence for tradition. She worked in Escanaba as a dental hygienist, while Dusty Destrampe was a utility worker at K. I. Sawyer Air Force Base in Gwynn, about thirty miles north. Broad and tall, thick-necked and strong-willed, Dusty clashed with Tara when she was a teenager, yet provided a strong foundation for his family. The two would hunt rabbit and deer every weekend during the season and Tara lived to please him, but the two, much alike in temperament, were often in conflict.

The Destrampe home was located two bumpy, curvy miles off the main road that extends north from Escanaba, State Highway M35, on twenty-eight mostly undeveloped acres, behind a dense grove of pines and some apple trees. Bought in 1974 for $20,000, the small gray frame house sat twenty yards off the road, its add-on back porch giving it a cared-for look. The home was flanked to the rear by a small pole barn, a larger wooden barn, and an animal pen where Tara tended to her livestock—goats, chickens, and a few cows they kept for fun rather than profit. To the immediate south of the home was about eighty acres of open pasture and forest, and the closest neighbors were about two hundred yards away.

And fifty yards to the south, on the same side of Beaver Lane, obscured completely by forest, was a small encampment dubbed "Dusty's Sugar Bush," his pride and joy.

The main structure was a barn built in 1991, a large place that Mary had decorated to look almost like a home. The green outhouse, a small brown barn with green plastic containers for gathering sap, and a portable trailer for selling the maple syrup made the little compound quite an operation every spring.

As an annual tradition, the family invited friends over to help tend to the sturdy groves of maples, collecting the raw sap, boiling it, and finally bottling the syrup to be given as gifts and, sometimes, sold to make a buck or two.

The young Tara wore two curly pigtails, a nonstop smile, and liked to talk. About anything and at all times. So chatty and forceful was she as a youngster that her parents rewarded her for keeping her mouth shut at school. Get through the day without a reprimand, they told her, and she would receive a stick of gum. One pack went a long way.

Tara attended Mid Peninsula School, a long, single-story institutional building to the north of the Destrampe family home. The school district covered over three hundred square miles, and kids in the area went from grade school to high school together in the same building, all 250 of them. Behind the school was a football field with a small set of bleachers that could hold about a hundred or so hometown fans who supported the Wolverines on chilly autumn Fridays—including Tara, a cheerleader—under a bank of lighting trusses that cast a cold, dim glare. The football field, ringed today by a modern, rubberized track, is surrounded by thick Michigan forest.

By high school, Tara had distinguished herself not only as a cheerleader; she was active in a range of school activities, including playing clarinet in the school band, and she graduated third in her class of forty in 1990.

Melissa Elliott, one of Tara's childhood friends, met her in the second grade. "My mom had a beauty shop in Perkins and her mom was there and Tara came out to the swing set behind the shop and we swung together," she recalls. "And we were friends for a long time after that."

Tara was her classmate, her cheerleading teammate for four years, and her confidante. Although graduation ended their close friendship, in their school years they were an inseparable pair who confided in each other in long notes they exchanged during classes.

Every August the two would exhibit their 4-H projects at the Upper Peninsula State Fair in Escanaba, sleeping in a trailer on the fairgrounds. After a day spent in the stalls and exhibit barns, the two would repair to their trailer and prepare for a night on the midway, where they could watch the boys from neighboring towns, meet up with their friends, and eat bad fair food.

"Tara was boy crazy. We all were," Melissa says. Yet for all her adolescent pining for the opposite sex, Tara spent plenty of time outdoors, enjoying the rough-and-tumble of the wilds. She was a tomboy of sorts who loved to skeet-shoot at the Mead Rod and Gun Club in Escanaba and ride her gray-spotted Appaloosa named RJ's Broken Fingers. She was a good rider, with a streak of mean. One day, RJ bucked her off. Tara got up, dusted herself off, slapped the moody horse across its long snout, and got back on.

Because of her mother's work as a dental hygienist, Tara became obsessed with her own dental care, brushing her teeth a predetermined number of times each way. She wore braces in the tenth grade, but by the time she was a senior, her fastidious look was fully developed, with a perfect grin offset by a mane of fluffy brunette hair.

Melissa's mother, Candy, owned a beauty salon in Perkins and she would cut Tara's thick locks. Tara was particular as a teenager about her look: a late-eighties hairdo, curly—she didn't need the spiral perm standard at the time hers was natural—with bangs that stood up high and tall. She would measure exactly five inches of length where she wanted those perfect bangs trimmed. Then she'd spray them vertically in a look her pals called "the wall."

Her fastidiousness not only with her looks but the way she lived, was something that she carried throughout her life.

Melissa's younger sister, Jennifer, who was also friends with Tara, recalls, "We did everything together as we grew up. All of us always knew that we were loved by our parents, who went out of their way to get us involved in things."

Jennifer and Melissa, typical of UP natives, both married soon after high school and attended college in Marquette, fifty miles to the north. Today, Jennifer works as an accountant at her family's siding business, and Melissa teaches at Soo Hill Elementary in Escanaba. The two sisters and their families live across from each other on a remote road with plenty of woods around them, and their parents live on an adjoining lot. It is a cozy life defined by a familiarity that Tara did not care for.

But Tara may have had more pushing her than just ambition and an adventurous spirit. While her accomplishments were admirable on their own, they were fueled by competition with Alicia, her younger sister. Most people thought that the two were close, but in Tara's view, at least in some regards, they were also rivals.

Later in her life, Tara wrote a journal entry that explains her ambition.

"For as long as I can remember, I hear my mom telling stories about she wasn't good enough for her mom and for as long as I can remember, I have always felt in competition with my sister because I felt I wasn't good enough. I have always been striving for the attention/recognition I thought my sister was always getting.

"I made the decision to go as far in state as I could to go to school," she wrote in 2006. "I think I was making a statement to my parents that I feel on my own, so I am going to go on my own."

Life at the Destrampe house was not boring, Jennifer says, and loud arguments punctuated by expletives were as much a part of the family fabric as was the closeness.

As she grew older, Tara's personality took on the vibe of the wilderness, determined, willful, and strong. She was raised without a lot of boundaries in a family that let her know she could do anything she set her mind to.

The family watchword was *frugality*, fully at odds with Tara's love of material things. She yearned for loftier things than the limited, practical wares that made good sense to the locals. Dusty was a thrifty man who actually enjoyed collecting empty cans and bottles, which he cashed in for the deposit money, alongside highways and in Dumpsters on his drive to and from his job at the air-force base.

"And he'd brag that he bought the last round of groceries with that money," recalls one family friend.

For all the love Tara had for her father, the two strong-willed Destrampes were never shy about waging a little domestic war.

"Dusty was a bad-tempered man, quick with an expletive but deeply in love with his wife and two daughters," Jennifer says. "Tara would tell Dusty to fuck off. I'd hear them talking to each other and she'd let the f-bombs fly and I couldn't believe it—I could never talk to my father like that."

Yet for all her harsh words, Tara always left people with the impression that she cared about them. Even though she would frequently befriend someone and then go without much contact for years, she was always known for touching people emotionally.

A note from Tara to Melissa in their senior-year yearbook—Class of 1990—reads: "Remember I will always be there for you no matter how far apart we may be. Take care of yourself and have a fabulous life. Love you! (Terrible)—remember."

———

Terrible. Terror. Those were Tara's nicknames and she earned them for the force with which she ran her world. Smart, verbal, and controlling, Tara was a type A from her youth onward, and that attitude spilled over into her first serious high school relationship with classmate Jamie Hanson. He was head over heels in love with her from the time they hooked up in high school, and the two were an item on and off during the two years she spent at Bay de Noc Community College in Escanaba, and later when both left the area to attend Michigan State University in East Lansing. Their quarrels fed Tara's legend for having a temper.

"Tara was definitely the head of that relationship when they were together," recalls Jennifer Elliott. "And she was hotheaded. She would tear into him."

Tara would unleash her wrath on her boyfriend with no regard as to who was around, on one occasion bursting into Jamie's home, with his parents sitting there, to give him a loud scolding. As these episodes grew to legendary proportions, the Elliotts dubbed her "Terror," a play on her name.

It was not that Tara was unlikable, just that she wanted things to go her way. In high school, she had a group of pals who joined her for drives around the area after she got a used maroon sedan her father helped her buy. They loved to drive the back roads, and sometimes ended up at Camp Ridgerunner, a property owned by Melissa Elliott's now-husband Mark, a police detective.

Melissa and Jennifer lost touch with Tara as high school ended and the world of adult life began. Melissa and Tara would talk on the phone occasionally, and Tara related stories about attending Bay de Noc. And there were more boys.

"She met a guy at the community college," Melissa recalls, "and they started dating." He was quite an operator, it turned out.

He had presented himself as a beginner in the field of romance, and even claimed that he had never dated before. Shortly after their courtship began, however, Tara learned that the boy had fathered a son.

"And she asked us if we thought she should break up with him," Melissa Elliott recalls. "She was a little naive in that way."

———

Tara had a job in high school at the Ranch Steakhouse, a restaurant in Escanaba, which she kept when she enrolled at Bay de Noc, where she completed two years of undergraduate courses. She also worked in the men's department at the Fair, a small clothing shop in the heart of Escanaba.

Escanaba sits on the shores of Little Bay de Noc, a thirty-thousand-acre haven of fishing, where walleye, bass, and perch are plentiful in the chilly waters that open onto Lake Michigan. Downtown Escanaba, once the center of action, was a fading beauty in the early eighties. The former lumber town had been a commerce center for points north in its 1800s heyday, but it had now settled into an archetypal small town of thirteen thousand, with some small mom-and-pop motels, the Delta Plaza Mall, anchored by a JC Penney, and a healthy dollop of bars, for the nights get very cold in upper Michigan and natives are known to pass the time with a shot or six when things get a little dull.

In the middle of Escanaba's main drag, Ludington Street, sat Manning's Shoe and Ski Shop, something of a landmark in the small town. A family-owned business for 113 years, in early 1992 it was mostly run by Pat Manning, son of Jack Manning, who had taken the business over from his father.

One afternoon Pat and his wife walked into the Fair to browse its upscale line and were waited on by a cheerful, obviously well-informed Tara. It took no more than a few minutes with the bubbly girl for Pat to know that he could use some of her good-humored help at Manning's.

"She was very energetic and stood out, and we were looking for good personalities," Manning recalls. He asked her if she would consider a job change. "She was the type we wanted."

Tara showed up the next day at his store, still wearing her Ranch Steakhouse uniform, to ask further about the job.

"She was so interested that she didn't even take time to drive home and change, just came in and asked. She was more than interested, and nothing was going to stop her. We paid better than minimum wage and we had a computer system and the employees worked hard and learned a lot. We gave them plenty of responsibility."

Tara quickly fit in with the rest of the employees and latched onto a group of older girls who worked there. "It was like they were working in the heart of fashion, at least for this part of the state," Pat says. "These girls became good friends and trained each other."

"The first thing I saw was the smile," former coworker and friend Amy Sabourin remembers. Two years older than Tara, Amy had immediately been taken with the younger girl's charm.

"Then it was the hair. You couldn't miss either of those. But it was also her outgoing nature. She made me feel very at ease right away. She was so confident. I couldn't help but love her."

During slow times at work, the two got to know each other.

"I felt like a big sister to her," Amy says. "We always talked at work and she talked about her dreams and I coached her about her schooling.

"She was always looking for counsel. She talked about what she wanted to be and the things she liked. She always knew—even then."

Yet despite her chattiness, Tara revealed little about herself. As much as she and Amy talked, and spent time together, they never got really deep.

"It was strange," Amy now recalls. "You could feel close to her but there weren't a lot of deep conversations."

In fact, most of their conversations, as is often the case with teenage girls, were about boys. Jamie Hanson was her on-and-off boyfriend, Tara told her.

"He was a really nice guy, a local farm kid and very

good-looking," Amy says. Tara explained that they had been together for a long time, but that she wasn't looking to settle down. "She let me know that she was looking for more."

A string of employees came through Manning's during Tara's days there, and most of them were captivated by the ambitious young lady who was obviously going places.

Tara was "unforgettable," says Jane Veeser, who also worked alongside her. She and Tara, of course, had talked about boys.

"I was just out of the high school," Veeser says. "She was dating one of the guys I had known there."

Tara also told Veeser about her on-again, off-again romance with high school sweetheart Hanson. "I don't recall them being an item, but more of an issue," Veeser said. "She seemed like she was on to bigger things. I would have never expected her to stay in Escanaba. That was not her personality."

And as for guys—she liked them a little wild, Veeser says.

"She was not going to end up with a boring guy."

That fall of 1992, Amy was planning her wedding to Todd Sabourin, a local boy, and she asked Tara, who was now downstate at Michigan State University, to be a bridesmaid.

"I wanted her to be in my wedding," Amy says.

Held in April 1993, the wedding was a beautiful event, and Tara looked striking in a deep purple dress. Her corkscrew hair was pulled up and piled on her head, with wispy curls dangling down on either side of her face, and she wore a small gold locket around her neck.

Also part of the wedding party was Todd's brother Scott. Although Tara and Scott had never actually met,

Tara had caught his eye back when she was a cheerleader at Mid Peninsula School and he was an athlete at Bark River, a Mid Pen rival.

As with Amy, it was Tara's smile and energy that captivated Scott. They made a connection and began dating when Tara came home from college.

Scott Sabourin visited Tara at her home in Perkins and she proved quite a match as they competed in shooting at a makeshift range she had constructed with Dusty.

"Her parents owned a barn there and she was very into shooting," Sabourin recalls. "She was very proud of the way she could shoot. She had a competition rifle and was a very good markswoman. I wasn't as good as she. She had a little shooting range set up at the back of the property. We shot at targets. When she first told me how well she could shoot, I disregarded it and made it playful, like 'I am better,' but she made me eat my words in the long run."

The summer courtship had gone well, but in August, Scott went to Western Michigan University in Kalamazoo. Tara, meanwhile, was back to Michigan State for her senior year. They both tried to bridge the eighty miles between the two colleges, with Sabourin visiting MSU as often as he could. When he did, Tara would don some "spirit" attire, something in the MSU colors of green and white, and take him to Spartan football games.

"We just kind of hung out, went to the movies, walked to some places to eat," he recalls. "She came to visit me at Western and we'd go out to the bar at night. She liked to dance and we went to Rick's Café in East Lansing, the Knollwood Tavern in Kalamazoo. We hung out for about six months."

Tara was always interested in business, while Scott, practical and analytical, was more interested in science.

At college, he studied paper science and engineering, while she focused on marketing.

But their future plans didn't jibe—Sabourin was planning on returning to the Upper Peninsula—and it became increasingly difficult for the couple to maintain their long-distance relationship. Both were living on college-student budgets and neither had the most reliable of transportation. With school and work schedules, not to mention the cost of gas, "It got to the point where it wouldn't work anymore and we lost contact after that," Scott says.

It was clear even at that point in her life that Tara was a climber with no intention of returning to the Upper Peninsula permanently or letting anything stand in her way.

Pat Manning takes credit for having persuaded Tara to check out MSU in the first place. She had visited every summer in her 4-H days to deliver and pick up animals at the university, and those were forays into civilization, as far as Tara was concerned. Now MSU could be her home.

It was founded in 1855 as a land-grant college, which focused its curriculums on agriculture, engineering, and home economics. It is now regarded as a top institution, jammed with liberal-arts classes and a strong business school.

"I know that she wanted to be a businesswoman, and I twisted her arm a bit," says Manning, himself an MSU alum. "She had taken 4-H trips down there but I told her it was a good school as well. For many kids up here, it's easy to feel buried when you get away from here and go to a place like MSU. Tara was wide-eyed, no doubt, when she went there. When you grow up shooting a twenty-two and farming, you have a lot of catching up to do."

Which is exactly what Tara did. Upon arriving in the fall of 1992, she immediately became friends with her roommate, Christine Willis, at Abbott Hall, one of the older dorms on campus, complete with steam heat, an ivy-strewn exterior, and a stand of thick oaks out front.

Christine, a senior finishing her degree in art history, had also grown up in a farming family—she was from the small town of Bellevue, in the southern part of the state—and with their similar backgrounds, they quickly bonded. Soon Tara found herself rushing at Sigma Alpha, an agriculture sorority that Christine belonged to.

Tara also ran into someone else with whom she had something in common: Jamie Hanson, the boy from home who never seemed to be far from Tara. Jamie had become a resident assistant on the men's side of Abbott Hall. He was ROTC, preparing to serve in the military, and, in the interim after graduation, to move back home.

As always with Tara, much of her talk with Christine was about boys.

"She still had feelings for [Jamie] then," Willis says. "They were still friends. I always thought there was more to that and she had deep feelings for him. I thought they would end up being married."

Oddly, though, Willis notes, Tara never spoke of a dream of matrimony. For all of her interest in men, she never mentioned getting married or having children, a cornerstone of grown-up life to many.

Tara continued to explore her dating options. She hung out with another guy on campus at the time, a good friend of a girl who lived next to her in the dorm. But it was nothing serious.

As her relationships with Jamie Hanson and Scott Sabourin faded, college life was becoming more about the studies than anything else. She took a part-time job at a local Limited clothing store, but found that even those few hours hampered her studies. She stayed in more than the average student, the bars of the town's main drag, Grand River Avenue, offering her little.

"We went out, but not every night, mainly on weekends," Willis says. "She wanted to do well in school and thought a lot of her father. She didn't want him to be disappointed in her."

Always in the back of her mind, what her dad thought was key.

"She would always talk a lot about him and everything, in the choices she made. If she thought it wasn't right, she would say, 'What would my father say?'"

Christine Willis graduated that May of 1993 and left for her own adventures. She and Tara kept in touch sparingly for about a year and then lost track of each other. Tara, Christine said, did not keep many ties to the university. While some members of their sorority updated their personal information on the sorority's Web site as a way to stay in touch, Tara did not.

By the end of 1993, Tara was well on her way to a degree in business administration. Nothing could stop her now, and she was thinking that she maybe needed to expand her horizons in terms of men. Perhaps someone a little more worldly. After all, there she was at a Big Ten university, full of young men with a degree of worldliness that she had not yet experienced.

CHAPTER 4

As college towns go, East Lansing, Michigan, is easy to get around in and filled with students who ride bikes, toss Frisbees, and walk from dorms to classrooms in an easy flow. The town is a safety net for those not yet ready to make their move into a grown-up world.

Adjacent to Lansing, the Michigan state capital, "EL" (as East Lansing is affectionately referred to by locals) provides enough cheap beer and eats to sate restless students who prowl Grand River Avenue, the main drag, in search of coffee and connections. While the university's campus sprawls across farmland and boasts more than forty thousand students, it is friendly, casual, and quintessentially Midwestern. Students there embrace academics but never forget how to have a good time, whether cheering on the Spartans on a beer-infused football Saturday or at local watering holes. Here was the place where both Steve and Tara forged their independence and got to know themselves.

Summer is when East Lansing is at its relaxed best. Rent

is cheap and most kids are working jobs and partying. It was in the summer of 1994 that Tara Destrampe, deeply involved in wrapping up her business-administration studies and fully focused on her academic aspirations, met Stephen Grant through her roommates.

Steve had moved out of an apartment he'd shared the previous nine months with some friends, and was living in a small complex called the Oaks with two female friends, while Tara was living in a student settlement called Cedar Village with one of Steve's old roommates and another friend.

Some evenings the whole crew, including Steve and Tara, would hit the local watering holes.

While Steve was instantly attracted to the petite, assertive farm girl, Tara did not initially share the same feelings for the talkative, boastful boy from Detroit. Steve liked Tara's moxie, her big hair, her fresh-faced UP innocence. But his cocksure, know-it-all persona, his city skills, put her off at first, and when he asked her out, she turned him down. He was much too different from the small-town guys she'd grown up with, and too far outside her comfort zone. She was used to being the one in charge of her personal relationships.

"She didn't want to go out, but we did like to talk to each other," Steve recalls. "We would always talk about Detroit. She said it was all one big ghetto and I'd tell her that there were some good places."

Steve's then job in the office of State Senator Jack Faxon, though, was enticing to Tara, planting the idea that there might be more to Grant than met the eye, that he might provide entrée into the more upscale political life and have some credibility beyond his blue-collar background. And he often talked of his aspiration to become a lawyer. Maybe Steve was a guy who finally had it together and was pointed toward a goal.

Whereas Tara was lukewarm on the idea of a relationship, Steve was persistent. He was not someone who liked to hear no. He was sure she was the right girl for him and he let it be known that he was not backing off.

One of her excuses for not going out with him was her on-again, off-again relationship with Jamie Hanson.

"This is what she told me, but I just wanted to go out with her," Steve says. "I was asking her to just give me a chance."

Tara was flattered by Steve's attention and desire, even if others viewed it as cloddish. And she was intrigued by his possibilities and by the fact that he was a guy who sought a life outside his own upbringing—similar to Tara's own hopes.

Finally, she allowed a date.

"I gave her a tour [of Detroit], to let her know there were some nice parts," Steve says. "We went down I-696 all the way to Lakeshore Drive, down through Grosse Point and all the mansions. Then we got down to Jefferson and had lunch at Fishbone's in Greektown. Then we went to the Detroit Institute of Arts."

It was a beautiful day, Steve recalls, enough to earn him another date. They went to a small bar and eatery in a Lansing suburb. Again, they had a nice time.

The tipping point in his quest for her affections came, unexpectedly enough, several weeks later at the funeral for Tara's paternal grandmother, Mary Jane Destrampe. Even though at the time Tara was again seeing Jamie Hanson, Steve appeared unannounced at the Crawford Funeral Home in Escanaba, having driven six hours from Lansing to be there.

"I felt it was the right thing to do, I really cared about her already," Steve says. "I called her when I got to town and told her I was there. She was surprised."

His presence created quite a scene in the small, close-knit town. Who was this outsider who entered their world at such a sad time? What about his fancy sports car, a 1985 Mazda RX-7, which garnered attention in those parts just by driving down the street? Shouldn't someone know who he was? They didn't.

It was a surprise not only to Tara, but also to her family. None of them had ever met Steve—had no clue really as to who he was—and greeted him tentatively as he muscled his way in to pay his respects and show his devotion to Tara.

"It was awkward," Steve said. "But it wasn't terrible."

He said he went to dinner with the family, "but I felt really out of place. So I drove back to Lansing. The next day, Tara called me and told me she was in love with me."

"He came and introduced himself as her boyfriend," Alicia would later say. "That was [at the funeral] for my father's mother, and I think all I even knew about him at the time was that Tara had just started dating someone at State."

The grand gesture, while hardly endearing to most of those gathered, had thrilled Tara, who dreamed of living life large and being swept away from the small-town world of her youth. She ended things with Jamie Hanson that very night, and officially placed her faith in Steve, heading back to campus to pick up with her brash new suitor.

It was more dramatic than that to some.

"Tara broke up with Jamie almost in front of everyone," recalls Melissa Elliott, Tara's childhood friend, who was present at the service. "She was there from MSU with

Jamie and Steve drove up and he comforted her—with Jamie right there."

Returning to East Lansing, Tara and Steve were wildly happy in their newfound bliss, a relationship that quickly turned domestic. The two got an apartment in Okemos, a suburb to the east of Lansing; they split it with another friend, though Steve and Tara shared one bedroom. A few months later, Steve proposed to Tara on the steps of the Detroit Museum of Art, not long after she graduated in December 1994. She said yes.

Early in 1995, leaving behind MSU, they moved to the Detroit suburbs, close to where Steve had grown up. Steve's job prospects had dried up, and when his father offered him a job with a good salary, he felt he had to take it.

"The job in Jack's office was gone, but I had another offer, but it was only for twenty-four thousand a year," Steve says. "But my dad called me and offered me eight thousand more a year. We had to take it."

Tara had balked at first at the idea of moving to Detroit, but Steve persuaded her once again to abandon her small-town way of thinking. Seeking to appeal to her growing curiosity for the world outside the UP, he assured her that his area of town, about twenty miles north of the city center in the coveted suburbs, was far removed from the bad stuff in downtown. She went along with the idea, appreciating that the town was miles away from the staid life of her childhood and could be a place to launch herself into the world of business. She was eager to find real, meaningful work.

They moved to an apartment in Auburn Hills, a prosperous Detroit suburb, where upscale meets blue collar on the way to the top. Located just a minute off of the main artery of Interstate 75, which bisects Oakland County, the complex was a good start for the couple. With a population of around seventeen thousand people at the time, the area was caught up in an upturn in the region's economy and it would grow 20 percent in the nineties. In addition to being home to a number of auto-related companies, including the U.S. headquarters for both Chrysler and Volkswagen, the area was also host to a number of engineering, technical, and educational-services companies, giving it an economic diversity that was rare in the state.

The move was upscale, to be sure, and while Steve and Tara were living in an apartment complex, it was far different from the college-town dwellings they had just come from. Almost everyone in the development was a professional. Tara was impressed, and eager to become one of them.

Tara began a job as a Kelly Girl at an established engineering firm in Troy called Morrison-Knudsen, which soon became Washington Group International. Although she was inexperienced, her coworkers quickly took notice of her potential. She was focused and determined, a natural-born leader, which caught the eye of management, then in need of some skilled help in writing proposals. Pretty soon Tara had moved into a full-time job with increasing responsibilities—finally in the spotlight and on track for the career in business she'd always dreamed of. She was eager to learn and fit into the corporate culture. It didn't hurt that she was vibrant and pretty.

It was a solid job with decent pay and provided Tara with plenty of room to grow.

In one inside corporate assessment, Tara was deemed an employee who was "quick on her feet, decisive, able to hold her ground, able to take circumstances into account and act on them quickly."

But while Tara's new life as a professional was charmed, Steve had joined his father at the small tool-and-die shop in Mt. Clemens, where he toiled in grimy obscurity, albeit for decent wage.

Stephen and Tara married on September 28, 1996, at Bethany Lutheran Church in Escanaba in front of one hundred people. Tara's maid of honor was her sister, Alicia, and Steve's best man was his college pal Bryan Rellinger. The wedding announcement that ran in the Escanaba newspaper stated that Steve had graduated from Michigan State University in 1993, although he was, in fact, twenty credits shy of his bachelor's degree.

The wedding itself was a little confusing to some of those in Tara's family. The party dressed in burgundy, but many at the event were seeing red. Frankly put, Steve appeared to be a mismatch for Tara's strong-willed personality. He seemed ill at ease, talking nonstop and giving orders like a drill sergeant. To the laid-back northerners, he was a classic downstater in the same way some Southerners view Yankees. To others, he appeared a somewhat worldly guy with the gift of gab.

"He was a jerk," says Amy Sabourin, who was Tara's bridesmaid, as Tara had been hers in 1993. "He was very outgoing, but I wasn't used to confrontation. You would think that at a wedding everything and everybody would be nice, but I was not happy with it. I would have slapped him, but no one else seemed to think giving orders was out of the ordinary."

Kelly Utykanski, Steve's sister and also a member of the wedding party, remembers things differently. She says the wedding came off smoothly.

"We enjoyed ourselves; it was a nice wedding," she recalls. "My dad and I were there and it was just fine."

It appeared that there was a divide as to what was considered appropriate behavior. And it got worse as the day progressed.

Amy recalls that after the ceremony, "Tara and Steve were going to come back up the aisle [for a receiving line] and we were in the back and couldn't get Tara's train buttoned up. Steve was freaking out and it was already tense and he was making things tough—he was at the back of the church screaming at us, telling us we had to get her skirt up and one of our nails ripped and he was yelling. My husband and I, it was the first time we had met him and we would look at each other as if 'what's going on?' We didn't know anyone at the wedding besides Tara and Alicia. We couldn't figure out why he would act like that, so bossy."

Whatever it was that led Steve to come undone at the end of a long day, Amy didn't like his tone, his moodiness, or his making the precious moment into a crisis about his own needs rather than those of his new bride.

After a honeymoon on the Gulf Coast of Alabama, the newlyweds settled into married life in their Auburn Hills apartment. Tara was already moving up in her job, and she was marked by her employer as an achiever.

The following July Fourth, ten months after their wedding, the couple returned to Escanaba, and some of Tara's childhood friends got to meet Steve. Again, he left a poor impression on the locals.

"I thought he acted like he came from money," says Melissa Elliott, who had not attended her former best friend's wedding the previous year. "He was uppity and I thought she could do better."

Tara, however, seemed happy with her choice, so her friends wrote off his repellant behavior in the hope that she knew what she was doing.

He was seen as an outsider, someone who had taken Tara away, even though it was Tara who had elected to get out of the UP in the first place.

When Tara and Steve returned later in the year for Alicia's wedding, it was evident that Tara had changed, shedding virtually all of her UP sensibility.

"Tara was laying it on thick, talking about what she had done, what she was buying, and the car they had, which I don't even remember," Melissa's sister Jennifer Elliott recalls. "She wanted to impress people, it was very obvious."

Melissa concurs: "It seemed like a competition when I talked to her this time, as if she was trying to be better than everyone else, with all the money she told us she was making. I was perfectly content with my life and it didn't seem worthwhile to talk to her about this stuff."

Recalling a trip to Florida that she and Tara had made in 1993, Melissa says, "We would go to the tourist shops and look at sunglasses, but all she cared about was the label on the glasses, not what they looked like. This was Tara."

———

In late 1995, Steve picked up the phone just as he had reached out to Pam, his former workmate at Faxon's office, a year before, and tried to plug into a happy memory of the past.

"Do you remember me?" he asked. On the other end of the line, a high school mate who hadn't even thought of Steve in years considered the voice. It was higher pitched than average, a bit assertive.

"Yes, I do. How are you, Steve?" Paul Buss answered. After high school graduation in 1988, Paul had gone into the navy and then come home to Macomb County with a very marketable skill in electronics. Along the way, he had married his high school sweetheart, Becky.

"Congratulations on your daughter," Steve said. "I heard about it. I'll bet you didn't know I still followed our class."

The conversation was the catalyst for a renewed friendship. Once again, Steve had reached out to someone from his past. His social skills, while still a bit prickly, were astute and convivial. Steve made friends easily, and Paul was happy to be back in touch with him. Steve invited Paul and Becky over, and upon seeing Tara, Paul was instantly impressed.

"She was very beautiful, and I had to look twice to see that Steve was with her," he says. "We went to their apartment in Auburn Hills, and she was very cordial and doting on him."

Tara showed the Busses the new furniture they had bought, and later, Steve cooked some dinner. It was obvious to Paul that Steve had fared well, despite his sometimes abrasive nature. The newlyweds complemented each other beautifully, Paul said to Becky on the way home after this meeting. "We talked about how perfect they seemed together, the way they got along. Tara was so easy to talk to, and the whole time with them was very easygoing."

After that, the couples would meet monthly for some function or another, perhaps a wine tasting or maybe just Paul and Steve going to the North American International Auto Show at Cobo Center in downtown Detroit.

One year, Steve threw a surprise party for Tara's birthday and the Busses were among the fifteen or so invited guests. They showed up an hour early, misunderstanding the time of arrival. Steve was flawless in his handling of this mishap.

"Hi, good to see you," he said, looking absolutely perplexed at the couple as Tara stood behind him. "What are you doing here?"

If Tara deduced that a surprise party had just been messed up, she never showed it. Steve's innate acting skill had paid off again.

———

By 1997, the Grants were ready to move into their first house. They had banked some money and needed some more space for their growing number of possessions.

Their new home was a two-bedroom single-story house of reddish brick in the suburb of Utica, a starter home in the classic sense, with a huge oak tree in the front yard. The small neighborhood they chose was filled with quarter-acre lots and had been built in the mid-1950s, with single-car garages and no sidewalks.

Most of their neighbors were elderly couples and the Grants' arrival was welcomed by one of the few younger couples on the block, Jim and Diane Harrington.

"We got to know them shortly after they first moved in because they were next-door neighbors . . . [Tara] always had something nice to say, she was always able to be funny, and she was just beautiful," Jim Harrington recalls. The two couples became fast friends, despite the Harringtons' initial dislike for Steve. It was all that talking he did, they would say to each other, and how he seemed to have an opinion on everything.

Steve made sure that the Harringtons knew he had worked for Jack Faxon, that he had graduated from

Michigan State, and that he had gone to work at USG Babbitt as a favor to his father in order to help save the business.

"I believe him to be one of the most arrogant people I've ever met," Jim states. "He was sure of himself at all times; regardless of what he was working on, he assumed he was doing it better than anyone else could, and anyone who disagreed with him was just wrong."

Steve was an adept handyman, having grown up around tools and influenced heavily by his father's do-it-yourself ethic.

"Steve took care of property values. He made some great improvements on that house, which was nasty to begin with," Diane says. "It was run-down, had paper bags stretched over the windows. He put in French doors, added a deck on the back. And converted that garage."

In that spirit, Grant set about turning the garage into a master bedroom, which would free up the other two bedrooms for guests, office space, or whatever else they needed.

Steve was beaming when he finished, and the job he'd done on the new room looked quite professional. Yet as he tended to do, he'd overlooked the formalities and had failed to get the necessary permits from the township. It would later cause the couple trouble, but for now, the new homeowners were proud.

When Jim set about putting a deck on the back of his own house, Steve was ready to take charge. "He thoroughly pissed off my father-in-law, who was an engineer for years at GM, when Steve was directing him how to lay decking."

But at the same time, Grant could be a generous and kind soul, Jim found. When Al, Steve's dad, came over to work on a soapbox-derby car, a hobby he had picked up over the years, Steve asked if Jim's seven-year-old son, Jonathan, would like to race in the annual Mt. Clemens Grand Prix, an autumn event. USG Babbitt would sponsor the car, he said. All Jonathan had to do was drive it.

"He would go and pick up Jonathan from school and take him over to the shop to do some trial runs with the car," Diane Harrington says. "He was really good with kids, and he seemed to genuinely enjoy them."

And it was clear that Tara adored Steve.

"Steve is the smartest man I have ever met," Tara told Jim one day as the two were making small talk in the Grants' driveway. Harrington later shook his head over that one.

Tara taught Diane how to plant perennials and "that a chick can look good wearing a baseball cap, because she sure did.

"And the meals we had! We would go over there and Steve would cook—he was a great cook—and he was the kind of guy who always had the best wine, the best beer, the best ingredients."

The Grants had money, or so it appeared. Shortly after moving into the house on Cardinal, they bought a Mazda Miata for Tara. They had no children—although were now speaking of family plans to friends and relatives—and Tara's increasing workload also meant more income.

By the time the couples sat down in February 1998 to watch the Super Bowl at the Grants', Jim was wondering, "How did this dude get with this fantastic woman and get into this kind of life?

"Steve did far better than he should ever have done," he says. "She was beautiful and intelligent. I could not understand what she saw in him—but I would never have asked that."

The two couples lost touch when the Harringtons

moved away in the spring of 1999, although they touched base a few months later, when Tara and Steve invited them along to a fancy charity event.

"The Garden Party is, if not the charity do of the season, arguably the best fed," one local society magazine in Detroit crows. It was perfect for the upwardly mobile Tara and Steve. Tara had scored four tickets from Washington Group, which generally run $150 apiece, and while the Harringtons were more of a beer-drinking kind of couple, they went because, well, it was the Grants who'd asked them.

It was a boiling June 6, a Sunday that was made for drinking, as it turned out. All four of them got drunk on the generous wine pours, Diane recalls, and it was one of the best times the two couples ever had together.

"We all got 'schnockered,' then went to someone else's place, who Steve and Tara knew, and they made margaritas, then back to our house," recalls Diane. "It was one of the most wonderful memories I have of Tara, just great conversation all day. And it was the last time we got together."

Diane also recognizes this as the day she realized that Tara was attracted to Steve's penchant for bypassing the law. Steve's confidence in himself, his ability to get away with things, like speeding, or circumventing the township ordinances for building, were ingrained and they made him appear, to Tara, a bit dangerous. And she was obviously drawn to his risk taking.

"Steve had that little mischievous, 'I'm going to break the rules' thing going for him. While the other three of us were more, I don't know, kind of redneck in some way. Not that he thought he was better than us, but he just had an interesting manner and approach. Even that day, I mean, someone had to drive. And that was Steve. He would do that."

———

Tara gave birth to daughter Lindsey in November 2000, as the couple considered a move to a bigger house. For a time, the home on Cardinal had served them well, thanks to the additional bedroom. By now, Tara's family had firm opinions about Steve; some, including Tara's mother, admired his handyman skills, his embrace of family, and his chatty demeanor, while others were put off by his boisterousness.

"He manipulated people to think a certain way of him," says Carla Lanaville, Tara's aunt on her mother's side. She and her husband, Rod, initially visited the Grant family early on in their marriage, but halted the visits as the years passed, primarily because she didn't like dealing with Steve.

"We saw early on that he was manipulative, but we never told Tara what we thought. It sure wasn't the same way she saw him. He doted on her excessively. And with her, the way she was, she thought it was special."

There is no doubt that Steve also thought Tara very special. Five years into their marriage, they had a healthy daughter, and Tara was earning a salary that kept them both in new cars, good food, and some exotic trips abroad. Steve was one lucky guy who had married well. Where would he be without Tara?

CHAPTER 5

The house on Westridge represented a new life for the Grants. Its price tag of $242,000 meant they were moving up. But not everyone thought it was an improvement.

When Tara drove back to Perkins for a visit in 2000, her aspirations to luxury living and an executive lifestyle were apparent to her old friends. And they didn't like what they were seeing.

By then the relationship between Tara and her old friend Melissa Elliott was cordial but hardly approximated the closeness the two had shared in their teenage years. Melissa was happy in her Up North world, while "Tara had changed in ways that we could never understand." Now Tara was an executive in Detroit, with a much-stamped passport.

"A lot of us who knew her could not believe she chose that kind of life," Melissa says. But in some ways, she was still the same.

"I went over to Alicia's to see Tara and she was making a salad, and there were grapes involved. And Tara was the same in one way—she was checking each grape to make sure it was a good grape. Examining it."

Tara's tastes had changed as well, adds Jennifer Elliott, another high school pal.

"I was surprised to find out that she knew about wines, for example. Tara was already materialistic. I think when they first got together . . . she believed that Steve had some money."

That was a notion Steve cultivated, driven in part by fantasy, in part by feelings of inadequacy, his friends say.

He always gave the impression of having money, and that working for his dad paid pretty well. A listing for USG Babbitt notes that while the business had excellent credit, it also had two employees and annual sales of less than $500,000.

So it was Tara's money that went a long way toward the new house on Westridge in the upscale suburbs of northern Macomb County, in Washington Township.

The township sits on land that was once primarily agricultural, gently sloping hills with apple and peach orchards framing the landscape. But despite earlier charms, development has destroyed much of the area's natural beauty, with five-thousand-square-foot houses carrying $1-million-and-up price tags, many situated behind the red-brick walls of gated communities.

At the same time, the residents espouse the Midwest kindness and goodwill that makes the region such a draw. That familiarity, generosity, and willingness to reach out has touched many a hard-hearted city dweller, and it's no surprise that Steve was willing to stick around the area in which he grew up.

Adding to the township's allure for the Grants was the 4,500-acre Stony Creek Metropark, a rolling, heavily forested swath of land with bike and running trails, a nature center, an eighteen-hole golf course, a five-hundred-acre man-made lake, and plenty of room to roam. In the summer, it was a boating center, and in the winter, kids would hit the hills with snowboards and sleds.

The Grant home was just a few blocks off 28 Mile Road, which, to the west, ran right through the northern reaches of the park.

Steve and Tara closed on the Westridge house on March 15, 2001. They launched their lives in the former orchard turned three-hundred-home settlement, and threw themselves into community life, both serving on the Carriage Hills subdivision board. Steve eventually became president of the group, while Tara's work schedule and travel precluded her from continuing.

As head of the board, "You could see he had a kind of short fuse," says one former neighbor who was part of the group. "He got frustrated and took the job pretty seriously. But in those situations, such as a disagreement in a public place, people can keep control of themselves. And he did."

The Grants fit in well with the other families in the subdivision, though many of them were older couples who had left Detroit when its urban ailments became too dangerous for them to weather. "Most of the folks here come from the east side of Detroit or some other parts of Macomb that were growing too quickly," says Frank Perna, who was one of the first to build in Carriage Hills back in 1972. At first, the development attracted middle-management types from the auto companies, including designers and a few line workers. By the time Steve and Tara arrived, neighbors included established doctors, lawyers, and executives. Tara was delighted to be in that kind of company.

The Grants had their second child, Ian, in November 2002. He was, like Lindsey, healthy except for a slight heart murmur. Once again, the Grants were blessed. Meanwhile, Tara had worked as hard as anyone could in order to get to the top and she was fast approaching it. Her salary was nearing the six-figure mark—it would eventually reach nearly $170,000—and although she was traveling, she was able to take Steve along on occasion. The two were seeing the world, but with children, it was starting to become a little burdensome. Things would have to change, they decided. More time at home, more devotion to the family unit.

Steve, for his part, knew he would be delegated to a supporting role. And nothing drove this home more than his seventeen-mile commute to USG Babbitt. The drive took him from his new, esteemed neighborhood into the heart of industrial Macomb County, blasting down Van Dyke Road, onto the suburban autobahn that is Hall Road, and onto Groesbeck Highway. If the rest of the county was growing up and sprouting dollar signs—and it was—Groesbeck, where his father still lived, was part of yesteryear, an area jammed with tool-and-die shops, liquor stores, fly-by-night motels, repo joints, and greasy spoons, places with names like American Production, the Flamingo Motel, Masonic Auto Electric, and Fairlane Tool. Every morning, Steve motored past the Du Pont plant that provided paint to the auto industry, and, on his right, the 1,450-bed Macomb County Jail.

USG sat at the end of a short street off Groesbeck in an industrial den of the old-school variety—it was one of several businesses in a battleship-gray cinder-block building. USG was about 1,600 square feet, with bay doors on each side and a railroad track about fifteen yards behind it.

It was a labor of defeat, both the drive and the work. After seeing his wife off to a week of business in Russia, Germany, England, or some other exotic locale, Grant would report to work at 8:30 A.M. at the dingy shop in a crummy part of town.

It was not simple work, and it took some strong technical skills. But it was not what Steve had dreamed of.

———

"Wherever her job required, she would go," is how Tara's sister, Alicia, described Tara's fealty to her job. Tara was a dedicated employee of the Washington Group, Alicia said, and would do whatever was necessary to deliver.

From the start, Steve was unhappy about being left alone. He told his friends, quite simply, that he missed his wife.

In 2003, the Grants contracted for their first au pair, a decision that allowed Steve to both work and also have some free time without having to ferry the kids back and forth to school, medical appointments, or wherever else they needed to be.

But the Grants had a hard time keeping the au pairs. Some stayed for weeks, some for months, their names running together, Stephanie, Victoria, Lonnie. Some got to the United States and partied too much, others weren't up to the rigors of the work. The Grants had seven au pairs in all, though they still felt it was cheaper than day care. It was a system that worked, at least for the time being. Maybe sometime soon, Tara would cut down on the travel; but her driven nature would not allow it.

When Tara was home, the Grants were as tight as any family unit could be. Tara would take Lindsey for manicures, while Steve took Ian and ran errands to the bank, the grocery store, the Nino Salvaggio International Marketplace (an upscale market that rivaled Whole Foods for fresh, gourmet foods), where he could score some ingredients for a home-cooked meal. Steve loved to cook—"one of my favorite hobbies," he says—and the new home had a large kitchen.

"He was a great cook, and we looked forward to going over there for dinner," says Paul Buss, Steve's friend from high school who, with his wife, Becky, often visited the Grant home. "He would whip up these off-the-wall recipes with mushrooms that I had never heard of and vegetables that I didn't know existed."

The couples, often with their children, sometimes headed to downtown Detroit for a meal at the Soup Kitchen on Franklin Street, or maybe to a local trade show—boats, cars, camping gear, it didn't really matter.

"Steve was really into his family. We talked about family and kids and he was so good with kids," Buss says.

The one thing that he never talked about, though, Buss notes, was his work at USG Babbitt.

One day in December 2003, Steve walked into the post office a couple miles from his house and ran into his old friend Martha Anaud* from their childhood neighborhood. She was now married with two children, and an

*Denotes pseudonym.

executive at a Web development company in Royal Oak, a couple of suburbs away.

Like Tara's, Martha's career was playing a big part in her life. After graduating from Michigan State University, she had spent several years in Washington, D.C., working for a Democratic congressman. Like Steve, Martha's husband, Tim,* also coached soccer, and he traveled frequently in his position as a Web consultant. And their children were the same age.

It was enough to launch a full-on family relationship. The couples started getting together every couple of months, usually with all the children present. "Steve was coaching soccer, and he had practices on Wednesday and Thursday afternoons," Martha says, "and it worked into our schedule so that we could put our daughter on his team."

The Anauds were sending their daughter to Krambrook-Griffin Academy, a seventy-student private school in the township that accepted kids from early childhood through eighth grade. In the fall of 2004, the Grants moved Lindsey and Ian to the academy, which had a tuition fee of around $6,300 a year.

The Grants were nothing if not doting parents, essentially, it seemed, tripping over themselves to ensure that Lindsey and Ian had the best upbringing possible.

"Tara and I would volunteer for field trips and class parties and she was very involved when she would return from her business trips," Martha says.

The Grants moved Lindsey into Indian Hills Elementary in the Romeo School District when she reached kindergarten, though, not so much to save money but to ensure that she was around a more diverse group of kids and had access to the organized sports she would inevitably want to play. It meant a daily school-bus trip, and

Steve dutifully walked her to the bus at the mouth of the Carriage Hills subdivision. He was the only dad among the mothers there, who discussed among themselves what a strange sight it was to see this tall, youngish-looking man in their midst. If he minded, Steve never said a word to anyone.

The Anauds thought they had lost the Grants to career moves in late 2005, when Washington Group was putting together a construction project with General Motors in Germany. The Grants began telling their friends that they would be moving to Germany so that Tara could be closer to the project, and that Steve might land a job with Washington Group in the move as well.

"They had an apartment and furniture in Germany already," Martha recalls. "Steve was real excited . . . he had taken the lead in getting things set up over there and he was hopeful about working for the Washington Group. They sent out their Christmas cards that said 'this will be our new address in Germany.' "

But the move was scrapped—the planned operation that Tara was to be part of never went through—though Tara continued to commute to the region several times in her capacity as an operations manager. Steve would sometimes go with her, but more often not. And Tara still came home as much as she could to take part in the lives of the kids.

"We would take our girls to get manicures and go ice skating, and all kinds of things," Martha says. "But one thing I did notice: I never spent any time alone with her. It was always with her and Tim and Steve or some of the kids. I don't think she did anything alone. When she was home, it was family time."

In November 2005, Tara went to Phoenix. It was a business trip, but it wasn't related to her job, per se, but rather to a Landmark Forum conference that she hoped would help in her quest to be the best employee she could be. While in Arizona, she would also take some time to visit Steve's mom, who was living about twenty minutes outside of Phoenix.

The Landmark Forum, part of a curriculum from Landmark Education LLC, has endured considerable controversy since it rose from the ashes of the confrontational est awareness seminars of est guru Werner Erhard, from whom Landmark purchased its intellectual basis when it formed in 1991.

But the Forum has persevered and prospered, despite its critics. Tara was sold—and she dutifully prepared with notes written to herself in a spiral notebook.

"Write down specifically what I WANT," she wrote on the plane en route to the seminar. "What do I care about? By answering this above question this is how I authentically market myself and address my career ambition."

Tara returned home invigorated by the Landmark program, so inspired that she inked rare, heartfelt letters to those closest to her, though she never sent them.

She wrote a letter to her parents, declaring her love for Mary and Dusty but calling herself "inauthentic."

"Dad . . . I have greatly suppressed the events and constant verbal abuse you rendered," Tara wrote, and said that the seminar had taught her to forgive and that life has no meaning without the "self." It is a variation on the est teachings, and the seminar clearly had a profound impact on Tara's way of thinking, at least temporarily.

She addressed her mom, telling her that she had harbored resentment against her and it had not allowed what they deserved from their oldest daughter, which was "authentic" love.

Issues about her parents' often-fractious relationship were not fully resolved in her own adult mind. With the opportunity to write her true feelings—to be authentic, as the Forum's script prescribed—she not only let them know that she had been hurt, but that she hoped to turn a corner.

She aimed that same recommitment to honesty at her sister, Alicia, whom, friends felt, Tara often resented because Alicia was more diplomatic and received credit within their family as the "good" daughter who somehow managed to keep the peace.

So in her letter to Alicia, Tara said, "I have always given the illusion that we are close, but I guess in reality that is not accurate. I have in reality spent as much of my life as I can remember in constant competition with you, compared myself to you, and to some extent resenting the fact that I thought I could never be as good as you in the eyes of our parents. This I realize now is a story that I have created, and have spent my time collecting evidence to justify my story."

It was an honesty that showed how confused Tara was in her feelings for others, those whom she was supposed to love but for some reason had been unable to. Tara and Alicia were close in one sense—pictures of the two, smiling, were displayed at the Grant home—but they never shared the intimate bond that typifies so many sister relationships.

Tara closed the note with, "I love you very much and want a genuinely close and sharing relationship with you. I am truly sorry for not sharing this with you sooner. Love, your big sis."

In her transition from closed-off professional to newly open and emotionally available spouse, Tara also penned a missive to her husband, which struck at the imbalance within their relationship. She acknowledged that he had not come first in her life and also referenced a previous relationship in which, for once, she had fully opened her heart, gotten it broken, and therefore had shut herself down, even with Steve.

"I have not been present in much of our marriage," Tara confessed. "I have further invalidated you by always needing to make you wrong, for me to be right, and dominating you to avoid being dominated and in doing so not really loving you at all. These actions have not allowed me to see you and hear you for what you really are . . . someone who loves me unconditionally."

She refers to having her heart broken by a guy named Pete whom she had dated while attending Bay de Noc Community College in the early nineties, a guy who friends noted had been rather immune to her considerable charms.

Tara admitted that she had not given all of herself to the marriage and that she had even pushed Steve away in an effort to avoid being hurt. It was quite a realization to arrive at after almost ten years of marriage and two children.

"The impact of this has essentially been pushing away the one person who has fully committed to me to love me unconditionally," Tara wrote to Steve. "What became very clear to me is that you have been the only committed party in this marriage . . . you have made the efforts to change and I have simply created more stories . . ."

Tara asked that the two renew their wedding vows on their tenth wedding anniversary the following year and pledged to love Steve in a more emotionally open way.

"I love you for the human being you are and for not giving up on me and supporting me in the possibility I have created for myself. Love, Tara."

Tara's letter to Steve also hints at trouble behind the scenes. The loving relationship that had been so admired by their friends and colleagues was perhaps not all that it could be or seemed to be. "For almost as long as we had been married, Tara had told me that I was worthless, that no one else would want me, that she was the best thing that ever happened to me. I believed her," Steve says.

Steve later told friends that Tara's continued obsession with her past, including Pete, had sent them into counseling in 2005. With her letters to Steve, Alicia, and her parents, it was apparent that Tara was trying to reform her controlling ways and release her attachment to the past.

There had also been some bumps in the road for both Steve and Tara's extended families. K. I. Sawyer Air Force Base had closed in September 1995, and Tara's dad, Dusty, took a job at Fort McCoy near LaCrosse, Wisconsin, until he could retire. In 2003, the then-retired Dusty suffered a stroke. In the meantime, Tara's sister and brother-in-law, Alicia and Erik, had moved to Chillicothe, Ohio, where Erik had found a new job.

Alicia "was always trying to make sure things were okay," notes one friend of the family. "There was talk about how to help care for Dusty, and she stepped up and just told [her parents] they should move to Ohio to be near her and Erik. I don't think Tara would have done that."

In February 2006, Patty, the third wife of Steve's father, Al Grant, passed away from a brain aneurysm. It was one more blow to Al, who had also lost his second wife, Peggy, to cancer in 1995.

———

To his few friends, Steve appeared happy with his life, and for the most part, his bent for trouble was abating. But there had been a troubling circumstance in early 2004 that developed into a drama, one in which Steve again may have made difficulties out of something that should have been resolved fairly easily.

Steve had made plenty of improvements on their former house on Cardinal Street, which they'd sold in 2001 to Barbara Horn. The optometrist worked at an eye clinic a half mile from the home, and she and her husband were pleased to find a place so close and for what they considered a bargain.

By January 2004, the Horns were ready to move on and they put the house up for sale. Not so fast, said the Shelby Township inspector who came in to do a preliminary check to ensure that the house was up to code. When Grant converted the garage to a master bedroom, he had failed to obtain the proper permits; therefore Horn could not list the place as a three-bedroom, which was a blow to its sale chances in an area by then selling almost exclusively to growing families.

Horn, sensing a problem, wrote a letter to the Grants and told them of her situation, noting that if they could cover the costs of the code violations, there would be no further issue.

Steve said that he could fix the problems and do the upgrades himself, coming to the house and talking with Horn. But Horn declined his offer. "I told him no, I would get it all done professionally," Horn recalls. "He was very nice and he was looking at the problems and trying to figure it out. He was a little nervous, he stutters quite a bit."

On January 16, Horn filed in small-claims court against

Grant, asking for $2,317 plus costs, and alleging "misrepresentation on seller's disclosure statement and purchase agreement regarding open permits."

But Horn had also not checked to see if there were any open permits when she'd bought the house, instead taking Steve and Tara's word for it.

"He had his lawyer write me back, which is a bad start," Horn says. "He said that he had reviewed the listing history and noted that there is a room conversion listed on there. And they claimed that since we didn't catch it, it wasn't his fault."

The Grants then filed a countersuit, alleging "attempted extortion by Ms. Horn [which] required us to pay for legal services (6 hours) and to miss work to investigate the matter costing us paid time off (two days—1 each, Stephen and Tara)."

A judge ruled in Horn's favor, and on appeal lowered the total to a flat $2,000. Steve's displeasure at the minor defeat was obvious. He refused to pay the whole amount in a lump sum, insisting instead on paying $150 a month for the first three payments, then $200 a month thereafter. He said the family did not have a credit card, "and that he just didn't have a way to give me all the money at once," Horn says. The amount should have been easily paid, but Steve appeared set on making it drag on.

"He paid with a cashier's check. I don't know why, maybe so I didn't have his bank-account number. And it was always dated that same day," Horn recalls. Court records show that he was late with all of his payments, beginning with the first in July. Finally, he insisted on bringing the payments by Horn's office. After several uneventful drops, Grant walked into her office on a winter afternoon with his cashier's check in hand.

He was late again and he asked the clerk at the counter

if she would be so kind as to predate the receipt so that it wouldn't look like he was tardy. He had been recently warned by the court to make the payments on time, and if he was late again, the entire amount would come due.

The clerk told him she couldn't do that. Steve became bellicose, refused to sign the receipt, and reached over the counter to grab it from the woman, who was cowering away from the agitated Grant, who towered over her.

"He didn't yell, but he was loud and I heard it from the back and came out," Horn says. "One of the ladies said she was going to call the police, and he said, 'No, I'm going to call the police.' Everyone was very shaken up, and I told him that he could not come to the office again to drop the check. From then on, I would meet him in a very public place."

That place was the parking lot of the Old Stone Bar and Grill, a small pub and eatery not far from Grant's house. Horn arrived promptly for the 5 P.M. exchange with her mother and infant daughter in their SUV and backed into a parking space, giving her room for a quick getaway and room on either side so that Grant could pull over, jump out, hand over the check, and leave.

"But he was twenty-five minutes late, and when he got there, he blocked us in, pulled right in front of our space so that we couldn't get out, and had to get out of his car, a Jeep something, and come all the way around to get to my passenger window," Horn says. "I know he was doing this to intimidate me."

This was not the quiet gentleman who had helpfully followed Horn and the Realtor around the house on Cardinal in 2001 when the Grants were selling the place.

"When we were buying, Stephen was walking through the house with us and kept talking, telling us about the house [while] Tara sat on the couch," Horn says. "Stephen, he just wouldn't stop talking. But he was really nice about things. I liked him."

Steve doesn't deny that he'd purposely made things tense with Horn: "Tara and I were pissed that we lost [the small-claims case] and were *very* sore losers. We dragged out paying her and made her life as miserable as possible."

There were other episodes; things that might make some think that Steve was a little peculiar. In 2002, he sued a man, Kevin Bilske, after he and Bilske were involved in a traffic accident.

In a lawsuit, Grant claimed that the accident had caused him "pain, suffering, disability and mental anguish" and asked for relief in excess of $25,000. Bilske's lawyer noted that Grant had failed to wear a seat belt, which played a part in his injuries. Grant later settled for $12,500.

He had won, this time. For Steve, it was often all about getting the upper hand.

CHAPTER 6

Marriage, while it often starts with a burst of wedding-day flamboyance, is at its essence a very private institution and a grand stage at the same time, a place where misfires are magnified and where rancor is often veiled.

But it can be a tough road jammed with potholes, and if a divorce rate in the United States that hovers around 40 percent isn't proof enough, shelves of books with titles like *The Proper Care and Feeding of a Marriage* and *How to Improve Your Marriage Without Talking About It*, embarrassingly candid television and radio talk shows, and myriad courses on how to rescue those troubled unions all speak to the difficulties wedlock can bring.

If there was ever any trouble in the Grant marriage, it was apparent to no one.

"Tara wasn't the type of person who would ever talk about something like that," Alicia said later. When the two sisters spoke, it was always about the families, she says. "It was about work, it was about the kids."

And the two never discussed Tara's apparent wedded bliss.

"She didn't speak about the marriage but about herself and the travel and how it tired her out sometimes."

Still, if Tara was worn out, that wasn't evident to observers either. Friends who saw and interacted with the Grants were impressed by their playful banter and the confidence each brought to the other. Neither Steve nor Tara was one to merely sit back and watch, and they led an active life. Steve encouraged Tara to bike with him, and she gladly complied. When time permitted, the Grants enjoyed trips to northern Michigan, some weekends just jumping into one of their SUVs and taking the family up to Wilderness State Park or renting a cottage at Lake Houghton. For a time the two had a boat, and Steve was an avid runner. In the winter, there was ice skating at a local rink or indoor rock climbing.

———

Beginning in October 2006, Tara was given the job of handling the Washington Group's office in San Juan, Puerto Rico. The company was hoping to come to an agreement with the Puerto Rico Electric Power Authority to coordinate repairs of a recently damaged power plant. Tara would be part of that team, and she was now gone at least three weekdays out of each week.

"She always traveled, from the time we met her," Martha Anaud remembers, "but it really increased then."

Tara was the office manager for Washington Group International's San Juan office, and the office staff was being whittled down. Tara would be making some decisions on who would go and who would stay. Her schedule varied, but generally she was back in Michigan on Fridays, and sometimes she had a shorter week on the island, maybe Tuesday through Thursday, and then somewhere else for a meeting before heading home. At the same time, she would work an occasional weekend either in San Juan or somewhere else.

Her schedule was flexible, though, and Tara was never shy about asking for time off when she needed to do things with her children, her supervisors said.

Being in charge of the downsizing in San Juan served to increase Tara's worth to the company. "She was a good manager and a good leader," Lou Troendle, Tara's supervisor over the years at Washington Group, said later.

In Tara's mind, it seemed to Lou, things at home were stable.

The most recent au pair, Verena Dierkes, a teenager from Germany, had been a godsend, combining true affection for the kids with a willingness to do whatever the Grants asked of her.

Some of their friends questioned—inwardly, for interfering with Tara's business was a no-no—whether allowing Steve to be home alone for a week at a time with a beautiful young girl was the wisest thing to do.

Alicia, friends say, wouldn't ask Tara about leaving Steve alone with Verena for fear of Tara's reaction.

"I'm not sure that they were close enough for Tara to talk to her about things like that," says family friend Melissa Elliott. "And I think I failed Tara in that regard as well. We just stopped talking."

Still, Tara's old pals talked among themselves when they heard about the arrival of Verena, and Tara's new workweek.

"We wondered why she chose a good-looking nineteen-year-old blonde to do her job while she was gone for a week at a time," says one friend.

Perhaps it was purely Tara's instinct to trust.

At Halloween 2006, Tara's maternal grandparents came for their annual visit on their way from the Upper Peninsula to their winter home in Weslaco, Texas, in the Rio Grande Valley. Fritz and Mae Gould were always "treated so well" when they came to the Grant home, Mae says.

"[Tara and Steve] were in love, they really were, and he was always very nice, very friendly. They loved to get the kids together for things and we would all go out for dinner."

During the visit, Tara, Mae, and Verena hopped into Tara's car in a drenching rain and went over to the soccer field to watch Steve coach his team. That evening, Mae and Fritz, Tara, Steve, and the kids all piled into Steve's Jeep Commander and went to dinner at the Shogun Japanese Steak House in Shelby Township, one of Steve and Tara's favorite places.

"And Tara surprised me by telling them it was my birthday," Mae says. "She said, 'Is it your birthday?' and I said, 'No, of course not, you know that.' And she said, 'They're going to take your picture because they think it is and that's what they do here.'"

On Monday, Tara was out early to catch a flight to San Juan, Steve was off to work at USG Babbitt, and the Goulds moved along toward the sunshine of South Texas. The visit had been extraordinarily good this time, with the great-grandchildren getting older and their personalities beginning to develop—Lindsey was quickly becoming an image of Tara, with her long curly hair, quick smile, and assertive nature.

And Steve was, as always, good with the kids and the picture of a loving husband, Mae thought. And that little prank at Shogun, that was very Tara-ish.

It was a playful surprise that exemplified the good humor the family was in at the time. The Grants certainly seemed happy, there was no one around who would deny it.

———

As the year wound down, Tara, a meticulous list maker, jotted down her goals for 2007, both professionally and for her family life. She listed possible vacations: February in Arizona, where they would visit Steve's mother outside of Phoenix; March in the Upper Peninsula, of course, for the maple-syrup gathering; and November to Disney World for the kids' birthdays.

And she jotted a list, in her looping, precise penmanship.

- Buy piano
- Take 2 adult vacations—Europe—(Sept–anniversary) Paris—Caribbean (end of March/April)
- Plan Walt Disney trip for November (B-day—Thanksgiving)
- Sit w/a financial advisor in January
- Plan life better
- Look into buying new car
    - Chrysler 300
    - BMW5 w/Euro delivery (Sept.)
- Start college savings account for kids (529)
- Get 'SMART' about finances
    - look into stocks
    - other mutual funds
- Steve's retirement plan has no plan
- One weekend night a month is date night
- Become a better communicator to Steve—stop being angry (therapy if needed)
- Stop yelling

- Start doing 15 min. a day meditation
- Start yoga again for my soul
- Have once a month girls night w/Lindsey
- Get reconnected w/family
- Start exercising again
- Revise and stick to budget
- Track spending on computer
- File and box old bills/receipts
- Keep office organized
- Start a card night
- Plan dinners out w/friends or parties @ house
- Plan once a month kids date night (movies, musical, dinner, sports event, etc.)
- Look @ balanced activities for kids
  - music (piano)
  - foreign language (Spanish)
  - sports (no more than 2)
  - soccer, swim, gymnastics, baseball/football
  - yoga, karate

That Tara wished that she could "stop yelling" allows that she may not have realized all the resolutions she'd made after taking the Landmark Forum the previous year, although that wish and several others, including the yoga and meditation, also hint at a desire for a more peaceful state. She had always had a problem with her temper. But her hopeful goals portray a woman who was trying to reconcile the disparate parts of her world, one in which business meetings collided with her duties as a wife and mother.

On Thanksgiving 2006, Tara and Steve loaded up the kids and Verena and headed to Ohio for a large family gathering at Alicia's home in Chillicothe, south of Columbus. While the two families did not get together a lot, there was a general air of festive competition when they did.

"We were getting ready to leave the night before and Verena was coming with us," Steve recalls. "And she asked me how many clothes to pack, or how long we were going to be there. And I said, 'We might leave Thursday and we might leave Sunday. You can never tell when these two get together,'" referring to Tara and Alicia.

This visit was no different, with a battle between Alicia and Tara over "family issues," as Alicia stated later. On Thursday, Tara announced she wanted to cut the visit short, but Steve, who was hoping to go bike riding, calmed her down.

The next day, Friday, the two families met for lunch and the bickering between Tara and Alicia continued throughout a visit to the Columbus Zoo.

Early Saturday, the Grant contingent piled into the Jeep Commander and headed north.

"Tara and Alicia did not get along," Steve says. "I'm not sure if Alicia even knew that Tara didn't like her at all."

———

The Grants hosted a small party during the week of Christmas and several couples turned out. Lou Troendle and his wife were there, as were Mike and Leanne Zanlungo, Martha and Tim Anaud, about a dozen people in all.

The house was festively decorated both inside and out, with a green wreath on each side of the front door welcoming visitors.

It was unremarkable but pleasant, the type of event where neighbors get better acquainted and chat about the neighborhood. The Grant home was always jammed with people, it seemed, from au pairs and their friends to neighbors and their kids. And it seemed that the talk at the functions always revolved around children.

Later in the week, Tara sent a Christmas card to her estranged high school friend Melissa Elliott.

"We will be up in March for Sugar Bush season. It would be great to see you. Take care and warm wishes for a wonderful holiday," Tara wrote, and enclosed a picture of Lindsey and Ian.

There were doors opening for Tara, drawing her closer to family and friends. Yes, 2007 would be her year, all right.

————

The New Year started beautifully, in fact. Tara and Steve spent January 17 through 22 in Puerto Rico, celebrating Steve's thirty-seventh birthday, riding horses on the beach, indulging in the local food and culture, and soaking up some sun. The kids stayed with Verena in Michigan, where they went to a bowling party with the Zanlungos and their children.

The following week, Tara flew to London on business and Steve stayed home. On Friday, January 26, Tara found herself sitting near Tim Anaud on a plane heading back from London to Detroit. The two decided to gather up the families and grab dinner at Shogun, the Japanese steak joint. It was a wonderful night, Martha Anaud recalls, and Steve and Tara were especially vibrant.

"At one point, they just stopped everything they were doing and kissed," she recalls.

CHAPTER 7

In the thirteen years since Steve had ended his relationship with Deena Hardy, the hometown girl from around
the corner in the old neighborhood, he'd kept in touch.
They were, after all, childhood friends, ex-lovers, and
had even been domestic partners for a time. Deena had
moved on to other things, although she was hardly thriv-
ing. She'd met a lawyer in Lansing, and, while not married, they had a child and were living in a tiny apartment
in one of Lansing's run-down rental neighborhoods. He
wasn't bringing home big money, while she aspired to a
career as a dental technician. Compared to Deena's situation, Steve was the picture of success, with his large home,
kids going to two of the best schools in the area, and a
beautiful, professional wife.

Steve had made annual calls to Deena for the past decade, asking about her plans, dreams, and family.

"Every year, he would call me, ask if I were married,
what was going on in my life," Deena said later. That
annual call came in January 2007, a week after Steve's

birthday. Only this time, it was different. It was "more flirtatious . . . it seemed like he wanted to hook up."

And for the first time, the two exchanged email addresses. While Deena was willing to continue along these lines, she can't recall who asked for whose address first. She was aware that Stephen was married with children, and of course knew of Tara.

Steve, dealing in some fanciful thinking, told her that he was now traveling quite a bit as part of his job, taking down work sites. His fictional occupation revealed a man experiencing some career envy, transposing Tara's bright career onto his own day-to-day grind. In turn, Deena told him that she was considering a career in nursing.

During nearly a dozen phone conversations that month, Steve laid out a scenario in which he claimed that Tara was having an affair with a man he referred to as "the old geezer," a guy who, he insinuated, was her boss. On Thursday, January 25, one night before the evening the Grants joined the Anauds for dinner at Shogun, Steve became sexually suggestive to Deena as they conversed via email.

"I hope you keep at the nursing thing," he wrote. "You never know when I might need a sponge bath."

He also waxed eloquent on his views of marriage that night: "I like being married," Steve wrote. "I just think of marriage vows like speed limits. Sometimes you have to break them . . . you just need to keep an eye on the road to avoid detection." He added that "I don't care about being married, I never have. It is that no conscience thing, I think!"

And they discussed the "old geezer," and Steve implied past indiscretions on Tara's part. In his wife's e-mails, Steve told Deena, "She says things in code. And because of that, I don't know what is actually going on. Also . . .

about two years ago, she did the same thing with some guy she used to know. Nothing physical, just text and email and phone calls."

Steve asserted that he knew it wasn't physical because of "the magic of intercepted email and phone calls." This was accomplished, he said, because his old friend Bryan Rellinger, the best man in his wedding, was a vice president at a computer company "and one of his techs helped out a bit if you know what I mean. Straight up NSA shit if you get my drift."

Deena later said that "it seemed he was fed up with Tara . . . He didn't say whether he was going to divorce her, though in fact he implied he didn't want to get a divorce because he didn't want to mess up his kids."

The two set up a meeting for Tuesday, January 30, with Deena mindful of what Steve intended—two ex-lovers, both communicating some boredom with their respective lives, perhaps in need of some spice. But then Steve canceled the dinner plans, citing obligations to his children.

"Look I can't do it," he told her in an email. "I can't ruin my kids' lives over a stupid relationship."

"[Deena] was pissed, but she understood," Steve says. "It was the second time I had done it. A couple years before I had stood her up . . ."

———

Verena Dierkes was an intellectually curious nineteen-year-old girl, and her pursuit of learning knew no bounds. She had already achieved her goal of coming to the United States from her native Germany.

Verena, with her long shag of dirty-blond hair, looked much like a typical Michigan coed, dressing casually in jeans with tank tops that showed off her toned frame. She possessed the sort of sidelong glance and shock of thick bangs that reminded one of the young Princess Diana, who, before her royal coming-out, had also hidden shyly behind thick golden locks.

Verena's work schedule was flexible as long as her prescribed duties were carried out, and the Grants were a kind and accommodating couple. As per her contract, they provided her with a cell phone and suitable transportation, a red 1991 Mazda MX-6 sedan.

On the evening of January 30, Verena went to her Spanish class at Macomb Community College in Clinton Township. Her English was already stellar—the accent that she had carried with her from Germany was fading fast—and she wanted to broaden her language skills even further. When her class let out at 8 P.M., she met her close friend and fellow au pair Anna at a Starbucks not far from the Grant home on Westridge.

Tara had left for Puerto Rico that morning, and Steve was at home with the two kids. He had returned around six, pleased with himself for not following up on his meeting with Deena. It gave him some confidence to know that despite all his boasting about his light opinion of the marriage vows, he didn't need to fall into bed with an old flame just to prove his masculinity. He was just as pleased to know that Deena had agreed to meet him as he would've been to bed her.

Satisfied, Steve tended to the kids, fed them, put them to bed, and then jumped into the shower. Tonight he was going to clean the hard drive of one of Tara's older laptop computers and hand it over to Verena to use. He had initially thought the computer, an aging Dell, should be taken to CompUSA to have the existing files erased, but Tara had protested, saying there might be some private data on there that a stranger shouldn't be privy to.

Grant sat down on a wooden stool at the kitchen counter and began to go through some of the files, mostly work-related things. He was not averse to some snooping, and through some password manipulating, soon found himself in Tara's private files, which she'd saved as documents.

Steve was astounded as he read the missives dated two years previously, in February 2005. They were copies of e-mails between Tara and Pete Brancheau, the guy from Up North who had broken her heart fifteen years earlier. These were clearly notes between two people who had been together sexually in the past and were approaching something close to being so again.

Steve sat stunned, even though the communication was two years old. The hypocrisy of the situation was lost on him—in his mind, while he may have been guilty of some flirting in the past week, he was innocent. But he felt this was different. The e-mails were remnants of a scare that had occurred in the Grants' marriage two years before, after Tara had reached out to and reconnected with Pete. It had sent the couple into marriage counseling and had bothered Steve ever since.

Perhaps for good reason.

"Tara and I would have been together if it hadn't been for our age difference and two thousand miles," Brancheau says. The two had met in the library at Bay de Noc College in Escanaba in late 1991, where he was taking classes before entering the U.S. Navy. He was twenty-five and brushing up on his math skills in hopes of entering flight training school. Tara was nineteen.

"I spent a lot of time in the library and would see her there. We sat in the same area, and she caught my eye, but I never had the guts to say anything to her until the last day of the term, and I offered her a muffin."

The two talked for some time, forging an instant connection.

When he came back to campus on a break from his basic training in Chicago, he went back to the library. And there she was. The two set out to finish what they started, "mostly friends, never really intimate," Brancheau says.

He left again for San Diego, where he was to be stationed, and Tara bought a plane ticket to visit him several months later. But when she called a few nights before her flight, asking what the plans were for her time there, he had none.

"I had no reservations, no plans at all, I'm just not like that. We had just planned on her visiting me here, on her coming out. I like to just let things happen."

Tara didn't. And the morning she was to arrive, she called and said she never got on the plane. She was in tears.

"I saw her again a couple years later when I was in town not long before she left for MSU," Brancheau says. He went to her parents' house and they played cribbage. Both he and Tara were on to other things and they fell out of touch, but neither ever forgot the other.

In summer of 2004, the Grants, with kids in tow, visited Escanaba and attended the Upper Peninsula State Fair.

"We were walking through the grounds, and Lindsey was three and Ian was one and I was handling the kids, you know, and we run into Pete's mom," Steve says. "Tara talked to her while I tended the kids, and Tara handed her a business card. She handed everyone a business card, and I never thought anything of it. Pete had never come up, really, before, as any kind of issue."

But running into Pete's mother reminded Tara that

Pete was out there somewhere. She followed up the card drop with a call.

"She left a message on my mom's answering machine and asked that I get in touch with her," Pete says. "She didn't even leave her name, actually. I sat on it, knew who it was, but this was in September 2004. I said to myself, 'Why would I want to call this person back?' "

But in November, he did call her back, on her cell phone.

"And it was like we never missed a beat, we laughed, we talked, it was really nice."

More calls, then e-mails, followed.

"I won't say we didn't care about each other. We did, even over the phone."

They talked about their lives and their feelings. At one point, Pete asked Tara why she had called him at his mother's house, why she'd reached out.

"She was a tough-minded chick," Pete says. "And she said she wasn't happy. There were trust issues in their marriage over finances. She told me there was a big issue with the machine shop that Steve and his dad ran, and that she had gotten a large bonus at work, forty thousand dollars, and Steve made her put it into the shop. Other than that, though, she was mum about Steve."

Late that year, Steve and Tara had agreed to take some time off between Christmas and New Year's. But then Tara told Steve that she would have to work; in actuality, however, she had planned a rendezvous with Pete.

"She was on the road and we had been talking here and there, and that December, we were going to get together. But I had been involved with the same woman for a long time and I just didn't see any use in meeting with someone who was married with children. There was nothing good that could come of that."

So he canceled the meeting. Both cried, Pete says. And they did keep on talking on occasion, until three weeks later.

On the Sunday before his thirty-fifth birthday in 2005, Steve tended to a chore in Tara's Trooper, putting a new, updated insurance certificate in the glove box. As he stuck it in there, he came across a holiday card. It was unaddressed, and Steve thought it was for him.

It quickly became clear that was not the case. It was a love note from Tara to someone who was not her husband.

"I didn't want to think bad things right off the bat, so I just kind of waited and thought about it," Steve says. But several days later, when Tara began acting suspiciously, taking long drives and not answering her phone when she was away, he confronted her. And she confessed.

"I was so hurt and so angry," Steve says. "This had not happened to me before. I told her to leave the house, I had to think about things. I told her she was never to talk to Pete again. I took care of the kids, I just didn't want to talk to her. She was gone for a week."

Before she left, though, he told her to hand over Pete's number. And the next day, Steve called him.

"He had found the card, and he had found out that we cared about each other," Pete says. "And he called me at work and threatened to put a bullet in my head if I continued to talk to Tara. He said he knew where I lived and where I worked. I can't say I didn't do him wrong."

Pete sent Tara an email letting her know of the threat. And that was the last he ever communicated with her, he says.

———

Now, on a bitter winter night, in his own kitchen, Steve was reliving a painful episode from the past. He flushed.

Into this scene walked Verena, pleased with another pleasant night with her studies and her closest friend. Steve, clad only in his pajama bottoms, looked up from the keyboard.

"How was your day today?" he said, somewhat distractedly.

"It was pretty good," Verena said, unbuttoning her coat, pulling a scarf from her neck, and dropping her purse on the counter.

"Well, at least yours was better than mine," Steve said.

"What's wrong, what happened?" Verena asked.

Steve stared at the screen, still a bit absorbed in his thoughts, saying nothing while Verena walked into the entry foyer and hung her coat up.

"Would you mind reading something for me?" Steve finally said.

"Yes, sure," she replied, thinking it was perhaps something in German that she could translate for him. He got up and she took his place at the counter, while he stood.

She began reading. It became immediately apparent that Tara and this person with whom she was exchanging e-mails had been intimate at some point.

"I couldn't imagine that Tara would ever cheat on him," Verena said later. "I didn't know what to say. I was kind of embarrassed because I was just the au pair and it was not my business what was going on in their marriage."

"Is Tara still in contact with this person?" she asked.

"I didn't read all of them, these are enough, so I really don't know. I don't know what to do. What can I do? What do you think I should do?"

"I would talk to her, that's the best thing you can do," Verena said.

"Well, one time I had a friend who was in a situation like this," Steve said. "He just got some people who would beat the other guy up. But I can't do that, I wouldn't do that."

Steve was still standing in the kitchen, and the house was quiet. He told Verena the same thing he had told Deena just five days earlier in their frenzied email exchanges.

"I never want to get divorced. I have always said that if I got married, I am going to stay married. My parents got divorced when I was a kid and it was hell on me. I can't have my kids experience that."

———

The next day, Steve called Tara. He had to know, he had to ask her what was going on. Even though he realized that the e-mails he had accessed and was obsessing over were two years old, they made him concerned about the question of Tara's fidelity now. She traveled a lot, she spent a lot of nights alone—presumably—in hotels all over the world, and right now she was spending her weeknights at a Marriott in a tropical paradise.

On Thursday, February 1, after several phone conversations that included his reading back some of the intercepted messages, Steve sent Tara a heartfelt email, explaining how he'd come across the messages and telling her that despite it all, he still trusted her.

"I will NEVER . . . this is in writing . . . say anything about him or that situation again. I did not and had not thought about IT in a long time . . . REALLY! I trust that you are true to me, but I do worry!"

He asked for her help in order to understand, and said he was proud of her work and "for all you have done and earned in this job.

"But you are on the road a LOT . . . and you do drink, sometimes too much when you go out . . . I of all people am not pointing fingers about the drinking, but when people drink . . . everyone . . . they sometimes forget who they are for a time and do things they might not otherwise do." He ended the message restating his love for her, but "I was just hurt by what I read and had to tell you."

It was off his chest, all of this worry about infidelity. Many marriages go through it, and it was now something that, for the Grants, was part of the past.

At least as far as Tara's conduct was concerned. As for Steve, he was just getting warmed up. Later that night of February 1, he came home from a work delivery around 10 P.M. and found Verena in her room. It was late, the kids were asleep, and the girl was beat. But Steve wanted to talk, and he stood in the hallway, leaning on the door frame.

"I want to ask you to remember not to act any differently when Tara comes home tomorrow," Steve said.

Verena shook her head, no, of course not.

"Tara deserves a kick in the ass," Grant added, not seriously.

Then: "I'd like to tell you something, but—" he said. "But maybe I should just keep my mouth shut."

A sure way to tantalize a teenager: hide information.

"Come on, tell me, it can't be that bad," Verena urged, now curious beyond measure. What could this man want to say that could be so bad? "You said there is something you want to say, now I really want to know it."

"Well," Steve began, "Okay. You are beautiful, I want to sleep with you."

Verena blushed as she tried to laugh off the come-on. Steve, not a bad-looking man, in good physical shape, was asking her to sleep with him. Verena felt a disparate combination of creeped out and . . . excited. She changed the subject quickly, to more neutral things like the kids.

Soon the two found themselves engrossed in talk about all kinds of things, about their lives, about their thoughts, with Steve appearing to be earnest in his hopes of knowing and understanding Verena. His chatter was peppered with compliments, more than once telling her how beautiful she was and how pretty her legs were. At one point, she looked at the clock on her nightstand. It was 2 A.M. They had been talking for four hours.

The next day, around 3 P.M., Steve called her.

"How are things going with Lindsey?" he asked.

"She is fine," Verena said.

Steve paused. "Well, I'm glad you're still talking to me," he said.

"Why shouldn't I talk to you?" Verena asked. She realized that some of their talk the night before had been frank, but, quite honestly, she was flattered. After all, a girl likes to hear compliments.

"Because of what I said last night. I actually expected you to call [your Au Pair America counselor] Sue and tell her everything. I thought you would pack your suitcases."

Steve had misread Verena's devotion to his family, although the fact that she hadn't done as he had feared only served to embolden him.

———

Tara returned to Detroit late that Friday, February 2, after 11 P.M., with plans for a routine weekend, capped by the Super Bowl on Sunday evening. She and Steve had bickered during her layover at Newark Airport, with angry back-and-forth calls.

Both Steve and Verena were worn out after staying up so late the previous night, talking. Tara had already put the flap with Steve behind her and was glad to be home and ready to start a weekend with the family. On Saturday, at Steve's urging, she and Lindsey went to get their nails done while he and Ian ran some errands.

On Sunday, February 4, the Grants watched the Indianapolis Colts defeat the Chicago Bears 29–17 in the Super Bowl. The family was gathered, and Verena checked in as well. At one point, Steve and Tara paused for a long embrace. *Good*, Verena thought. *They must have worked out the trouble over those e-mails.*

But when she returned to her room to prepare for bed, shortly after the game ended, she had an email from Steve.

"For what I'm thinking now, I would definitely go to Hell. Just thought I'd let you know," he said.

Verena was now really flattered, and in the glow of his attention, even with Tara sleeping in the next room next to Steve, she fired back.

"You know you're going to Hell anyway, so it doesn't matter . . . What were you thinking about?"

She received no answer that night.

The next day, Monday, February 5, it was Steve's turn on the keyboard, this time from work.

"If you don't know what I was thinking about then I'm sure you can imagine from my view I had from the sofa. I swear I looked once, ok, maybe twice . . ." Steve wrote, indicating that he'd been able to see Verena's cleavage from his vantage point on the couch as the family watched the Super Bowl. And that he was happy about it.

On Tuesday, February 6, Tara caught a morning flight back to San Juan and Steve went to work at USG Babbitt. But he wasn't done courting Verena. Not by a long shot. That morning, he called the phone company and changed Verena's cell service to allow her to send and receive text messages, even though she didn't really care about having that function. It didn't matter; Steve needed it in order to continue his overtures. And, Verena admitted to herself, she liked the way he was extending himself to gain her favor.

"I liked the way he talked to me and the things he said to me," Verena said later. "I liked the way he told stories and I liked listening to them." Naively, she added, "I didn't expect that later there would be more than just conversation and e-mails."

That evening, as she sat in her Spanish class, Steve began sending her text messages, at one point telling her that he needed a "hand to scratch my itch," a not-so-thinly veiled request for sex.

When she got back to Westridge around ten, Verena went up to her room, passing Steve on the stairs, and the two exchanged greetings. She put her schoolbook away, logged onto her computer, and was greeted by an email from Steve inviting her to come join him downstairs to talk to him and "open up." If she did as he asked, he said, he knows that she is his. If not, "I know that you hate me."

While such a dime-store lothario hustle would probably not work on any female over twenty, Grant knew what he was dealing with—a young girl just out of high school.

"I'm just here because I don't hate you, but you don't 'got' me," she said, walking into the family room.

Now Steve applied the full-court press, flattering her, asking her about past boyfriends, telling her how much he cared for her. Finally, as the two sat next to each other on the couch, he began to hold her, pushing his lips to her neck, then to her mouth, kissing her lips. Verena was not receptive, but she also was not about to push him away: "It was not that it didn't feel good, but I was thinking of Tara," she said later.

As things cooled off, the two went upstairs to their

respective rooms, which were next to each other. They prepared for bed with a vibrating sexual tension connecting them, bridging her closed bedroom door. Steve continued to text-message her, finally asking if he could see her face one more time before going to sleep.

Verena opened her door and poked her head out.

"Here I am, good night," she said, and closed the door then crawled under her covers.

Moments later, Grant quietly, timidly, opened the door.

"This looks like an invitation," he said. He walked in slowly and sat down on her twin bed. It was impossible for him, large-framed and gangly, to sit without being physically close to her. Steve began touching her shoulders, face, caressing her head, and Verena accepted his touch begrudgingly.

"This is wrong," she managed.

"No, no, it's not wrong at all," he said.

Finally, Steve left the room. Both slept the sleep of fledgling adulterers.

The next day, Wednesday, February 7, Verena awoke around the same time as Steve in the predawn. They chatted benignly about the upcoming day, he in the hall and she sitting up. Then Steve turned and headed back into his room to get dressed. As he peeled off his pajama bottoms and stood naked, Verena walked in to ask a question.

"It was uncomfortable for a second and I didn't know what to say and neither did she," is how Steve remembers it. Verena turned her head to look away, and Steve grabbed his robe.

During their many deep talks, Verena had voiced some reservations about being naked with someone, just part of the talk.

"Now there's no issue anymore," Steve told her. Then

he apologized, giving her a quick kiss as she moved to rouse the kids. But there it was. Steve was pushing full steam ahead.

That evening, as the au pair had coffee with some of her friends at Starbucks, she and Steve continued to text. At one point, Verena said she felt guilty about doing anything behind Tara's back.

"It was not fair, there was absolutely no reason why I wanted to hurt Tara's feelings," Verena said later.

A little stunned by Steve's disregard for his wife and what she might feel if she discovered them, she asked Grant, "You don't regret anything, do you?"

"It's not always right or wrong and it doesn't always seem black or white," he texted back.

Later that night, for the first time, the two spent the night together in Verena's bed. "Cuddling and kissing" is how Verena described the extent of their contact. On Thursday, February 8, Steve called Verena around ten-thirty from work and invited her to lunch. He came by the house at eleven-thirty.

"I've never been able to go to lunch with Tara," he said. "She asks me to go out sometimes, but she always wears such nice clothes to work and I have these dirty things on; it's embarrassing."

It was a simple lunch that day, at the nearby Buffalo Wild Wings, and the two chatted easily, she talking about her parents and their planned visit in the coming months, he about his work.

That night, as she sat in her room listening to music, surfing the Web, Steve came in. Verena thought he seemed a little looser than usual, and he confessed that he had downed a few drinks that evening. They talked, and Steve got up to leave. "Good night, love you," he said.

Verena didn't miss a beat. She broke into laughter.

The declaration seemed staged somehow, even to her young ears.

"Yeah, that was planned," she said. But Steve played it as straight as could be, stunned, and saying over and over, "Oh God, shit, oh no."

He sat back down on her bed.

"I know it's weird for you to hear those words and I won't repeat them, although I mean it, but it's right, I am falling in love with you."

Verena sat quietly. She said later that she could not say she loved him, because it wasn't so, but "I knew that I liked him more than I should." That night, the two again shared a bed, first Verena's, then, at Steve's insistence, moving to the bed he and Tara shared. Before they went to sleep, Steve performed oral sex on Verena. She didn't protest, but she also said she didn't reciprocate.

On the morning of Friday, February 9, the alarm clock in Verena's room began buzzing, as usual. It went on for some time without awakening the new lovers, but she finally got up from Steve's bed, went in to turn it off, and returned to bed with Steve, leaving the door partially open.

"Where's Verena?" came a little girl's voice from the end of the bed. "Her alarm clock went off, but she's not in her room."

Verena barely had time to pull some covers over her head.

"Maybe she's in the bathroom," Steve said to his daughter, motioning to the hall.

Lindsey looked over her shoulder. Verena's door was open and the light was off.

"No, she's not in there," she said.

"Oh, I forgot, she wanted to get up earlier to send some pictures to her parents, she's in the office," Steve said.

This satisfied Lindsey, so Steve got up and walked her back to her room to get her things together for school, giving Verena time to get out of bed.

Did Lindsey see anything? Of course it's possible that she could have seen Verena moving from her room after shutting off the alarm, and getting back into bed with Steve. Verena said later that she doubted it.

"She might have seen me but I can't imagine that she did. She never got up by herself, it was actually pretty hard to wake her up."

CHAPTER 8

On the last day of her life, Tara Grant awoke around 6:30
A.M. in Puerto Rico, after spending the evening at the
hotel bar. She had engaged an older couple in conversation, had a couple of drinks, and had slept easy in excited
anticipation of seeing her kids the next day. That Tara was
at the bar surprised Steve, "because she never goes to the
bar," he said later.

She made a couple of calls as she got ready to board
her plane home, Continental Flight 476, which departed
at 1 P.M. with a connecting flight in Newark. She spoke
during the day with Steve and touched base with the company's Cleveland and San Juan offices. Her sister, Alicia,
called once from Ohio and left a message, which Tara
didn't immediately return, and she spoke with Washington Group's human-resources office in Birmingham, Alabama. Upon landing in Newark, she spoke with friend
and workmate Kirby Lloyd. At 6 P.M., as she waited for
her connecting flight to Detroit, she called Alicia back
and the two chatted for forty-one minutes, records show.

During that chat, Alicia would later tell investigators that Tara said she and Steve "were on different career paths."

And in an interview with a Detroit paper two weeks later, Alicia said that Tara told her that the coming weekend at home would be short because she had to return to Puerto Rico a day early.

Alicia told another friend that things were coming to an acrimonious head in the Grant household. "Tara spoke to Alicia that day and gave the impression that things were over," says childhood friend Jennifer Elliott. "Alicia thought for the first time, [Tara] was saying that she had to end it."

Alicia later denied that was the case, instead portraying the conversation as routine, speaking about the kids, a planned family trip to Arizona the following week, and "just girl stuff, sister stuff."

Tara spoke with Steve intermittently during the day, and according to Steve, the two discussed her travel schedule, with Steve urging her to see if she could lighten it up a bit.

While most observers could see no cracks in the facade of the Grant marriage, others were beginning to see that Tara's success was fueling some animosity in Steve, and Tara was beginning to feel the two were growing apart. In fact, she had for some time resented Steve's jealousy, his snooping in her e-mails, his hints that her relationships with some coworkers were a little more than just friendships.

Flight 2763 to Detroit was delayed, but by 7 P.M., she was in her seat and ready to get home. The weekends had become her only real downtime, which she cherished with all her heart.

The plane touched down at Detroit Metropolitan Airport at around 9 P.M. Tara pulled her Isuzu Trooper out of the parking garage at nine-thirty and called Steve at home. The two were bickering again, and it wasn't good. They spoke for eighteen minutes beginning at 9:47 as she made the hour-long drive back to their home on Westridge. It was close to ten-thirty when she pulled into the driveway, pressed the garage door opener, and pulled her truck into the garage, then shut the door.

"There was a little bit of back-and-forth that the weekend before we had talked about, um, the fact that she travels too much," Steve said later. "And she told me then that she was gonna try to get things so [she wasn't] traveling so much . . ."

Tara, despite always giving the impression to others that things were going fine, was apparently ready to hand her husband some kind of ultimatum when she got home. Was she placating Steve when she told him that she would attempt to fix her travel schedule? Or was she just playing it tough for her little sister, who claims to have never liked Steve?

———

Not long before Tara landed, Steve made a call to Gary Mugnolo, a member of the Downtown Coaches Club at Michigan State University. The father of a friend of Tara's was being feted as part of a basketball alumni ceremony at the February 17 basketball game against Iowa, and while the Grants held two season tickets, Steve was looking for two more so that he could bring some friends to see the event.

"I have no idea why he called me, but it was perfect timing. I had two spare tickets," Mugnolo says. "[Steve] said he'd buy them, I sent them off, and he sent me a check, even putting in a little extra for my trouble."

There was another thing that struck him about the caller: "He was very polite, very appropriate."

Grant never used the two tickets he purchased that night.

At around 9 P.M., Steve placed four calls to the reservation line at the Desert Pearl Inn, a gorgeous resort set on the Virgin River in Springdale, Utah. However, the records show that he didn't make a reservation.

"The plan was for the next week, we were going to stop in Phoenix, the whole family, and visit my mom for a few days," Steve says. "Then travel up through Arizona and into Utah and stay at Desert Pearl. Then fly back home out of Las Vegas."

———

After the call from Tara ended at 10:05, Steve put down his cell phone and called Verena from the landline in his house. She was out with some friends at a watering hole in nearby Rochester Hills called Mr. B's, a restaurant and bar with a party-time decor that married Detroit sports pennants and pictures from the Red Wings, Pistons, Tigers, and Lions with rock-and-roll memorabilia from locals such as Kid Rock and Eminem.

Verena heard the phone even over the blare of the jukebox, but was getting put out by Steve's constant texting as she was trying to enjoy the night out with friends and at the same time ensure that their suspicions about who was constantly contacting her were not aroused.

"It kills me to say that, but Tara will be home in five minutes so you can't call anymore or send any text messages," Grant said in a voice mail. "But I will send you another text message to tell you that again. Don't forget to give me a kiss when you're home. Make a noise and I will come downstairs so that I get my kiss. I will leave you a note on your bed."

He texted back once more, at 10:32. "You owe me a kiss," he said.

Verena was bursting. She was quickly falling for this man she worked for. Steve had wooed her, physically pleasured her, and now, she told her best friend Anna as they sat in the busy Friday night clamor of Mr. B's, she was in love with Steve.

———

It's possible that Tara walked into the house on February 9 determined in some way to initiate a discussion about the state of their marriage. But Steve would later say that she did not come in spoiling to continue their argument, but with her earbuds in and her iPod playing, her laptop case over her shoulder.

He says now that the disagreement between them was about cutting back her travel schedule. And then that evening she came in and announced that she would be returning to San Juan on Sunday, at least a day earlier than usual.

———

The final word on a dispute almost always boils down to the veracity of the participants' accounts and those of any witnesses. In the situation that commenced around 10:35 at the home on Westridge that night, the only people in the house were Steve, Tara, and their two children, Lindsey and Ian, who were presumably asleep, their eight-thirty bedtime long past.

Tara can never give her side of the story, so there is only Steve's rendering of the events and the work of investigators to go by.

Before giving his statement, however, Grant complicated the matter for three weeks, spinning a web of lies and deception that bespeaks a bizarre proclivity for dishonesty.

According to the detailed account Steve would eventually give, he was upstairs when Tara entered the house. He yelled down to her when she walked in, but when she failed to respond, he came down the stairs to greet her and found her with her iPod earbuds in, "and I kind of got disgusted," Steve said. He went back upstairs, and Tara followed shortly thereafter.

"I was getting ready to go to bed and Tara came in and we were talking more," Steve claimed in his statement. "Tara told me that she was thinking about leaving on Sunday morning and I said, 'No, not okay.' And she said, 'Well, I need to go on Sunday.' And she said Lou [Troendle, her supervisor] was going back down there on Sunday; she says, 'I need to go.'"

Steve said it was the point that launched another argument.

"I said, 'You spend too much time with him already and you don't spend enough time with us.' And I said something about Lou, that 'you're only going down there [because] Lou's down there.' And she said, 'Why do you always think Lou?'

"I don't know, it's just weird how you get to travel that much together. And she said, 'Well, what the hell do you think I'm doing?'" In his written confession, Steve admitted that he "wanted to say the meanest thing I could think of." So he pushed the issue, "and it somehow elevated to the point where I [said], 'Are you fucking him?'"

After that bombshell, Steve told officers that he asked Tara again why she was going back to Puerto Rico early.

"And she said, 'Fuck off.' She said, 'Too bad.' She said, 'I got to do what I have to do in my job and it's none of your business.' So she started to turn around and I grabbed her wrist . . . 'Stop' I said, 'just stop it. You're not going anywhere.' I said, 'We're gonna finish this conversation.' And she slapped me and I hit her back . . . As long as I can remember, she had belittled me and—and her one way—she knew, she knew if she hit me, I'd hit her back."

Part of this account, which was in Steve's hospital-bed statement to law enforcement, conflicts with his written account. In the latter, Steve said that when he grabbed Tara's left wrist, she said, "What, are you gonna start hitting me?"

"I let her wrist go and said I wouldn't do anything like that," Steve wrote in his statement. "She said she knew I didn't have it in me . . ."

According to Steve, when the two exchanged blows, they were facing each other in front of the door to the master-suite bathroom, just to the left of the entertainment center that held a large TV. Her weak punch left him with a scratch on the side of his nose about an inch long and deep enough to later scab over.

"I think I just, I went to hit her and I think I hit her on the side of the neck. And I kind of, I don't know, like knocked the wind out of her, but she fell backward . . . but she was fine. I know that she banged the back of her head on the floor." Then Grant said Tara "said something like, 'That's it. I'm gonna take the kids. You're gonna be fucking homeless. You're a piece of shit.'"

As Tara began to get up from the floor, "I put my hand on her neck because she kept saying that, that it was over, that she was gonna take the kids, and because I hit her, that was it. And I said, 'No, you hit me first.' And she said, 'It doesn't matter . . . cops aren't going to think that. I'm calling the police.' She started telling me . . . if a man hits a woman, he goes to jail and she gets the kids and the house and everything. And she said, 'Screw you . . . you'll never see your kids again.'"

As she lay in front of the bathroom, hurling threats, Tara was sitting "kinda halfway up . . . her mouth was going a mile a minute, saying, 'You're done, you're done . . . '" Grant said Tara told him he "was going to jail and I would become the loser I always was.

"I grabbed her neck. And at first I was only grabbing her neck to make her stop talking, to make her shut up."

In the statement, Steve said he was thinking, "Shut up. Stop it. Don't say that . . . she wouldn't fight right away, and I just squeezed and she, um, and that's when I realized that I was gonna go to prison for hurting her. She was gonna tell somebody. I gotta make her not tell."

Grant said he kept "squeezing, squeezing, squeezing, and wouldn't let go . . . I think at one point she realized that I wasn't stopping. She finally grabbed my hand at one point but it was too late then . . . and that's when I covered her face up . . . with a pair—with gray underwear or a gray T-shirt . . . I was only covering her face, just so I wouldn't have to look at her."

The choking went on for several minutes, and by then, Grant knew she was dead; he had strangled her "too long, too much time had gone by . . . I knew she was dead . . . I didn't feel a pulse. I didn't feel anything . . ."

Stephen Grant had murdered Tara, his wife of ten years and the mother of his two children.

And as he later told police, "Once she was dead, I started to panic."

As a freshly minted murderer, Steve went downstairs, sat at the dining-room table, and wept. The tears mixed with the blood dribbling from the cut just above his left nostril. After several minutes, he realized that his life was now changed forever, and he quickly began to concoct a story that he would have to believe and live if he were to remain a free man. It was now a little after 11 P.M. Verena would be coming home soon. The first thing he wanted to do was delay her, if he could. Steve quickly texted her, telling her that Tara was late but that didn't mean she had to come home, hoping it would persuade her to stay away. He had to buy some time. His mind, always fertile when it came to telling tall tales, was now racing with the effort to concoct one.

His wife's dead body lay in his bedroom upstairs, feet away from where his children lay sleeping.

Grant walked back up the stairs to the bedroom, and there Tara lay, the gray underwear over her face, still clad in the clothes she had put on that morning for the trip home: a silver Ann Taylor blouse, black striped pants, size six, a black Victoria's Secret thong, and a black bra.

She lay on her back, next to the armoire. Also near the armoire was one of Steve's belts, an old brown thing that he had worn that day.

"I knew I couldn't carry her. She was too big. So I grabbed a belt and wrapped it around her neck [and I used it] to pull her downstairs."

Tara's hips and feet hit the stairs as he dragged her down, clutching the belt in both hands. Steve was doing his best to remain quiet, although the kids rarely woke once they were asleep.

The stairs opened onto the living room, then the dining

room, then the kitchen and out a narrow laundry area and into the garage, which is where he was headed.

Grant tugged Tara's body along, struggling with the deadweight of his late wife, her feet flopping. He now had enough leverage to keep her head at about his waist level. Steve was aware that he was also struggling within a very finite time frame. His new lover, the teenage au pair, would be home any minute. What if she were to open the garage and catch him, as they say, in this morbid flagrante delicto?

As he reached the garage, intending to put her in the back of her truck, "I dropped her . . . the belt slipped or broke. And she fell and it was the most disgusting, like it sounded like dropping a watermelon on the cement . . . there wasn't any twinging [sic] or anything. I knew then that I had killed her. I didn't know what to do. I think that the only thing I could think to do was to hide her . . . I hid her in the back of the truck."

He stashed her body in the back part of the Isuzu, using a cargo liner meant for his Jeep to cover the body up.

"And she was in there kind of like laying on her side. And her one leg was pulled up, and . . . that was it."

As Grant stood there, breathless, terrified, he heard a click. It was the garage-door remote making its connection with the sensor.

Verena drove north on Mound Road toward Westridge around eleven forty-five, believing that her new paramour was very needy. She'd had to tell him earlier in the evening to stop bothering her with texts and calls, that her friends were becoming suspicious. At one point, she had told them the calls were coming from a persistent boy she had met at a local club. Most of her friends bought that, but of course her friend Anna knew it was Steve.

Verena was at the foot of the driveway when she hit the garage door opener. It was an older device that came with the house, and always took some time to fully raise the door, so she slowly eased up the driveway as it lifted.

"Oh, Tara's already home," she said to herself, seeing the white truck. She parked the car and walked through the garage and into the house, the door from the garage to the house making a noise as it shut.

"What the fuck are you doing here?" Steve shouted, bounding down the stairs clad in his pajama bottoms, meeting her in the kitchen.

Verena was puzzled. Steve had always been nothing but soft with her, and his angry demeanor took her aback.

"What did you say?" she asked, more than a little hurt.

"Nothing. I'm sorry. I thought you were Tara. Is she still out there?"

"Her truck is in the garage," Verena said, puzzled. "Where is she?"

Steve walked over and sat down at the dining-room table, dropped his head in his hands, and began to weep. After a few moments, he looked up at her and said, "She left."

Steve laid out a story for Verena that would evolve upon retelling over the next three weeks.

"I saw [Verena's] face just drop when I yelled at her, I couldn't think of anything else to do, and from then on, it all built on itself, the lie," Steve says. "Every day it got more and more and I couldn't stop it, it became more irreversible. It got to that point where I couldn't go back and tell the truth."

He laid out this story for Verena: He and Tara had argued over her incessant travel, and the discussion became heated when she said she was returning to San Juan a day earlier.

Verena later explained, "He told me that Tara had to leave on Sunday again instead of Monday, so she just would be home on Saturday. Steve said to her that she should just stay there over the weekend and come back on Wednesday, then she would have more time for the family."

Steve told Verena, and later everyone, that Tara had come home, unpacked her things, repacked a bag, kissed the kids, and left. He claimed to have heard her saying, "I'll be out there in a few minutes," believing her to be talking on the phone, and Steve said he saw her get into a black car-service sedan at the end of the driveway, possibly a Cadillac CTS.

"He was also talking about divorce," Verena related. "He said he'd expect to have divorce papers in the mailbox on Monday."

Steve also explained that there would be a custody dispute over the children, "and if people found out that he and I were having an affair, he wouldn't get the kids."

At one point, Steve said he had to check Tara's truck to see if she left something for him in there. After grabbing a flashlight and going out to the car, Steve returned with a card that he said he'd given his wife three months ago.

"Tara, I love you! Enough said," the card read.

"One thing we have to do is delete all of our text messages, because Tara could check them, since you and I have the same phone contract and she knows my code," Verena recalled Steve saying.

After the two talked for a while, they repaired to their separate rooms. Steve never asked Verena to join him. Instead he called his friend Bryan Rellinger in Grand

Rapids, at 1:30 A.M. It was Bryan who had helped Steve install computer monitoring software on Tara's old laptop when Grant had suspected her of infidelities. Three times it rang through, going to Rellinger's voice mail. The last time, Steve left a message: "The shit has hit the fan," he said. "Call me back."

CHAPTER 9

On Saturday, February 10, Steve got up and, like any other
Saturday, ran some errands, while his wife's body was
stiffening in the cargo area of her Trooper. Temperatures
had dipped into the teens overnight, and combined with
rigor mortis, external factors were exerting their effect on
the corpse.

He took his Jeep Commander to the bank, the post office, and then around the familiar streets of Macomb
County. He went out past Stony Creek Metropark, then
circled back home. He held on to the keys to the locked
Trooper, lest Verena get too curious, but he was satisfied
that she had believed his story.

Bryan Rellinger returned Grant's message at 9 A.M.,
but Steve's college friend was at a restaurant eating
breakfast with his father and kids, preparing for a trip out
of town, and could not talk much. Investigators would
later question Rellinger, who denied that Steve told him
Tara was dead.

Verena was worried about Tara's apparent departure,

and just as concerned that she had figured out something was going on between the au pair and her husband. She told Steve to call Tara's cell phone, once, twice, three times, standing there as he obeyed.

Steve left messages, acting the angered husband who had been deserted. He had called first at 2:17 A.M. that morning, shortly after leaving the message for Bryan.

"Tara, it's Steve. It's, I think it's after two by now, it's quarter after two. I just want to know what the fuck's going on. I think you owe me and your kids. At least you owe a little bit of an explanation. Call me. Just call and let me know what the hell is going on."

He would leave several other messages, well aware that eventually, law enforcement would be involved and checking her voice mail.

"Hey, it's me, I'm just trying to find out what's going on this morning or today, or if you're still leaving today, if you're leaving tomorrow, or if you are planning on coming by. Just tell me ahead of time so I can make plans, make sure the kids are here because they want to see you. Um, gimme a call, bye."

As he moved forward in this massive deception, Steve began to methodically construct a variation on the story that he'd told Verena, a tale that he knew even he had to be convinced of if he was to gain credibility.

Steve unpacked Tara's Travel Pro suitcase, backing up his story to Verena—and later, to family, friends, and cops—that she had had a second suitcase packed for her departure Friday night.

On Saturday, he also called back Gary, the man with the basketball tickets in Lansing, just to make sure the deal was done. He was set for the MSU basketball game on the seventeenth.

Verena's concern was heightened by the fact that Steve

had backed off somewhat from his amorous pursuits. While just the previous night he had been madly texting and calling her, there were no communications that day. But Steve had other things to take care of besides his crush on a teenager.

"I planned to get up Saturday night and hide Tara somewhere," he later said. "But it was too cold and I knew I wouldn't be able to hide her."

As Steve pondered how to dispose of Tara's body, Verena went out to a movie and for coffee with her friend Anna and confided to her that Tara had left, and that she was concerned that it was because of the affair she was having with Steve.

When she came home at around 1 A.M., Steve was in bed, but awoke when he heard Verena arrive. The two then spent the rest of the night in Verena's bed. Steve had come up with a plan, and he didn't have much trouble sleeping.

He had decided he needed to dismember his wife's body.

On Sunday morning, February 11, Steve got up around 7 A.M., as usual, and walked out to the garage. He grabbed a blue plastic tarpaulin, which he placed in the Trooper's backseat. He also took his bow saw, a blue twenty-eight-gallon Rubbermaid container, some clear plastic garbage bags and some clear plastic sheeting, and a pint of whiskey from the well-stocked liquor cabinet.

"I have a lot of work to do today," he told Verena. He explained that he had missed some time at his job the previous week and had to make it up, and was going to USG Babbitt for a few hours.

Steve then called his sister, Kelly, and his father to

make sure they weren't planning on coming by the shop that day. Both would occasionally stop by USG on weekends to visit or perhaps go over some paperwork. But they were both busy with other activities that Sunday. The coast was clear. Grant got into the Trooper and headed for the shop, prepared for the grimmest task of his life.

The temperature overnight had again dropped into the teens, which suited Steve's plans.

He backed the Trooper into USG Babbitt—the garage doors were wide enough for a vehicle even the size of the large SUV—and opened the back gate. Over the past thirty-six hours, Tara's body had distended in several directions. "Her body was stiff and in a weird position," Grant wrote in his statement. One of her legs was now sticking out to the side, and an arm was sticking up and out. And her body was as stiff as a board.

"She was much bigger then," Steve said later. "Very hard to move."

The shop was jammed with machinery, saws, drops, and steel inventory. Steve cleared a space to lay the tarp, weighing down the four corners with pieces of metal, and placed his wife's body on it. To ensure there was enough room, he moved the Trooper back outside the building, which was vacant early on a Sunday.

Plans hatched in panic can defy logic and even believability. On this cold day, while other people were engaged in family activities like ice skating, skiing, perhaps shopping at the area's many malls, Stephen Grant was preparing to carve up his wife's body like a butcher slicing up a chicken.

If murder turns the world against the perpetrator, dismemberment casts them into a whole other category, that of a macabre sicko. And that is what Grant, only days earlier an active suburban father, elicited in the eyes of many as he crafted makeshift blades at the tool shop and went about dismembering Tara with the coldness of a maniac.

Steve grabbed the bow saw, took one of Tara's arms in his hand, and started to hack at the wrist, moving the serrated edge back and forth. But the frozen flesh didn't give as he thought it would, so he halted. This was proving to be more difficult than he'd anticipated.

Steve walked out to the truck, where he took a few pulls on the pint of whiskey. Momentarily setting aside his plans for the body, he turned his attention to Tara's briefcase, which she had left in the truck.

Steve took the case inside the shop with him, emptied it, and using one of the industrial machines in the shop, shredded the case on the band saw. Next he took her laptop computer and did the same, in the process shattering the hard drive, sending glass scattering about the shop. As he cleaned up the mess, a piece of glass jabbed into his finger.

Steve continued his chore, putting the computer pieces into a box along with Tara's purse, cell phone, and computer bag. In the office paper shredder, he disposed of her business cards and work documents and placed them along with other shredded materials in a paper bag.

Steve later explained that he knew he had to get rid of all of Tara's things because "Tara's not going to travel without her computer. She's not going to travel without her phone. She's not going to travel without her computer bag, all these files."

Eventually, he turned his attention back to the prone, twisted form that used to be his wife, now lying in the middle of the shop floor.

He looked around the shop, searching for a blade that would cut swiftly and with the least mess.

"I remembered that my dad . . . needed a hacksaw for something [after] he had one of the band saw blades break," Steve recalled later in his statement to police. "They stay straight, perfectly straight. They're like an inch wide, and they're ten teeth per inch and they're high carbon steel. So I took one of the old ones and I broke it and I snapped another piece off and I wrapped a washcloth or a blue towel around it and I started cutting with that."

Armed with six blades with their ends swathed in cloth, Steve began hacking at Tara's body, cutting the limbs at the joints: the elbow, the wrist, the shoulder, the knee, the ankle, and, finally, the neck. It was rough going at the start and he vomited shortly after starting, he told officers.

"I cut her next joint and then the next joint, and at some point, I threw up . . . and I threw up again. And then I drank some more whiskey. And then I just told myself, 'Look, if you don't do this, you're going to prison for the rest of your life.' "

He told the cops there was "very little blood. And it surprised me, to be honest." The little blood there was, he said, "was real thick, like syrup."

And he couldn't remove Tara's pants, "so I just ripped the pant legs up to the waistband. And I cut as high as those, but the blade kept catching in the cloth."

When he was done, he had separated Tara Grant's body into fourteen pieces, which were spread out before him. He then wrapped the body parts in thick, forty-gallon plastic garbage bags and placed them in the twenty-eight-gallon container. Some bags had one piece, others two.

On top of them he placed the blades and some rags, then finally the headless torso, which he covered with more rags as well as a pair of blue-and-red-striped work gloves he'd worn as he toiled. The torso, Steve said, was wrapped in thicker green plastic. He had ripped some parts of the tarp as he'd sawed, and he also cleaned up some flesh and blood that had seeped through onto the floor of the shop.

After filling the container, he jammed it with newspaper to ensure that nothing shook around.

"I was kind of surprised that she all fit in there," Steve would later tell investigators. "When I first started looking at her, once I got her out of the truck, I thought, 'There's no way.'"

The deed done, Steve backed the Trooper into the shop and loaded it with the Rubbermaid container and the bags of Tara's shredded belongings. Rolling down the windows to prevent any possible odor of decay, he drove back to the house on Westridge at 2:30 P.M. and left the Trooper, and Tara's remains, locked in the garage. Then he rounded up Lindsey and Ian and put them into the Jeep Commander, and they all went to get some groceries at Meijer. Mom was mad but she would be back, he told them. Don't worry.

While they were out, Verena left to meet Anna. While she was waiting at a traffic light en route, Steve and the kids were sitting at the same light, going in the opposite direction.

"I see you," Steve texted her.

Verena returned home at 8 P.M., and Steve waltzed down the stairs and kissed her.

"I missed you," he said. "You were gone most of the weekend."

The two sat down in the family room and watched the TV show *Desperate Housewives*, which Verena usually watched with Tara.

Later, around eleven-thirty, Steve came into Verena's

room and lay down, caressing her, calmly and with tenderness. If he was worried about his missing wife, it wasn't apparent to Verena.

At 3 A.M., Monday, February 12, Steve awoke and, without rousing Verena, dressed, went downstairs, and eased the Trooper down the driveway. Before leaving, he also placed a red plastic sled in the truck, without a specific plan in mind. It was dark, twelve frigid degrees, and Steve was making it up as he went along.

———

After an hour of driving through mostly empty roads, with the red plastic sled and the blue Rubbermaid container holding the fourteen pieces of flesh and bone that were once Tara Grant, Steve began thinking of a hiding spot for the remains. He contemplated putting the container in a Dumpster, but realized that if the Dumpster was upended, a likely scenario, it would present a nasty surprise to whoever was around. Even though the parts were individually wrapped, there was some blood in the clear plastic wrap, and a human hand, for example, was quite easily recognizable.

Steve pulled the truck south onto Mt. Vernon from Inwood, into a sparsely populated portion of the county where mostly isolated homes sat thirty to forty yards off the road. Inwood Road, a stretch of mostly dirt road, marked the northern border of Stony Creek Metropark, the suburban wilderness oasis whose proximity had so appealed to the Grants when they bought the Westridge home. It was four miles from the Grant house.

Steve knew the area, he had jogged out there plenty, although in the pitch blackness, it was more difficult to navigate. A small incline, where, in better weather, county maintenance crews could park, offered him a track for the sled. The snow was several days old now and it stood about five inches deep, a good base for sledding.

Steve parked the car and removed the Rubbermaid tub and plastic sled. He placed the tub on the sled and pulled it behind him up the incline. As he reached the top, he moved the sled past a broken cattle guard that had been erected to prevent ATV and other motorized vehicles into the park. But when he paused, Steve later said, the sled took off on its own, sliding down a slight ravine into the woods, where it smacked gently against a tree, spilling body parts out into the snow.

"As soon as I started going, it was like Keystone Kops," Steve said later. "The sled took off and now I'm chasing after the sled with Tara's remains and cut up body in it down a hill."

Panicked, with the moon providing the only light for his macabre endeavor, Steve grabbed the largest piece, Tara's torso, and quickly buried it in a drift of snow. He buried the remaining body parts in another snowdrift. To his eye, in the darkness, they appeared satisfactorily covered. The scene was a flashback to the Mac-10 machine gun he had buried so many years before. But the stakes were now much higher, and this had to be done right.

Also in the Rubbermaid container were the makeshift saw blades he had used in the dismemberment, which he now dispersed with wide throws into the darkness. Same with the rags he had used to hold on to the blades; Steve tossed them as far as he could into the dark forest, along with a pair of black, size-twelve Rockport shoes that he had been wearing when he cut the body up, and the rubber latex gloves he was currently wearing to avoid leaving fingerprints on the parts or the sled.

"I was standing where the sled was and I would throw a shoe and I would throw a thing, just to make everything kind of disappear into the forest."

It was a lousy job of hiding the evidence, he knew. The nearest house was a half mile to the south, but the park was popular with the locals, and, well, he was sure an astute resident would soon make a grisly finding.

What would happen then? No one knew Tara was missing except Verena, but this would get him busted for sure. So he did what he had done for much of his life when things got to be too much.

He ran. This time, to the truck. He had to get out of there.

———

Steve hopped into the Trooper and drove back home, parked Tara's truck, and loaded the remaining evidence into his Jeep Commander. He wiped the Trooper down, sat down in the family room, and chatted with Verena as Lindsey and Ian began getting ready for school upstairs. Once they were fed and ready to go, he also got up to leave. But as he spoke to Verena, wishing her a good day, he teared up. Verena was sure it was because he missed his wife. But he also warned Verena that if Tara were to return while he was gone, she needed to phone him immediately. And if Tara were to head upstairs, where he told Verena he kept a loaded CZ 9mm handgun, she was instructed "to grab the kids and get out of the house," the au pair would later say.

"He said if she does come back, then I should call him and the police 'cause he didn't know what was going on in Tara's head," she said.

Actually, Steve was still trying to find a permanent hiding place for Tara's head, hands, feet, and everything else. As his family finished their morning at home, he got into the Jeep and headed back to Mt. Vernon and Inwood roads, this time pulling his vehicle up the incline, past the cattle guard, as far in as he could get to avoid detection.

As he reached the woods, he made another call to Tara's cell phone.

"Hey, it's me once again. It's quarter to seven and I'm going to tell you this: If I don't hear from you in fifteen minutes, I'm going to call Randy, get Lou's cell number, and find out what the fuck is going on. This is nonsense, Tara, you owe me a phone call, you owe me to let me know what the fuck is going on between us. Please call."

After making the call, Steve ran down into the small valley and pulled the sled out of the snowbank, unburied the plastic-wrapped torso, and, in the plain light of day, dragged it down into the woods a little farther until he found a suitable spot, removed the torso, and reburied it in the snow.

Steve then pulled the sled back to its original spot, loaded it up with the other dismembered body parts, and reburied them in the snow as well. He grabbed the blue Rubbermaid container, walked back to the Jeep, tossed it in, and backed down onto Mt. Vernon Road. There was more obfuscating to do.

But first, he called Lou Troendle at Washington Group. It was 8 A.M. by the time he reached Lou at the office in Troy, and Steve disingenuously asked if Tara had arrived in San Juan. Lou told him no, and Steve carefully recited much the same story he had already related to Verena. The bickering over travel, the yelling, the black car-service vehicle, and Tara's abrupt departure. Steve called once more at seven-thirty that night, again inquiring if Lou had heard anything. "He was reasonably calm, somewhat concerned, somewhat upset," Troendle would later recall.

As he called that morning, Steve was headed south down Mound Road toward the first home he and Tara had bought in Shelby Township. Three blocks from that home, at an apartment complex set on Lake Pointe, he tossed the blue container into a Dumpster. From there he headed to another familiar place, Riverland Drive, where he had grown up. A block from his old house was another apartment complex, with parking areas under the buildings and Dumpsters at the foot of every other stairwell. Pulling to the very last building, Steve shoved Tara's shredded computer bag and purse into a Dumpster, then drove on to work, where he discarded the cardboard box holding Tara's cut-up cell phone and filleted computer in a Dumpster just twenty feet from the entrance to USG Babbitt.

In all, Steve had driven twenty-one miles, scattering a trail of evidence that would never be completely recovered. He was still worried, though, about that torso. Tara's torso, headless, lay buried in snow, frozen stiff. Someone, he thought, was going to come by and see it if the wind blew away the snow.

———

Verena was worried as well. She was sure that Tara had discovered that she and Steve were sleeping together. And if Tara was angry enough to go for a gun, well, things had truly gotten out of hand. That evening, her friend Anna came over after dinner and the two were upstairs in Verena's room, talking about the missing Tara, when Steve knocked on the door.

"Today I called Lou and asked him if he knew what

was going on," he told the girls. "Tara's not in Puerto Rico yet."

The two girls looked at each other, Verena's anxiety inching up another notch.

When Anna left, Steve and Verena sat downstairs in the family room, watching each other and the TV.

"Does Anna know about us?" Steve asked.

Now it was Verena's turn to lie.

"No, she doesn't," she said. The two then repaired to Verena's room, where they hugged each other all night, according to Verena.

———

On Tuesday morning, February 13, Steve used the shop phone to call Mary Destrampe, Tara's mother, in Chillicothe, Ohio. He told her that Tara had stormed out on Friday and that he was having a hard time getting her to respond since then. He asked if Tara had contacted her. Mary said she had not heard from her and was concerned. In fact, the last time Tara and her mother had spoken was on February 4, when Tara complained of her treadmill travel schedule. After hanging up with Steve, Mary immediately called Alicia Standerfer, Tara's younger sister, who lived a mile away.

"Steve just called me and Tara's missing," Mary told her. "He hasn't heard from her in four days."

Shortly after 10 A.M., Grant received a call on his cell phone from Alicia. Again, he outlined the story that was now becoming second nature, with few variations. The argument, the private car, the end. Alicia was not as placid as her mother, and she lit into Steve.

"You are a terrible husband," she said. Even if Alicia and Tara had a fractious relationship—and they did, friends and family members say—Steve had always been persona non grata with Alicia.

"Tara would never leave her children and not let us know where she was," Alicia later told an interviewer. And in the case of an argument such as the one that Steve was describing, it was her family that Tara would reach out to, Alicia felt.

With two young children of her own, Alicia was also a very capable woman, and didn't seem to mind kicking ass when it needed to be kicked. And she told Steve that he needed to get over to the police station and make things happen.

Steve began to put out calls to friends asking if they had seen Tara. During the day, he called his friend Mike Zanlungo, he called Bryan Rellinger again, and he called Martha Anaud. He spoke several times to his sister, Kelly. He delivered the same story, over and over, until it was rote. Steve was doing an acting job that prosecutors would later call "Oscar-worthy."

But there was still work to do, and the slow traipse toward police involvement upped his worry level.

After work, Steve told Verena that he was going to take a run at Stony Creek Metropark. He frequently used the park for running and bicycling, and he knew the trails well. When he got there, he parked his Jeep at the nature center near the middle of the park and began a quick jog north toward the buried body parts.

Steve carried with him a gallon Ziploc bag, which he'd jammed with clear plastic wrap, and he wore rubber gloves under his regular gloves. Under his knit hat, he'd stashed a single-edged razor blade.

Daylight had faded, but guided by overhead power lines, he found the burial sites with relative ease. He exhumed Tara's body parts and loaded up the sled again.

Easing the sled onto a small trail, Steve moved to an area with an abundance of tree falls. He then methodically sliced through the plastic with the razor and unwrapped the parts, then placed them under the falls and whatever stumps he could find.

His actions were at once ghoulish, panicked, and nonsensical. Even Steve can't explain what he was trying to accomplish by unwrapping the dismembered body parts, although some have speculated that he hoped that animals would feast on them. Still, to consume a human body would take considerable time. And time was one thing that Grant was running out of.

As he cut the plastic wrap open, he would bunch it up and jam it into the gallon Ziploc.

Steve was satisfied that the parts were now hidden and unwrapped. He began to head back to the nature center, discarding items as he walked. The hat and his woolen gloves went into a small river that ran through the west side of the park. The gallon bag, with the bloody plastic wrap and also the rubber gloves, he stashed behind a large grove of trees ten feet off Mt. Vernon Road, where it would be unapparent to anyone walking down the west side of the road.

Once back in his Jeep, Steve stripped off his track shoes and the black fleece jacket he was wearing, as well as the outer of two layers of running tights he'd been wearing. He put them all in a paper garbage bag he had brought along.

––––––

He returned home in time to answer a call from Martha Anaud.

"Tara left me on Friday night, we had a fight," Steve said. "Has she called you?"

"No, what happened?" Martha said. "What did she say when she left?"

They spoke for forty-five minutes, with Steve handling most of the conversation.

"I asked him a number of questions, and he launched into this long elaborate story," Martha says. When she tried to stop him and ask a question, Steve would plow on, refusing to answer until he hit the part of the story that related to her query. To Martha, who had known Steve for years, it sounded like he was testing out an explanation and didn't want any interruptions.

––––––––

Verena came home from Spanish class around ten that evening and Steve was home, watching TV in the family room.

"I'm going to have to call the police tomorrow," he said. "I have to report her missing."

After letting that sink in, he abruptly changed directions.

"How do you feel about me?" he asked. "I really need to know. I need to know now."

Verena looked down, away. She could not answer the question directly.

"Do you like me?" he asked.

"Yes," she said shortly. She was ashamed but could not lie.

"Are you in love with me?" Steve persisted.

She knew that she liked him much more than she should and way more than was appropriate. But love, that was a tough one.

"It's too early to say," she managed.

"Are you falling in love with me?" he came back.

"Maybe."

"Well, I love you, Verena," Steve said.

The couple went to bed. It had been a long day for Steve. And the next day was the start of his achieving a celebrity status that no one on earth would want.

CHAPTER 10

Macomb County has had a tempestuous affair with law enforcement over the years, one that has often been marked by precipitous tumbles from grace and braying accusations of malfeasance.

At the helm of the county's law enforcement chain is Sheriff Mark Hackel, a dogged self-promoter with prime-time looks who was first elected in November 2000 in the Democrat-dominated county. His father, William, had served twenty-four years as Macomb County sheriff and was named Citizen of the Year at one point by the local chapter of the March of Dimes, only to have his reputation undone by a later rape conviction.

William Hackel was convicted in April 2000 on two counts of third-degree criminal sexual conduct in relation to an incident with a twenty-five-year-old woman in October 1999 in a hotel room at the Soaring Eagle Casino and Resort in Mt. Pleasant, Michigan. He was sentenced to three to fifteen years in prison and was released after serving three years.

Hackel, who was married, maintained that the sex was consensual.

Shortly after Mark Hackel's election, the county's prosecutor of twenty years, Carl Marlinga, was accused of trading judicial favors for political support. Hackel supported the accused Marlinga, who was acquitted in the case. But the stench of dirty politics, cronyism, and corruption made voters in the otherwise law-and-order county north of Detroit wary.

Nevertheless, Mark Hackel was reelected in 2004. As the Grant case unfolded, Hackel was whispered to be eyeing a position as county executive, a lofty spot that would give him great power, with a fat salary and perks galore.

The Grant case would give Hackel a national platform, one that he used to his advantage, regularly appearing on national television and holding press conferences almost daily.

It was a Valentine's Day gift of sorts, which began on the morning of Wednesday, February 14, when Stephen Grant walked into the Macomb County Sheriff's Department during his lunch break from USG Babbitt. When most couples were celebrating their love, Steve was about to report the disappearance of his wife as part of a murder cover-up.

Grant entered the main lobby and strode down the hall of the building with its institutional-gray tiled floor, sickish purple fluorescent ceiling lights, and cold, impersonal vibe. Steve walked into a small office, approached a desk sergeant, and simply said, "I need to report my wife missing."

In a ninety-minute conversation, Grant told sheriff's deputy William Hughes the entire fake story again, complete with the dispute over "family issues," Tara's departure, the car service, and so on. He kept talking, adding more details, and even editorializing, filling the rapt officer in on his opinions about his missing wife.

In a report filed later that day, Hughes said that Grant told him the kids would not miss Tara because he was more involved in their activities than their mother was.

"I don't know if I want her back," Steve told the officer, according to the report. "In fact, I don't care if she ever comes back." He tossed in the notion that he had contacted an attorney to discuss filing for a divorce.

Steve also related that he had told Tara's sister, Alicia, that at this point, he would even be pleased to find that she was spending time with a boyfriend in a motel. In his written statement to the police that day, he said that he had called Lou Troendle, Tara's supervisor, who had asked that he not do anything until Tuesday.

"After getting off the phone, I thought, I was certain that Lou knew where she was, otherwise he would be worried."

He reported that he'd had a couple of beers before Tara came home on the ninth. He said he owned a handgun. Steve was all about giving up information, especially minutiae.

Hughes, a veteran cop, was listening with one ear at times as he looked at the scratch on Grant's face, the one-inch gash over his left nostril that was now clotted and well into the healing process. It must have been a hell of a scratch when it was first administered, he thought.

The case was assigned to Detective Sergeant Brian Kozlowski, a squat, balding, serious-looking man in his late thirties who had been with the department since 1990 and an investigator since 1997.

That evening at around 7 P.M. after reviewing Steve's statement and reading Hughes's report, Kozlowski and

his superior officer Sergeant Pam McLean visited the
Grant home on Westridge.

Steve let them in through the front door, and the kids
came around, curious about their visitors, before they
were sent into the family room to watch TV while Steve
told the story again—the fight over travel, the private car,
Tara walking out.

McLean spoke with Verena for about five minutes,
and Verena told her about the night in question, her out-
ing at Mr. B's, and her return to find a depressed Steve
who mistook her for Tara as she walked into the house
from the garage. Verena told the officer that she believed
the two were having marital problems.

Steve, again, was expansive in his conversation. He
told the officers that he was sure Tara's family knew
where she was and "they were keeping it from him,"
McLean recalled later.

Grant spoke with Kozlowski as the kids broke away from
their TV show to escort McLean around the house, excit-
edly showing their visitor their favorite toys and pictures.

She noticed three pairs of glasses on the nightstand in
the master bedroom. Inside the nightstand drawer, she
found several envelopes of money. McLean noted that the
house was tidy, "very clean."

"Mom is at work in another country," Lindsey told
McLean. "She'll be home soon."

Steve told Kozlowski essentially the same story he
had told Hughes at the department several hours earlier.

There was a glitch in Steve's story, however, which
raised the detective's bushy eyebrows. Earlier, he had told
Deputy Hughes that Tara had decided to return to San
Juan on Saturday, the tenth. Now he pegged the day as
Sunday, the eleventh. Kozlowski then asked about the
scratch on the left side of Grant's nose.

"A metal shaving caught under my safety glasses at work," Steve said, then pointed to scratches on his hand and pulled up his pant leg to show a purple bruise on his leg. A police photographer came around later that evening to document Grant's injuries, snapping a series of photos of the scratches and bruises.

Kozlowski asked about the state of the Grants' marriage.

"Are either of you involved with someone outside the marriage?" he asked.

"I don't think Tara is involved with anyone, and I'm not either," Steve said. "There was a time in the past, Tara . . . but it's over."

The two officers looked at everything with a suspicious eye, and Steve's demeanor—jittery and high-strung even on his best days—was troubling to them.

After a walk through the house, during which they noticed Bentley, the Grants' golden retriever/shepherd mix, and commented on what a beautiful dog he had, the two officers sat with Steve, alone at the dining-room table. The more inquisitive the cops became, the more nervous Steve became, McLean said later.

"He wouldn't necessarily answer all our questions, he was changing topics," she recalled.

As they prepared to leave at around eight-thirty, Kozlowski asked Grant if he would be willing to come down to the department and take a lie detector test. Steve said yes, then: "So you think that means I'm going to be in trouble for any of this?"

"What kind of trouble?" Kozlowski replied.

"You know, I didn't have anything to do with this," Steve said, and he began to cry.

———

The two detectives left the house without checking the most crucial piece of potential evidence in any missing-persons case: the family computer, which could contain evidence as to travel plans perhaps made weeks in advance, e-mails to persons who might have reason to do harm to Tara, or myriad other possibilities. But Kozlowski and McLean left without even asking if they could take the computer to see if there might be some clues as to Tara's whereabouts.

A missing-persons report is often met with a certain amount of skepticism by police, who know well that oftentimes a dispute can spark a flight, and that flight is often used to blow off steam. In this case, though, Tara had been missing five days, too long for just cooling off. Kozlowski said later that he was suspicious of this case immediately. Yet, while he was in the house that first day when Tara was reported missing—the most crucial time that could have been presented given the five-day lapse—he never tried to get the computer from the home office.

"It is most compelling to get into the house immediately when there is a disappearance," says one Macomb investigator, who worked on the case. "Even if the husband is not a witness, you have to get in that house and grab the computers, because this could very well be a crime scene. This was a big screwup."

On the other hand, another source who worked closely on the investigation said the failure to remove the computer was simple: The two visiting officers had no warrant.

"She was a missing person, and stats show that in many of these cases, it's the spouse that is the suspect. But short of these stats, there's no reason to say, 'Let me have that computer.'"

Despite this possible oversight, the two detectives began their own investigation, tracing travel plans, including the discovery that Tara had had a seat on a flight to San Juan that past Monday. Kozlowski contacted Lou Troendle, Tara's family, and Joe Herrity, Washington Group's head of security. Through Herrity, the sergeant was able to check Tara's email, her American Express card account, and her cell phone. In a report, Kozlowski noted that "no activity was recorded on any of these since February 9."

Phone records were pulled, showing that the last call from Tara's cell ended at 10:05 P.M. on the ninth. The detectives called twelve car-service operations in the area, and none had ferried Tara.

Things weren't adding up. Maybe it would be good to keep an eye on this Stephen Grant, the two detecetives thought. Shortly after their visit to the home, officers began to routinely cruise by the house, and within days, an undercover car was assigned to follow Grant whenever possible.

The line of questioning the night of February 14 spooked Steve enough to prompt him to begin looking for a good lawyer. After talking to a couple of people and doing a bit of sleuthing on the Internet, he settled on David Griem, an accomplished attorney based in Detroit. Steve's lawyer friend in Lansing, Tom Munley, had recommended Griem, so first thing Thursday morning, February 15, Steve placed a call to him, and within hours, he was sitting in Griem's twenty-fourth-floor office at the Guardian Building, a historic Art Deco edifice in downtown Detroit that could be reasonably deemed one of the few remaining architectural beauties in the long-dead city. There were several things that Griem was nailing down for his new client. No lie detector test would be given by the police. And no more police interrogations or visits unless Griem approved.

———

David Griem had served as the top trial attorney in the Macomb County Prosecutor's Office from 1973 to 1979, losing just one murder case during his tenure. It was the local boy's first professional job after graduating from the Detroit College of Law. Although he had initially aspired to a career in advertising (which had been his major at Michigan State University), he attributes his change of heart to Atticus Finch, the famous fictional lawyer from the book *To Kill a Mockingbird*.

Over the years, Griem switched sides to become a top-flight defense attorney, landing a number of high-profile cases. In 1992, he represented a Detroit Police Department officer, Sergeant Freddie Douglas, in the case of Malice Green, a black man who'd been beaten to death by two officers. Douglas, the sergeant on duty the night of the death and present at the scene of the crime, was acquitted of felony charges for failing to halt the beating and convicted only of neglect of duty, a misdemeanor.

In 1998, Griem represented accused Mafia chieftain Jack Tocco, charged with racketeering and conspiracy. A jury acquitted Tocco of the harshest charges and Tocco was out of jail in less than two years.

Steve came to Griem and appeared for all the world to be genuinely concerned about the whereabouts of his wife, Griem says, calling Steve "a very, very convincing individual."

"I came away from our first meeting convinced that this was a man who was frantic about his wife's situation," Griem says. "He wanted to do everything he could to find his wife and at the same time was trying to keep his family ship afloat."

———

While Steve sat talking about his missing wife with Griem, Verena pulled out of the driveway and headed to Krambrooke-Griffin Academy to pick up Ian. She spotted marked Macomb County Sheriff's Office cars sitting at each end of the street, just a hundred and fifty feet away. As she drove past them heading up toward 28 Mile Road, one of the cars fell in behind her and she stopped.

"Who are you?" the officer asked the shaken girl, who had rolled down the window.

She told him she was the au pair at the Grant home and was on her way to pick up one of the children from school.

"Do you know where Stephen Grant is?" the officer came back.

"I think he is talking to a lawyer but I don't know where," Verena said.

"Are you sure he's not at home?" the officer asked. Deputies had been trying to reach Grant on his cell phone, he said, but he hadn't answered.

"I do not know where he is," Verena repeated. It was clear that the officers were suspicious of the mild-mannered au pair, and they had succeeded in scaring her. After fetching Ian, as she pulled the boy from the car in the driveway, Steve called. "There are police cars watching us, watching the house," Verena told him, starting to cry. "These officers scared me. They said they are looking for you."

"They knew where I was, I was at the attorney's," Steve said. He considered what they could want and it hit him: "They probably want to search the house."

Which was fine with Grant. There was no evidence that he felt would give away his deed. The body was gone, and on Tuesday, two days previously, the region had been blanketed with another five inches of snow. That would provide a nice cover over the pieces of Tara that he had scattered, he assumed.

Steve had gone back to the shop for a bit after his meeting with Griem before heading home. Meanwhile, Griem faxed a note to Sergeant Kozlowski.

Because of the tone of your February 14, 2007, interrogation of Mr. Grant at his home . . . it is my humble opinion that it is necessary for me to provide a buffer between your department and Mr. Grant.

Just as Mr. Grant answered all of your questions last night, he will continue to answer all of your questions in the future. I believe it is necessary, however, so there are no misunderstandings, that all of your future questions be submitted in writing, which will, in turn, be immediately answered in writing.

It was enough to send the already-testy officer over the edge. It was going to be that way, eh?

Working quickly, police discovered that Steve had been driving on a suspended license. Three squad cars pulled him over not far from his work at 2:15 P.M. that day. According to a police report, he was stopped for turning without using a signal. The suspended license got him arrested. He was held for six hours as officers attempted to quiz him about Tara.

Tara, as a bridesmaid in the April 1993
wedding of her friend Amy Ritenburgh.
—*Courtesy of Amy Sabourin*

Tara returned every spring to her childhood home in Michigan's Upper
Peninsula to help her father, Dusty Destrampe, tap for maple syrup.

—*From the collection of the authors*

USG Babbitt sponsored a car in the Mount Clemens soap box derby for several years. Stephen is on the left, and his father, Al Grant, and Tara are on the far right.

—Courtesy of Diane Carroll

Steve on the boat that he and Tara briefly owned, 1998.

—Courtesy of Kelly K. Utykanski

Stephen Grant and his dog, Bentley, at Wilderness State Park c. 2000.

—Courtesy of Kelly K. Utykanski

Macomb County Sheriff Mark Hackel held a press conference on March 2, 2007, announcing the executions of search warrants on the Grant home and USG Babbitt. —*Todd McInturf*/The Detroit News

LEFT:
USG Babbitt, the metal shop where Steve worked with his father.
—*Courtesy of the Macomb County Prosecutor's Office*

BELOW:
The Grant house on Westridge, in Washington Township, Michigan.
—*From the collection of the authors*

Detective Sergeant Brian Kozlowski, Stephen Grant and Detective Sergeant Pam McLean checking the camera in an interview room. The officers had hoped to get Grant to repeat his confession on video, but he refused. Grant is clad in a Velcro "suicide suit." —*Courtesy of the Macomb County Prosecutor's Office*

ABOVE:
Evidence technicians carry bags from the woods of Stony Creek Metropark on March 4, two days after the torso of Tara Grant was found in the garage of the family home.
—*Brandy Baker/*The Detroit News

RIGHT:
Sheila Werner was walking through Stony Creek Metropark when she found a plastic bag that Grant had discarded as he attempted to hide Tara's body parts. —*Dateline NBC*

Steve, age two, and sister, Kelly, age four, 1972.
—*Courtesy of Kelly K. Utykanski*

Kelly and Steve lock eyes as they see each other for the first time since Grant's arrest and confession, 2007.　　—*Todd McInturf*/The Detroit News

Gail Pamukov and Stephen Rabaut, Grant's attorneys, confer during a pretrial hearing.
—*Todd McInturf*/The Detroit News

Verena Dierkes, the Grant family's nanny, testified against Stephen Grant at his trial, telling of their affair.
—*Dateline NBC*

David Griem, who defended Grant before the confession, testifies at a preliminary hearing for Grant.
—Macomb Daily

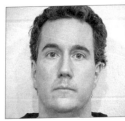

LEFT:
Stephen Grant, inmate #674421
—*Courtesy of Michigan Department of Corrections*

BELOW:
After a break in the trial, Steve is escorted back to the courtroom.
—*Todd McInturf*/The Detroit News

Therese Tobin, Bill Cataldo and Eric Smith, who prosecuted Grant, were pleased with the sentence handed down that would keep Grant in prison for fifty years before a shot at parole.
—*Todd McInturf*/The Detroit News

Alicia Standerfer, Tara's sister, leaves the courtroom, trailed by one of her lawyers, Mike Smith.
—From the collection of the authors

LOVING MOTHER DAUGHTER SISTER
TARA LYNN GRANT
NEE DESTRAMPE
JUNE 28, 1972   FEB. 9, 2007

Tara's grave, Gardens of Rest Cemetery, Escanaba, Michigan.
—Paul F. Blewett Photography

"I get why they stopped me," Steve told the *Detroit News.* "They thought I was going to be a little girl and go down there and cry and confess all my sins. But there's no sins, though."

The local NBC affiliate, WDIV, reported that Steve told the officer who approached him upon being stopped, "I know why you're pulling me over. It's because of my wife."

According to a police report, "[Grant] stated that his wife had left for San Juan approximately five days ago and he had never heard from her since. He further stated that the police were at his residence conducting a search," which, of course, was not true.

Griem called the traffic stop "cowboy tactics" to the press the next day.

"Many police officers can't make a case without a confession," Griem says now. "And one idea is to catch [a criminal] at a low time and hope he'll blurt out a confession. Put him behind bars, hope he'll fall apart. It didn't work [with Grant]."

But Steve got the message loud and clear. The cops were not going to play around.

———

That evening, Verena sent Lindsey and Ian to spend the night with their aunt Kelly while she went over to a friend's house. The next morning, Friday, February 16, shortly after 9 A.M., her cell phone rang. It was Sergeant McLean, asking if Verena could spare some time that day to talk. Verena put her off, saying she had to take care of the kids.

———

Verena was upset by the call. Things were getting sticky.

"The police called me this morning and they want to

talk," she told Steve. "I'm very afraid they are going to find out about us."

Steve had told her one evening that such a discovery would doom him. The cops would jump on it and assume he'd been trying to get Tara out of the way in order to pursue his new romance, he told her. Now he restated this concern.

"There are a lot of innocent people in jail," he said. "I don't want to be one of them. If the police find out that we are together, I'm going to tell them it started after February ninth, that Friday. And I'll just say that we kissed once."

Now Steve was reciting his own fears as Verena listened, rapt. He had concocted a story about the text messages he and Verena had exchanged.

"He said that if the police know anything about the text messages and they are somehow able to read them, he will tell the police that he and Tara had sex with a third person when they were in Puerto Rico and they liked it," Verena later told investigators. "He said he would tell them that they decided they wanted to do the same with me and that Tara had told him he should flirt with me."

It was an elaborate ruse, and Verena, for her part, thought the idea was stupid. It didn't temper her growing fondness for Steve, though. The two again spent the night together in Verena's bed for what turned out to be the last time.

While they slept, Tara's sister, Alicia, and her husband, Erik, were preparing to make the five-hour drive from their Ohio home to Macomb County to help find Tara. Carla Lanaville, Tara's aunt, and her husband Rod joined them, making the eight-hour trek from the Escanaba area.

Alicia and Steve had spoken by phone numerous times

over the past several days, and Alicia was thoroughly worried about her sister.

She was intent on doing something, anything, to ease her anxiety. Even before the deluge of publicity over her missing sister hit and cast a national spotlight on her, Alicia was the picture of grim resolution. While Tara was relatively thin, Alicia appeared breathtakingly slender. With her ultrafair skin and too-dark hair, cut in a spiky crow's-nest shag, she looked perpetually starved and angry, wearing a pulled expression that said she was devastated and out for justice. Erik, her husband, tall and balding, was also thin and looked like he, too, had missed out on meaningful sleep over the last couple of nights. Already the stress of the case was taking its toll on the family. Tara had left Steve once before, for twenty-four hours, after a particularly nasty spat. But this time something was seriously wrong.

Alicia had missing-person posters made and began making the rounds down the main arteries of Macomb County, placing them in gas stations and hotels. Erik took a trip to Detroit Metro Airport and checked hotels in the area. Nothing. And they were frustrated that Steve wasn't intent on helping, but in fact was an emotional wreck, oscillating from anger to despair to virtual incoherence.

On Saturday, February 17, a small item appeared in the *Detroit Free Press* about the missing person, near the bottom of the metro page. Other news outlets were starting to pick up the story by the end of the day, and Sheriff Hackel was eyeing this as a good chance to get the word out about Tara's disappearance.

That afternoon of the seventeenth, Verena left the house on Westridge for good, ordered out by her Au Pair America counselor, Sue Murasky, whom she would stay with temporarily.

First, however, Verena and Sue sat down at the sheriff's office with Sergeant Kozlowski, where Verena again told the story of the February 9 events.

When Kozlowski asked her point-blank if she was having an intimate relationship with Steve, she flatly denied it.

"She told me she believed Stephen Grant was a good father and husband," Kozlowski said in his report. "She also said she believed it unlikely that Tara Grant would not talk to her children for this long. Verena said Tara spoke with the children every day when she was traveling."

A few days later, Verena flew back to Germany. Steve called her periodically, professing his love for her and asking her if she felt the same way. Most of the time she did.

Back in Macomb County, on February 18, Alicia and Erik went over to Steve's and they all went out to dinner, Steve insisting on driving. They took Tara's Trooper. It was roomier, he said. When they returned from dinner to the house on Westridge, a satellite truck from Channel 2, the local Fox affiliate, was sitting on the street. Steve was irked, but Erik went out to speak to the camera. He tossed out a couple of generic statements and the trucks left.

Alicia and Erik returned to Ohio the next day with plans to come back to Macomb the next weekend. Carla and Rod drove home as well, feeling they had done everything they could.

Meanwhile, David Griem wanted to test the waters on the polygraph. The sheriff's office had contacted him once more and asked if Steve would take one, and of course Griem had refused. But what if Steve could pass one? One afternoon, it was set up with a local firm, and Steve sat down, had the electrodes connected. On some parts he fared well, on others he failed.

"They never asked me if I killed Tara," Steve now recalls. "They would ask, 'Did you have anything to do with your wife's disappearance?' I was surprised that I passed any of it."

The test came back inconclusive. No one was going to get to see the results.

———

On Tuesday, February 20, the *Detroit Free Press* blared a front-page story, WHERE IS TARA LYNN GRANT? It quoted Alicia extensively, who asserted that Tara had told her during that last phone call during the layover at the Newark airport that she had changed her typical weekend plans.

"Standerfer said her sister told her that her visit home that weekend had to be cut short because she had to fly back to Puerto Rico a day early," the story reported.

Sheriff's Captain Tony Wickersham said in the story that Steve was not a suspect.

The story launched a love affair between Alicia and the media, one that never foundered. But it also fed Steve's love of drama, with the picture of him on the jump page, 8A, tearing up as he spoke to a reporter.

By the end of the week, Steve would talk to any reporter who called him, and there were plenty of them. The questions came at all hours, in all places. He spoke with reporters and TV crews in parking lots, at the sheriff's office, or on their cell phones, sometimes calling them back three or four times a day. The conversations were generally about the case, but as the weeks passed, Steve would want to just chat, about hunting, haircuts, other things in the news, whatever. It was clear to reporters that he was loving the attention.

When it was revealed that Steve had worked in the office of State Senator Jack Faxon in the mid-nineties, the retired politician was deluged with calls. Faxon claimed to barely recall one of his top-ranking office staffers, but Steve felt bad that his former boss was dragged into the media melee.

"He called me and apologized," Faxon says. "He ran down the whole story of his wife going missing, in fact. I listened and barely said a word. It seemed funny that this fellow would call me and tell me about his wife's disappearance in such detail. This was a guy who really liked to talk."

Grant's attorney, David Griem, refused to take to the airwaves himself, instead firing off polite letters of refusal to over a dozen national TV news entities that sought his face on their networks.

> While I appreciate your invitation, I cannot appear on your program. My duty to my client, Stephen Grant, requires me to take a different approach from that being taken by the Macomb County Sheriff's Department. The police are trying Stephen Grant in the media, holding daily press conferences filled with innuendo about my client. While acknowledging that they do not have probable cause to believe that a crime has been committed, much less that Stephen Grant is implicated, police spokesmen miss no opportunity to question his actions, motives, and the extent of his cooperation . . . It would not be a service to my client to succumb to the urge to debate the sheriff's department and rebut the misstatements about my client that are being made daily. Frankly the focus of the police is not as concentrated as it should be on finding Tara Grant.

"We kept a list of every national news show that requested my presence," Griem says. "We did zero. The sheriff did every single one. Tara's sister did many of them. I did not, for several reasons. One, there was nothing to gain in doing these shows for my client. Two, I didn't want to be portrayed as beating up on Tara's sister. And number three, I love beating up on the sheriff, but no good would come of that for the client."

———

Steve, though, even gave interviews outside USG Babbitt in the days after the investigation began. One morning, Chad Halcom, a reporter for the *Macomb Daily* newspaper, went over to the shop with photographer David Dalton in tow. But Steve would not let the two into the shop. Dalton's delicate task of shooting Steve had to be done outside with no gloves on the winter day.

"It was freezing, bitter cold, one of the coldest, windiest days of the month, and he came out and met us as we pulled up," Dalton says. "Then he never asked us in, but stood out there for about twenty minutes. I shot pictures, Chad asked him questions. I had my hood pulled up, my fingers were freezing. And Grant looked cold, but he never wanted to go inside."

"He actually had his Jeep pulled up blocking the door to the business," Halcom says. "It was a strange thing, but we never imagined why he was doing it."

As Steve was giving every reporter the time of day, Griem's task of defending him was becoming more difficult.

"He had a habit of giving interviews and then telling me afterward," Griem says. "It made things hard for me when I was telling the sheriff's department that any interviews had to come through me."

In fact, Sheriff Hackel was poking at Steve via the media every chance he got. He defended the traffic stop—for failure to use a turn signal—and claimed that Steve would not cooperate with his office.

Griem told the *Macomb Daily*, "My client has been very cooperative and helpful with police. But sometimes an investigation is done by gathering all the available facts and then seeing if a theory of the crime fits all the evidence. And sometimes, certain investigators will have a theory first and try to find some evidence to fit it."

———

Deena Hardy was reading the stories about Tara Grant online from her South Lansing home, mortified. She would go back and revisit the email exchanges she had with her ex-boyfriend Stephen Grant, and then again check the growing number of stories about the missing Tara, whom Deena had referred to as the "cheatin' wife" in an email less than a month earlier.

Deena knew a reporter at the *Detroit News* who advised her to report the email exchanges to the police. While it's hardly the place of a reporter to aid any kind of investigation, it happens from time to time, and in this case, it was a convenient caveat that the *News* would get to print some of the e-mails, which it did on Wednesday, February 21. The paper repeated Steve's flippant comments about marriage and the notion of fidelity, including comparing marriage to speed limits, which "sometimes you have to break."

Steve explained away the e-mails as exchanges with a friend of thirty years, ex-lovers and current pals who could speak freely and with some humor and looseness to each other. And most failed to note that Deena had been fully prepared to meet with Steve for dinner on January 30 despite what she later said were, in her eyes, overtures to "hook up."

Still, it was a setback for Steve's fading public image, one in which he was slowly becoming, at least in the eyes of armchair detectives, guilty of *something* in relation to the disappearance of Tara.

A reporter called Alicia at her home in Chillicothe and asked her what she thought about the e-mails.

"I was absolutely flabbergasted by what I read," Alicia told the reporter from the *Daily Press* in Escanaba. "It was completely inappropriate . . . I've taken a turn about how I feel about my brother-in-law."

Later, though, Alicia would claim that she'd never liked Steve even a little and claimed that he wrecked many a family gathering with his "drama." But for the moment, she was playing the shocked relative. This would soon morph into a virulent hatred.

That day, Steve did another round of TV interviews.

TV REPORTER, DETROIT STATION WDIV: Did you have anything to do with her disappearance?

STEVE: No, absolutely nothing and I've told anyone who would listen that exact thing. I've had nothing to do with it.

TV REPORTER: If Tara is out there or someone who knows where she is, is out there, what would you say to them?

STEVE: Call the sheriff's office.

TV REPORTER: Don't you want her to call you?

STEVE: I'd rather her call the sheriff's office, because if she's been gone this long, then obviously there's some problem between her and I and I'd rather her call the sheriff's office.

Starting on that Monday, February 19, Alicia also began making repeated appearances on any station that would have her, pressing the same message: Her sister would not just up and leave her kids like this. By omission, she was implying that Tara perhaps would ditch Steve, admitting that at one time her sister had done just that for a twenty-four-hour period.

Alicia became a regular presence over the next week, hitting all the major-network morning shows, including the *The Early Show*, *Good Morning America*, Fox's *Greta Van Susteren*, and *Nancy Grace*.

Sheriff Hackel, too, was presenting press briefs to the media, advising them on his investigative team's every move. The tone of his rhetoric gradually increasing, he began noting with puzzlement that Steve did not seem to be interested in the fate of his missing wife. Hackel appeared on many of the same shows as Alicia, sometimes in the same segment.

On Thursday, February 22, clamor over the e-mails between Steve and Deena was giving his client a real black eye, and Griem set up a sanctioned press conference at his office, seating himself next to Grant but out of the camera range.

Clad in a white-and-brown-striped button-down shirt and khakis, Steve delivered a tearful, masterful performance.

"I hope Tara walks in that door right there," he said, his voice low, his face scrunched into crying mode, then going to full-on sobbing. "Right here. I hope she knows we're here and comes right in. That's what I hope. If not, I hope she calls my cell phone. I left ten messages for her. God, please, please, call anybody, call the police, call me, call my in-laws, call someone. If you see her, tell me. Please."

Griem says he allowed the local interview for one reason.

"If, God forbid, she comes up dead and God forbid he

gets charged, we've at least got a somewhat even picture portrayed to the people who are going to make up the jury panel. That is the only thing I ever care about with media coverage, is to not have a potential jury panel poisoned because the only thing out there is the other side of the story."

But Griem's sound strategy backfired in this case. Steve was convincing in his desperate pleas for information on Tara, but when the truth was discovered, it painted him as a masterful manipulator, and this made his foes despise him even more.

That afternoon, shortly after 1 P.M., Kozlowski faxed Griem a wish list of access to Grant's property, reading:

1. Can we have your client's computer hard drive? (Will only take approximately one day)
2. When can we have access to the Grant home?
3. When can we have access to Grant's vehicles?
4. When can we have access to USG Babbitt, 145 Malow, Mt. Clemens?
5. Can Steve tell us what clothes Tara packed and if he now remembers what she was wearing?

Griem was incensed, and responded shortly after 4 P.M. via fax, bypassing Kozlowski and directing his answers to the superior officer, Captain Tony Wickersham. Griem denied access to the computer, stating, "There is no legal basis, obligation, or reason to do so." Searching the house was also out, "especially in light of your words and actions (including the arrest of Mr. Grant on February 15)." Access to the vehicles would have no bearing on Tara's whereabouts, Griem said, and without a "satisfactory explanation of how access to the shop on Malow would help find Tara," no dice. Finally, he said, Steve does not know what clothes Tara packed as she left.

Two hours later, Kozlowski came back with another fax, asking for two laptop computers that Tara had used at some point, as well as the Grant home computer that was in the home's office.

Griem agreed to have Steve drop off the laptops, but refused to allow access to the home computer, stating that legal correspondence between Griem and Steve could be accessed.

It was a cat-and-mouse game that made it obvious Steve was the one and only suspect in Tara's disappearance. At an afternoon press conference that day, Sheriff Hackel announced a massive search would take place on Saturday, one that would cover all of Stony Creek Metropark, a three-mile radius.

The week of the eighteenth, a front from the south brought up some unseasonably warm temperatures, with sunny highs every day in the mid to upper thirties. That would melt much of the snow. And things that might have rested unnoticed under a frosting of winter would make their appearance. Steve had a problem.

Tara was in there, and the team of nearly a hundred and fifty officers, parks people, reserve officers, and general volunteers from the community on foot, horseback, helicopter, and ATVs would find her. Or whatever was left of her.

CHAPTER 11

*"It's a nightmare, it's truly a nightmare, and I keep
hoping I'm gonna wake up and it's not gonna be this.
I'm gonna wake up and Tara's gonna be laying next to
me and it's going to be a Saturday . . . and I'll go,
'Wow, that was a bad dream.'"*
  —Steve Grant, interview with Detroit TV station WXYZ

It was one more TV interview for Steve, one more performance. But in reality, he was probably speaking from his
heart when he gave that line to the local ABC affiliate in
Detroit. For him, the world would never again be the same,
and while he told himself at one point that he may have
gotten away with murder, deep inside, he knew it wasn't
going to go away. Now a planned sweep of the Stony Creek
Metropark by police at the end of a sunny, warm week was
sure to uncover the torso and other body parts that lay in
the woods at the northwestern part of the area.

On his lunch break on Friday, February 23, Steve
made his way to the sheriff's office and dropped off the

two laptops that had been requested by detectives. As he chatted with deputies, he asked if he could help with the large-scale search of the park, being familiar with the area as a mountain biker and runner. His lawyer, David Griem, told him it was a good idea and advised Macomb County Sheriff's Captain Tony Wickersham via fax that his client had his permission to do so, provided Steve was not questioned as he worked alongside law enforcement.

But shortly after Griem's 2 P.M. note to Wickersham, Sheriff Hackel, again delivering his message via the media rather than man-to-man, told a reporter at the *Detroit Free Press* that Grant's presence would be a hindrance.

"He keeps portraying himself as a suspect, that puts us in a weird situation," Hackel said. "We don't need him there, unless he happens to know where she is at."

The story hit the *Free Press*'s Web site, and by 6 P.M. Griem fired back another note to Wickersham on the increasingly busy fax machine.

"I'm bewitched, bothered, and bewildered why the sheriff would say such a thing. Mr. Grant wants to do anything and everything he can to help find Tara. Despite this article, Mr. Grant still wants to help. However, I have advised him that I will fire him as a client if he participates in the sheriff department's search tomorrow."

Steve had more pressing issues, in fact, although Griem was unaware of them. The search was to start Saturday, February 24, at 8 A.M. Steve, dressed in running gear, walked out his door at 5 A.M. The two miles to the park were an easy run for him, the combination of adrenaline and fitness serving him well. Even in the darkness, he had no trouble finding what he was looking for, right there near the corner of Inwood and Mt. Vernon roads. It was the largest part of Tara's dismembered body, her torso. It had frozen into the ice by now after lying there for twelve days with the sun melting some of the snow by day then freezing it again at night. It was still wrapped in the green plastic wrap and newspapers, unbothered by animals.

"The weirdest thing was when I walked in there, there were snowshoe tracks right next to it like literally somebody walked through in snowshoes," Steve later told officers. "It was exposed . . . The snow that was on top of it melted away and you could see completely. You could see the blood and the newspaper and everything in there."

He had to get that torso out of there, hide it better. After brushing away the remaining snow, he pulled the torso up, perched it on his shoulder, and began walking down the trail toward Inwood, the road to the north. Staggering under the weight—most of a body's weight is in its middle, and this piece of Tara measured a foot across and two feet horizontally—Steve moved west along the road and found a large wooden spool used to transport electric wire next to a tree. He temporarily laid the torso down behind the tree, shielding it from the view of anyone who might be driving down Mt. Vernon or Inwood, and placed the spindle over it.

"I tucked it in there and I ran all the way home," Steve said later.

By then, it was nearing 7 A.M., and Steve's mother, who had come back to Michigan from the Phoenix area earlier in the week to help her son during this stressful time, was up and about.

"I'm going to get some coffee," Steve told her. He grabbed two black garbage bags from the garage and hopped into Tara's Trooper. He sped to the spot where he had stashed the torso, parked on Inwood, and left the truck running. The sky was just starting to glow blue with the advent of dawn as he pulled the spindle back and stuffed the torso into one of the bags, and then the other.

As the search started, Steve drove down Van Dyke to 26 Mile Road, where he pulled into the parking lot of Caribou Coffee. He had to get his coffee and return home to show his mom that he had, in fact, done as he said. His paranoia was surging, and as he lived the bad dream he had created by murdering his wife, he turned irrational, seeking to justify every move lest he look as guilty as he was. The coffee shop was packed and Steve got spooked. What if someone saw him and knew what he had been up to? He left and instead drove to a nearby Speedway gas station for a newspaper and arrived home at seven-thirty.

"No coffee, the place was too busy," he told his mother. She didn't say anything about it. If Steve was having a meltdown, it wasn't evident to her. In fact, he'd been remarkably calm and normal during the entire time Tara was presumably missing. He paid bills, cared for the kids, handled his end at work, and called friends as if he were simply a bereaved husband.

"I never noticed a thing about him at all," says Kelly, who saw her brother several times a week at the shop. "If any of us would have suspected him, we certainly would have said something to him, if not the police, about it."

The search of Stony Creek that day was a bust, but it was admittedly a haystack/needle situation with no specific tips. Still, they never came close. The team of a hundred and fifty deputies, reserve officers, and park rangers gathered promptly at 8 A.M. in the parking lot of nearby Powell Middle School. It was to be a two-mile sweep, and the corner of Mt. Vernon and Inwood was four miles from the staging area. The effort was doomed from the start.

While spotters in helicopters hovered overhead, the searchers dispersed across the snow-covered acres of the park, moving from established trails into the thick woods on foot, ATVs, or horses, with search dogs in the lead. Tara's sister, Alicia, rode in an SUV with Sheriff Hackel, while Kelly was taken around the property by a deputy.

After four and a half hours, nothing had been discovered and the search team broke up at twelve-thirty. Steve heard about it on TV and started thinking that he might have gotten away with murder.

As the search at Stony Creek wound down, Steve got back into the Trooper and headed for the shop. He was haunted by the possibility that he'd again be pulled over by the sheriff's department, who would then find his missing wife's body in the cargo hold.

The sheriff's office later said it had assigned officers to tail Steve during the time that Tara was missing. But they never appeared to be around at times like these, when Steve was moving body parts. Or when, several days later, he slipped out the door as deputies searched his home.

"I couldn't believe that that morning I was able to run out there, dig up that torso, and hide it in the back of the car. You have to understand I was shocked," Steve later told investigators. "I thought I got away with it."

———

Steve arrived at the USG Babbitt thirty minutes later, parked the truck, opened the back, and pulled the black bags out of the cargo area as if they contained a carefully wrapped machine part, covered to avoid getting grease all over himself. He cradled the frozen-solid torso as he walked into the shop and locked the door. From a carton sitting on the table in the middle of the shop, he pulled out three more black plastic bags, heavy-duty thirty-three-gallon Iron Built bags, and kept sticking one inside the other. The shop was warm, though, and Steve had a troubling thought: What if the torso thawed out while it was here in the shop? His father would notice the smell for sure. He consoled himself with the multiple bagging. And the placement he had arrived at was ideal.

USG Babbitt was an aged shop, cluttered with metal lathes, drill presses, compression tanks, a band saw, and a sandblaster. The entire place was dusted with metal shavings and black powdery dust, refuse from the parts that were cut there. Ceiling fans attempted to whisk away some of the detritus, and the thirty-six-inch fluorescent lights on the ceiling cast a sick purple glow. Cleaning the place was clearly a zero priority; it was filthy. Rooms were crudely sectioned off, with two bathrooms, two small offices, and a break room. The rooms were shabbily constructed, more like small huts with their own roofs that extended only ten feet high, while the rippled, corrugated metal ceiling went up at least fifty feet. Steve propped a ladder against the side of the wall of the offices and placed the torso toward the back of the wooden office roof, hidden among cast-off metal parts.

On Sunday, February 25, he adhered to routine, taking the kids to Nino Salvaggio's International Marketplace, the specialty grocer in nearby Clinton Township, to buy groceries and have lunch. He also continued to talk freely to any media outlet that called. He talked about how the kids were doing, and how his life was now different.

Verena was home that day in Germany and had been reading every inch of news about the case that she could find on the Internet; her anxiety was ratcheted as high as it could go. She shot an email to her friend Rebecca, to whom she had also confided everything about her romance with Steve.

"Don't forget about that ONE thing," the terrified teenager wrote. "You have to promise!! You can't say anything!! Cause if you do you know what's going to happen to him . . . I'm scared."

But when Detective Kozlowski came calling on Monday, February 26, Rebecca rolled on Verena immediately. Kozlowski had contacted the girl through her Au Pair America counselor, claiming he had reason to believe Rebecca might be able to help him find Tara.

Rebecca showed Kozlowski the email she had received the night before from Verena. On the night of February 9, Verena had spilled the whole thing to her, she told the investigator.

"Verena told me that she and Stephen Grant were in love," Rebecca told Kozlowski. She said Verena had also been exchanging phone calls and text messages with Steve over the course of the evening at Mr. B's, the drinking joint in Rochester Hills.

"Who are you talking to?" Rebecca asked Verena at one point.

"Stephen," Verena replied.

After seeing the February 25 email, Kozlowski asked Rebecca what she felt "that ONE thing" was referring to.

"It was the affair she was having with Stephen Grant," Rebecca said.

But there was also something else curious about Rebecca's statement. She told the detective that while she and Verena were in Chicago for the New Year holiday, nearly two months earlier, Verena had confided in her that she and Steve were "in love." Yet at that time there had been nothing romantic exchanged between them at all. Had Verena entertained fantasies of Steve, perhaps hopeful dreams, before anything actually began? It remains a curious omission that has never been explored.

As Sheriff Hackel ratcheted up the typical cop rhetoric about "no suspects" in his daily interviews, Kozlowski was engaged in a full-court press on Steve, who was being tailed by officers in his drives to and from work. The whole thing stank, as far as Kozlowski was concerned. He was now convinced more than ever that Grant was involved in Tara's disappearance.

A national hotline was created to help encourage tips on February 26. People called and reported seeing Tara on *The Price Is Right*. She was seen at a local restaurant and spotted in Florida. One woman called and claimed that Stephen Grant had poisoned her dog. It was the typical nutcase heaven that such high-profile cases often draw. Yet each tip had to be checked out, coming in at a rate of fifteen to twenty a day, cops said.

More and more national media attention was being drawn to the case, and on February 27, Alicia went on Greta Van Susteren's *On the Record* show on the Fox News Channel.

Alicia claimed that in her last talk with Tara, "We had a very lovely conversation, actually. We talked about a variety of different things. We talked about my daughter's birthday coming up in April and, you know, that was about it."

There was no mention of the "different career paths" that she had told investigators of, nor of the Sunday flight rather than the usual Monday departure that she had told the *Detroit Free Press* about.

The trail was cold. Deputies were reduced to watching in-house security videos of Steve stopping at the BP gas station to buy a Reese's Peanut Butter Cup and a bottle of Propel flavored water. His convincing news conferences continued, as did Sheriff Hackel's relentless TV presence. Nothing was moving anywhere.

After two months of frigid and often single-digit temperatures, Wednesday, February 28, arrived unseasonably bright and warm, some respite from the bleak darkness and chill that defines Michigan in winter. The news of the missing woman from Washington Township was all the talk in Macomb County, from the hair salon to the local Meijer store. Sheila Werner had followed it on the television news. But she was hardly a news junkie, and it was not on her mind that midday as she walked her six-year-old daughter Olivia to the end of the driveway to catch the school bus.

Werner was a married mother of two and a part-time dental technician in her early thirties. She was also the proud sponsor of a mile's worth of dirt road that was Mt. Vernon, which paralleled Stony Creek Metropark. She had paid $150 for the privilege of adopting the roadway, and for her money got her name on a sign denoting her generosity. Indeed, she took her sponsorship seriously, frequently picking up trash along the narrow road, from where 28 Mile Road crosses it all the way down to Inwood.

On this day, with the snow melting a bit in thirty-six degrees after a spate of snowy, icy weather, Werner, a fine-boned brunette with a ready smile and a warm demeanor, finished some tidying up around her stately two-story brick house, tucked down a long, unpaved driveway surrounded by forest, and tugged on her boots.

Around 1 P.M., Werner set out north on Mt. Vernon, taking in the sun, sloshing through the watery melt on the road for about ten minutes before angling up a slight incline toward a cattle fence that had apparently been busted through. It was rare that any such vandalism happened in these upscale suburbs, but, she knew, kids often did silly things in their spare time. Oddly, though, she had never been up this incline, which opened onto a wide field of browned weeds.

She walked up the incline about forty feet and stopped. Werner looked around the hilly area, obscured from the road, observing the tree falls and the melting snow dripping off the leafless branches of the stout oaks, maples, and evergreens that filled the woods.

It was dead quiet. It was a little troubling and, inexplicably, she got the creeps. Best to get out of here, she thought. But instead of heading back down to the road, Werner trotted on north under the power lines, following a vague trail that was covered with fallen branches and withered shrubbery. The snow, about four inches deep, gave easily and she saw that she was the first person who'd been up there for some time, if the lack of footprints meant anything. At least, that's what she thought.

Fifteen minutes later, Werner decided to cut back west to hit Mt. Vernon and, as she proceeded, ran into a taut wire fence about five feet high, enough to make her follow it farther north to look for a break. All fences in these parts have breaks, because most suburban woodsmen aren't limber enough to just jump over the barricade. Just like they aren't tenacious enough to obscure things properly, Werner thought. She had found personal items out there, things she imagined someone might want to hide, some stray clothing, a well-used porno mag.

And then there was the trash she kept seeing and picking up. A bottle here, a piece of paper there. Werner clutched them as she finally found an opening in the fence line about a hundred yards south of Inwood. She could see Mt. Vernon Road just twenty-five feet in front of her.

But then she spotted something that made her crinkle her brow. There was a plastic bag sitting at the base of a large oak tree just ten feet off the road, facing her, obscured by the tree from passersby on Mt. Vernon.

It was an odd item really, a transparent gallon Ziploc job, apparently pushed into the snow with little concern for hiding it. Inside were several clear plastic bags, a wadded-up plastic 7-Eleven bag, a smaller Ziploc bag, and a pair of rubber gloves turned inside out. And at the bottom of the bag pooled about two inches of blood, gleaming crimson in the stark midday sun. Werner's mind froze. Her stomach dropped. Maybe it had been left by a hunter? But then she let herself wonder the unthinkable: What was that missing woman's name? Tara, that was it. Could this have anything to do with that?

Little did Werner know at the time that she had found the piece of evidence that would prove to be the undoing of Stephen Grant. And all she had really wanted to do was tidy up her little one-mile stretch of road. She took the bag and walked home, careful not to disturb the contents as she placed it on a refrigerator in her garage, unsettled, shaken, and unsure of what exactly she had found. Whatever it was, she'd better call the police. People don't just toss bags of blood into the snow, do they?

Macomb Sheriff Deputy John Warn arrived at Werner's house within the hour to retrieve the bag. They met in the garage and Warn held up the bag, looking at the melting blood in the bottom, noticing some small sticks and clumps of dirt and what looked like dog hair and metal shavings mixed in with the blood. He recalled having seen mention of a dog in one of the Tara Grant reports . . .

"I took him right down the road to the tree where I found the bag," Werner says. "And very quickly, there were other police cars there and I realized that this was something important."

An evidence technician arrived and shot pictures of

the area around where Werner had found the bag. Then there arose a dispute about what to do with the evidence.

"The sheriff's office wanted to test the blood for DNA to make sure it was Tara's," says one law enforcement agent. "A captain there tried to tell us that it would take only five days. But we knew that can take weeks, and it would be just stupid to let this go."

The case had already gone on way too long without a single break and time was starting to favor someone getting away with murder.

"We now started to know the end was getting close," the law enforcement source says. "And the sheriff's department had no idea how to handle it."

Clearer heads prevailed and the bag and its contents were transported to the Michigan State Police lab the next day, already a bit late. If the perpetrator were to find out about this, it could trigger flight, resulting in a costly chase and a debacle that could embarrass anyone involved in the case, especially if the suspect had been under their nose the entire time. But the bag arrived at the lab in Lansing and the blood tested positive as human. So far, no one in the press had any hint of what had been found.

———

The more he mulled it over, the less Steve liked the idea of the torso sitting up there on top of the small office structure at USG Babbitt, which could get quite warm. The metal roof pulls in the heat. Even though he had stuffed it into four garbage bags, expressly to prevent any leakage of body fluids, he wanted to move it again. This was no time to make a mistake.

His concern focused on the torso simply because it was the largest part of the dismembered body and one that was the most difficult to obscure. It was also the most awkward to move.

During the late afternoon of Thursday, March 1, he was poking around in his garage on Westridge and decided to put the part in another Rubbermaid container. He spotted just what he needed, a thirty-five-gallon job marked KIDS CLOTHES, filled with garments that were meant to be part of a garage sale. He moved the clothes into a bag and placed that in the basement, then loaded the container into the Trooper and drove back to USG Babbitt.

Once there, Steve again fetched the torso from its hiding place, placed it in the green Rubbermaid container, and walked it out to the truck, sticking it on the backseat.

Steve returned to the house after dark and parked next to his Jeep Commander. He took the green container out of the Trooper and placed it on the floor on the north side of the garage, behind the Jeep and closer to the street. He looked at it and was unsatisfied. It was sticking out a little bit, and looked out of place. Steve shuffled some other containers and some boxes holding some old clothes, and slid the green Rubbermaid into a space against the north wall. He slid a bag of salt in front of it slightly to the left, and there it was, just another storage container jammed with black plastic bags. It fit perfectly.

————

The next day, Friday, March 2, Detective Sergeant Brian Kozlowski received word that the blood in the bag found by Sheila Werner was human. He began to write his affidavit for a search warrant to gain access to both the Grant home and USG Babbitt. He recounted his interview with Verena's friend Rebecca in which she told of the sexual relationship between Verena and Steve. He noted the bag found by Werner, with the light animal hair, and mentioned that "affiant observed a light-colored dog in the Grant home on 2-14-07." He also listed the presence of metal shavings in the bag, and the shavings at USG Babbitt.

"Affiant believes that Tara Grant may have been a victim of foul play, and that evidence to this will be recovered from the search of the Grant property." The warrant for the residence was cosigned by Bill Cataldo, chief of homicide for the Macomb County Prosecutor's Office, while the USG Babbitt warrant was cosigned by Assistant Prosecutor Therese Tobin. Magistrate Richard McLean of the Forty-Second District Court in Romeo okayed the warrants.

While the warrants were being put together, another team of deputies was launching a search of the area of Stony Creek Metropark near the tree where Sheila Werner had found the bloody bag. The team went up and down both sides of Mt. Vernon and, like the fruitless search of the previous week, turned up nothing. They might not have known it yet, but there were thirteen pieces of a woman scattered in the snow and trees in that park, and yet, even with the location narrowed down to a square mile, they couldn't find a thing.

As they prepared the warrant, Steve gave an interview to a reporter at the *Detroit News* during the afternoon. Considering what he had done with his wife's body, it was jolting in its condemnation of her. It was also clear in retrospect that Steve felt he had gotten away with murder, or his statements against Tara would not have been so brazen.

"I was a better mom than Tara was," he told the reporter as, unbeknownst to him, officers prepared to search his home. "There's no other way to put it. I was the mom in the house—she was gone all the time. If the kids needed someone to take them to swimming, or school, or soccer practice, I took them.

"Some of her family has said in the media how much she loved her kids, and how she would try to fly back in order to attend their functions," Steve continued. "But that's not true. I can't recall one time when she did that.

"To be honest, as weird as it sounds for me to say this, I was the perfect mom—not Tara."

Power struggles—those that were hinted at in Tara's letter to Steve that she had written after attending the Landmark Forum in 2005—were part of their world, he said, with Tara "trying to show who's boss, and who's going to run the household. It didn't need to be that way."

For ninety minutes, Steve chatted, tossing out sound bites that would later make him appear to be a remorseless killer, providing prosecutors with credible ammunition.

"I know people think I had something to do with why Tara is missing," he said. "But I didn't do it."

An hour later, as he was headed home, three Macomb County Sheriff's Department squad cars pulled him over a mile from his house. There was going to be a search of his residence, Steve was told. He allowed a growing cadre of law enforcement agents to enter the house, grabbed a leash and the family dog Bentley, and with a TV camera taping, walked down the driveway and away from the investigations. The camera caught him looking back at the commotion as he walked away quietly into the street with the dog. After tailing him for weeks, the cops just let their quarry go.

The idea that deputies, and Sheriff Hackel, who was en route, simply allowed Grant to leave, was outrageous to some observers.

"That's what the back of patrol cars are for," says J. D. Gifford, a former FBI agent and now an investigator for a number of law firms in the Detroit area. "You just ask him to have a seat, let him know he's not under arrest. Keep him comfortable and get the search done. You can't just let this guy leave."

"Letting him walk away with his wallet, so he has money and credit cards, what a dumb thing to do," says a local investigator with another agency.

At the same time, police were facing a man who lived in an expensive home in a well-to-do suburb, with two small children in school—one of them a pricey private school—and who had a reputable defense lawyer in David Griem. Captain Tony Wickersham and David Griem had enjoyed a good relationship over the years, and through that Griem gave the officer an assurance that his client was solid. No one was expecting to find a piece of the missing woman's body in the garage. What police had hoped the search would accomplish was to gain access to that home computer, which had so far been disallowed by Griem because it contained communications with his client and analysis of it would broach attorney–client privilege. However, when a search warrant is executed, anyone in or approaching the location specified can be detained.

Still, Hackel later told reporters that he couldn't hold Grant at that time, regardless of the circumstances. "We have to follow the law," he said. "I cannot infringe on people's rights."

In an interview with the *Detroit Free Press*, the sheriff also attempted to cast the blame on the prosecutor's office. "I'm not going to listen to Monday-morning quarterbacking. The bottom line is that we followed our legal advice from the prosecutor's office."

Prosecutor Eric Smith confirmed that his office did advise that Grant could not be held without an arrest warrant, but added that whether or not to maintain surveillance was the sheriff's decision.

The torso would be found ninety minutes later, and the one and only suspect not only had a good jump on officers, they had no idea where he might have gone. The search to find him would eventually cost thousands of taxpayer dollars and place dozens of law enforcement agents and passing citizens in harm's way.

It was clear that not keeping an eye on the main suspect had been a bad move, and everyone knew it.

CHAPTER 12

The morning of Sunday, March 4, dawned bitter cold in Petoskey, with temperatures clocking in at a brisk nineteen degrees, in the northern Michigan resort town. Stephen Grant had arrived at the hospital around 7 A.M., his vital signs weak after he was found at the foot of a snowy evergreen in Wilderness State Park.

His room at Northern Michigan Hospital overlooked the beautiful Little Traverse Bay. The bay was covered with thick ice and the view to the north afforded a good look at the Lower Peninsula extending toward the Mackinac Bridge.

After a brief stop in the emergency room, Steve had been taken up to the intensive-care unit, where he was handcuffed to his metal hospital bed, had an intravenous warming solution plugged into his arm, a bladder lavage to raise his temperature (which had plunged to eighty-seven at one point), frostbite boots on both feet, a cardiac monitor to alert nurses if his heart should seize up from the dramatic shock of the cold, and a pulse oximeter to keep staff apprised of his oxygen processing. In other words, he had just made it through his suicide attempt.

Nurse Michelle Gaudreau came into the room and saw that her patient, with Macomb County Sheriff's Sergeant Jeffrey Budzynowski and Deputy Mark Berger beside him, was groggy. She was working the 7-A.M.-to-7-P.M. shift, and had just gotten on when Steve was brought up from the emergency room.

On admittance, he had told staff in a disjointed ramble that he had taken sixteen tablets of an over-the-counter sedative called Sleepanol as well as a supply of Vicodins. He told them that he'd also been drinking whiskey. And he thought he was in Mackinac City rather than Petoskey.

As the day progressed, Steve became more aware of how his halfhearted suicide attempt had played out. He was now caught.

"He became a little bit more alert. When he first came in, he was confused," Gaudreau said later, describing Grant as able to communicate with her and returning to normal function. "He was able to feed himself."

He was feeling better, Steve said, but his feet hurt. The nurse turned the TV to a hockey game; the Colorado Avalanche was playing the Detroit Red Wings.

He had lunch at around 2 P.M., and as he ate, he looked at Gaudreau, a registered nurse with nine years of experience who had spent plenty of time in the emergency room, although her time around accused murderers was limited.

"Can I tell you?" Steve said.

"I don't want to know," Gaudreau replied, and one of the guarding deputies came over.

"Don't talk to anyone," Sergeant Budzynowski said. "Do you want an attorney?"

Steve refused to believe that he couldn't talk to anyone.

"Yeah, call David Griem, he's my lawyer," Steve replied.

"Griem fired you this morning," Budzynowski told him. Steve's face went blank. His intoxicated flight, the run in the icy woods, the capture, and his obviously impaired condition all affected his tattered mind.

Indeed, that morning, as Grant lay sleeping 240 miles away, Griem had announced that he was no longer representing his client. He cited irreconcilable differences, and says he actually made the decision on that Friday as he was driving south on I-75 after a court appearance for another client in Flint. But the call from Stephen, who was sitting in the back of a patrol car that day, had thwarted his announcement.

"The case was killing me," Griem says. "But I get back to my office at five-fifteen and the phone rings at five-twenty and it's Stephen from the back of a police car. I felt that I had to stick it out and see him through at least [that]."

Now Steve was alone and without any legal help at all.

As he sat considering what to do, Budzynowski took a call from Macomb. It was Detective Kozlowski. The sergeant stood in the hall outside Steve's room as the two chatted on the phone.

"Ask Steve if he wants to talk about the case," Kozlowski said. Inside the room, Grant was puzzled.

"Did [Griem] really fire me?" Steve said, looking at Berger. Yes, Berger said. Budzynowski came back into the room and asked Steve if he wanted to talk to Kozlowski.

"If you really want to talk, you should talk to Kozlowski, because he wants to talk to you," the officer said. "But you should stop talking about the case to us."

Steve went quiet for a few minutes.

Aside from the frostbite and the obviously dire situation

Steve was in, he was "surprisingly cordial," Berger said later.

Dr. Michael Johnson came in to check on him. Johnson, whose high forehead, wispy blond hair, and round spectacles gave him an especially gentle look, specialized in vascular surgery, but the frostbite didn't look as though it would come to that grim conclusion. The doctor asked Steve how his hands felt.

"They hurt," came the simple reply. Grant asked the doctor if he could send a message to his kids. While Johnson gave no promises, Steve went ahead.

"Tell them that I miss them, I love them, and I look forward to seeing them," Steve said, his voice retreating into a sob.

Later, as Duke was playing North Carolina in basketball on the room TV, the two officers and Grant watched the game together. Steve was upright and alert, the deputies would recount. The three of them chatted about the game, the view of the bay from the hospital window, and the outlandish sums of money pro athletes were commanding these days. It was like a night at a sports bar, except for the pending murder charge, the hospital room, and the handcuffs.

Occasionally, Steve would drift into talk about his situation.

"Do you think I killed her?" he asked Budzynowski, who remained silent on the subject.

"Don't talk to me about the case," the officer said again.

"I was going to kill myself," Steve said, apparently not hearing him.

His chatter was met with silence.

Later, he asked about deals in exchange for a confession.

"What would you do?" he asked the sergeant at one point. Again, no response.

"Will I be safe if I go to jail?" Steve asked. There were no answers, although both officers knew that a talkative subject like Grant was prone to giving a confession. And if that were the case, they also knew that Kozlowski would be receptive.

"Call Koz," Steve finally said, using the detective's nickname. "I want to talk to him."

"C'mon up, we'll talk," he told Kozlowski on the phone.

"C'mon up and we'll talk?" the detective repeated, sounding as if he could hardly believe his luck. His suspect had managed to evade officers for three weeks, hide evidence in plain sight in a park in the middle of the county, and slide out the door of his own home just as officers were about to find key evidence against him. And now he was ready to talk.

"Yep, me and you," Steve said. He already wanted to explain. "I apologize . . . I should have told you but I couldn't. I was scared . . . you got to understand that."

"No, I do, I do. I understand it completely," Kozlowski said.

They said their good-byes and hung up.

Steve asked the two deputies guarding him if they could stay. They told him, no, it wasn't their case.

"Well, thanks for being so cool," Steve said. "And treating me like a human being."

At the Emmet County Sheriff's Office, just three miles north of the hospital, Mike Zanlungo's yellow Dodge Dakota sat in an impound bay, its tires flattened by search officers who had disabled it in case Grant had managed to circle back during the capture effort.

Officers tallied the evidence they recovered during their

ordeal. It included Steve's wallet with $389 in it along with his credit cards, a black-and-gray Timex Ironman watch, a toy cap pistol with a wood-colored handle, its orange tip colored black with a Magic Marker. The search team had also found, as they pursued Steve, a pair of pliers, a Heath candy bar, and a green-covered spiral notebook.

In Macomb County, sheriff's deputies finally had hit pay dirt in Stony Creek Metropark, where before they were unable to turn up anything. On Saturday, over a hundred officers had combed the area. This time, they discovered Tara's hands, feet, and chunks of her flesh scattered all over that narrow stretch of land where Steve, weeks before, had stood and tossed them into the darkness.

"As I was walking through the woods . . . I observed something pink," noted Deputy Scott Lasky. "The closer I got, the more I realized it was a body part. The part that I found was up by a tree, not hidden. It looked like a foot . . . pink and bony, wrapped up in something."

Reserve Deputy Conrad Maday II noted some "fresh sand on the snow" as he searched for Tara. "The sand appeared to have come from the stump of a fallen tree. I approached the stump area and inspected in a hole under the stump. When I laid down and looked into the hole, I saw what appeared to be human hair. After using a flashlight to look into the stump area, I confirmed it was a human head."

A leg was found nearby. It was a field of horrors.

On the other hand, the list of evidence seized from the Westridge house was chillingly neutral except for one item. The one-page register notes that police took Steve's passport, $1,507 in U.S. currency, a Sony Cybershot camera, the home-computer tower, monitor, and keyboard, some financial documents and "one white female torso located inside a green plastic bin."

A warrant charging Steve with open murder and disinterment and mutilation of a body was issued by the prosecutor's office.

Detectives Brian Kozlowski and Pam McLean arrived at the Northern Michigan Hospital around 7:40 P.M., making good time after leaving the sheriff's office at five and driving through some rough patches of snow. It was Michigan weather at its worst, even in March.

They took the elevator to Steve's room and greeted their charge.

"Do you think that you're, uh, of sound mind to talk to us?" Kozlowski asked.

"Yeah," Grant answered. He appeared ready to confess. He signed away his rights on a Miranda warning and waiver statement, showing a time of 7:46 P.M. Steve initialed each item on the waiver, all seven of them, then signed the bottom of the sheet. A microcassette player was turned on and he and the detectives began talking.

"Obviously, uh, you know, we met under unfortunate circumstances, but, uh, you know, I'm not here to judge you. I'm just doing my job and—" Kozlowski said.

"I know," Steve interrupted. "I don't tell you I'm here to help you in a lot of ways, but I'm gonna do what I can to give you direct and honest answers."

Steve asked first about the difference between various murder charges, first degree, second degree, and so on, and the two detectives did their best to explain.

Then they directed him to start at February 9. And for three and a half hours, Stephen Grant told them everything in what law enforcement said was a full confession. He explained the events leading up to Tara's final moments.

"And then she went limp, quit moving," he told the officers, his voice flat. "[I was] just holding, squeezing as hard as I could. I wanted her to shut up."

He told of hauling Tara's body to the Trooper, then to the shop to chop her up, and the panicked movements of the torso right up until the final moment that Friday, just forty-eight hours earlier, when he walked out of the garage of his house and into the evening.

"Okay," Kozlowski said, after Steve had recounted his story twice to the rapt detectives, almost identically both times. "Steve, it's getting kind of late, um, basically what I want to do from this point . . . [I] want you to put in writing what happened the night of the ninth."

"Okay," Steve said, amiable, willing to please.

It was a clear and fairly focused confession, the officers felt, and when the two left to get some sleep at the Hampton Inn just up the hill from the hospital, they were exultant.

The media had swarmed Emmet County, filling the motels and giving the local economy a boost usually reserved for summertime when the population of thirty thousand doubles. Petoskey has six thousand full-time residents and every one of them, it seemed, was amazed that a big-time killer had fled to their tiny region for some reason. The town itself had not seen a murder in several years, and the front page of the Monday edition of the *Petoskey Press-Review*, which usually features items about the city council and weather conditions, ran a hastily shot photo of Steve being hauled into Northern Michigan Hospital on a stretcher.

Emmet County Sheriff Peter Wallin held a press conference on March 4, relating to reporters the ordeal of tracking Steve with the a local team composed of about forty officers—including members of the Emmet County Sheriff's Office, FBI, Michigan State Police, Mackinaw City Police Department, Little Traverse Bay Band Police, Northern Michigan Mutual Aid Emergency Response

Team, and a helicopter from the U.S. Coast Guard out of Traverse City.

"I don't think he would have lasted much longer than he did," says Wallin, a solidly built man in his early fifties, who had been appointed sheriff in 2002, when the existing sheriff died, and was then elected in 2004. He has been with the department for twenty-five years.

"[Grant's] body temperature was getting to a level at which he would pass out, then that would be it. It was also a situation in which our team had to be careful. He knew we were tracking him. We knew he was suicidal, we knew he could be armed." Steve was running through areas in which he would go from a two-inch snow cover to waist-deep drifts. Noting that his phone calls had led the authorities to him, Wallin says, "You know about Big Brother watching? We can tell where you are.

"This is a small county with not a lot of crime," Wallin says. "So we don't get much attention, which is good. But I will say one question I got during this press conference that I didn't expect was [when] one young lady asked, 'Was [Grant] in danger of being attacked by bears?'"

Bears, of course, hibernate in winter, as anyone with a basic knowledge of the wilds knows.

"I said, 'If that were to happen, that would be one angry bear.'"

Word that there had been a confession leaked quickly from Northern Michigan Hospital. Reporters who'd covered the case said they were contacted by law enforcement overnight, one receiving a call around five-thirty in the morning on Monday, March 5, telling him that Grant had squawked and the case was in the bag.

"With my limited legal knowledge, I thought, 'This can't be a good idea,'" the reporter mused. "I wondered how he could get a fair trial now."

If there was fear a jury pool had already been tainted by so much publicity, it was fully realized now that a confession hit the airways.

News of the confession led the early-morning newscasts in Detroit, with rapt viewers who had followed the case awestruck that Steve had admitted what many had speculated to be true all along.

Given that the cops had almost lost the case by letting Grant walk away from the house during the warranted search, they were no doubt relieved.

"He gave a very lengthy confession, laying out exactly what took place," Sheriff Hackel said at a news conference Monday.

Just to make sure the world knew, Hackel went on *Larry King Live* that evening: "He confessed to our detectives," the sheriff said. "He actually—once he parted ways with his attorney, his attorney quit the case itself, he indicated when he was at the hospital that he wanted to talk to our investigators because he wanted to clear his conscience."

At 1:40 P.M. on Monday, March 5, Steve did a perp walk in his wheelchair, moving from his heavily guarded hospital room to a black Macomb County Sheriff's Office Ford Expedition, one of three that would make the trek back to Macomb County. Clad in a black-and-white horizontally striped jumpsuit with PRISONER emblazoned in bright orange on the right leg, his hands and feet bound to a waist chain, Grant glanced briefly at a phalanx of reporters that waited for a glimpse of him outside the emergency-room windows.

His eyes were wide, his expression mildly surprised at first, before he retreated into passive resignation as he came through the doors and into the ER bay surrounded by five law enforcement officials.

"They told me there were a lot of reporters out there,

and they told me not to look at any of them or say anything," Steve says. Yet he had not quite grasped the significance of the story and was unprepared for the sight of the army of press.

"Did you kill her?" one television reporter yelled at him. Steve said nothing and continued to look forward as the chair stopped at the SUV and he was lifted by officers, gently, into the backseat.

His feet, wrapped in white bandages, barely touched the ground.

CHAPTER 13

His first night in jail behind him, Stephen Grant was wheeled into a conference room at 11 A.M. Tuesday, March 6, where Detective Sergeant Brian Kozlowski and Detective Sergeant Pam McLean were meeting him.

His arraignment was set for 1 P.M. at the Macomb County courthouse in front of Judge Denis LeDuc, where Steve would answer to the charge of first-degree murder and dismemberment of a body.

But first, the two detectives realized, they needed to nail down that confession that was sweeping the news in video form.

They had failed to accomplish this, it later came out, because the department's videotaping equipment was not working, and in their rush to get to Petoskey, neither Kozlowski nor McLean had been able to secure any gear. Videotaped confessions always play more credibly to jurors than tape-recorded ones and are considered generally unassailable.

So that Tuesday morning, Steve was transferred downstairs to the mental-health unit, where he'd been placed—and would stay for the entirety of his county incarceration—since he was deemed suicidal at the time of his arrest. He was clad in a black "suicide suit" (a bulky, quilted outfit extremely hard to rip so that it can't be torn into strips that could be turned into a noose), with a blanket over his legs and his wrists handcuffed to the arm bar of the wheelchair.

Kozlowski and McLean were ready to video the confession, and they let Steve know this as soon as he arrived.

"Just so you know, Steve, see that little black dot there?" Kozlowski asked. "That's where we're recording."

He went on, speaking breezily, as if he were talking to a neighbor about heading to the grocery store: "I'm just gonna remind you that you don't have to talk to us."

On a small table against one wall sat another Miranda waiver, like the one Steve had signed before giving his confession on Sunday. As he looked it over, Kozlowski sat fidgeting in his chair, chucking his chin, brushing some imaginary dirt off one of his dress shoes, then back to the chin. Once they got Grant's confession on video, prosecution would be much easier. But all of a sudden things went south.

"The only question I had is you said we should do this before the arraignment, where I would get an attorney, because he's not gonna let me do this after?" Steve said, his voice rising at the end of his query, as if he wanted to impart some innocence to his tone.

"Well, if you wanna talk to an attorney before we talk to you, I want you to know—" Kozlowski said, before Grant interrupted him.

"Well, I guess I'm just asking because I don't know,"

Steve said, holding out his hands in a supplicating manner.

"Well, it's hard for me to give you legal advice, Steve, I'm not going to," Kozlowkski said. "It's just that I can tell you, I know you will be appointed counsel. If you want an attorney here, if you do not want us to talk to you now . . . we will stop right now, okay?"

"I just don't know. I mean we talked already. I just don't understand why we need to do it again in video," Steve said.

"I'll be honest with you," Kozlowski said, his voice dipping into an "it's you and me, pal" kind of bonding voice. "You know what this comes down to is that you were in the hospital, we were up there, and there's a difference of . . . hearing your voice and seeing [the confession]. Everybody here, we live in a day and age where everybody likes to see everything as opposed to [just] listening . . . I don't want to say it's a formality. It's very important and I'm going to use this videotape as evidence. You need to know that."

Kozlowski was being as up-front as any cop can be, shooting straight with the confused Grant. Even if Steve had been of sound mind when he gave his confession on Sunday, and testimony would later indicate he was, by now he'd had some time to think things over.

"I don't want to talk to you if you want to invoke any of those rights on that piece of paper," Kozlowski said. It appeared that he was hoping that he could coax his prisoner into saying something.

"I'll leave that piece of paper right there out front of you . . . We're going to ask you the same questions . . . It probably will go faster because we won't have to stop and change tapes."

He was now firmly convinced that Steve had seen no

compelling reason not to commit his confession to video-tape. And the detective was trying to control the situation.

"You were of sound mind and health when we talked to you at Northern Michigan Hospital," Kozlowski said, both a statement and a question.

"Right," Steve said.

"Yes or no?" Kozlowski came back.

"Yes," Steve replied.

"I know that, and what you're saying is now on tape," Kozlowski said. "If you want to talk to an attorney before we do this again, then tell me now, yes or no." Steve held his hands out, as if to say, "I have no idea."

"I just don't know," he managed.

"If you don't know, then we can wait until after the arraignment," Kozlowski said, no doubt aware that no lawyer would ever consent to having his client give a confession.

"Is that all right?" Steve asked.

Both detectives were effusive, over-the-top reassuring, even through their disappointment.

"Of course it's fine," McLean said.

What Steve didn't know was that David Griem, the lawyer who had fired him two days before, had just an hour previously called the jail to attempt to set up a meeting with his former client.

He had been transferred to Kozlowski.

"I've spoken with Tom Munley, a friend of Steve's who's also a lawyer in Lansing, and we want to come down and talk to Steve," Griem had explained.

No way was the detective going to let that happen just as he was attempting to get the confession on video.

"Steve is very, very contrite," Kozlowski told Griem. "He does not wish to speak to anyone at this time."

Later, Griem would note in his file that "Munley was blown off by [Kozlowski] in the same exact fashion" as he had been.

Steve later said that he had asked to see Griem that morning, contradicting Kozlowski's account. By now it was apparent that no lawyer would be given access to Steve at this point, nor would there be a videotaped confession.

As they all sat in the office, Kozlowski pulled out his cell phone and attempted to call Grant's sister, Kelly Utykanski, so that Steve could talk with her and perhaps get some advice about what to do. He was unable to reach her and left several messages. But as they all waited, having now established that there wouldn't be any talk about the murder, the three tried to chat. It was uncomfortable, to say the least.

"So what's been your relationship with Kelly?" Kozlowski asked.

"Good," Steve said simply. He knew where this was going. They wanted to know if Kelly had covered up for him during the period that Tara was missing.

"How about before all this happened?" the detective asked.

"Good, good," Steve replied.

"You see her on a regular basis?"

Steve shrugged, yes. Kelly would visit the shop, but rarely came to the house on Westridge, mostly because she had her own life going on, and partly because she didn't want to run into Tara.

They began to talk about the kids, and Steve became a little more animated. A hearing to terminate his parental rights was scheduled for that afternoon at 3 P.M., after the arraignment. Steve noted to the detectives that "Tara couldn't stand her family" and had even wanted to leave their holiday in Ohio in November early after a dispute with Alicia.

"Tara couldn't stand her sister," he told the cops quietly.

It was said matter-of-factly, although it was clear that Steve was torn when Kozlowski asked him whom he thought the two Grant children should stay with. Steve suggested Alicia and her husband, Erik. He and Tara had agreed two years earlier that if something were to happen to both of them, Tara's sister would be best suited to care for the kids. But when the two cops explained that Steve could sign a form that would allow the couple to have temporary custody, he declined.

"It's a hearing to allow Alicia and Erik to take the kids," McLean told Steve.

"Out of Michigan?" he asked, his voice rising.

"It's just a temporary arrangement," she explained.

"I'd like to talk to my sister . . . so I can tell her what I'm thinking," Steve said.

He looked at a wall map of the county, turning his attention away from the detectives, who were beginning to get restless. It was obvious he wasn't about to open up as he had on Sunday.

"Please understand that I'm more than willing to talk to you guys, all right?" Steve said, sensing their dismay. "I have nothing to hide now."

"We understand, Steve," McLean offered. But twenty-five minutes after Grant had again signed away his Miranda rights, McLean and Kozlowski were about to walk away without a videotape of the confession.

The two got up to leave, and Kozlowski leaned over to Steve, pausing for a second to look at the man whom he had chased relentlessly over the past three weeks. The cop had forged a fake friendship with him, just as he had done during his days in the field as an undercover narc. Even now he pretended to care about Steve's well-being.

"You'll be all right, man," Kozlowski said, patting the prisoner on the back. The two officers left, and Steve was alone. He looked at the ceiling, the small window behind him, and then again at the wall map of Macomb County, the place where he was raised and knew every little street, where he had endured life's hurts and finally committed one of the county's most atrocious crimes. He looked at lines that were the streets he would probably never drive through again. As he told Kelly a couple of weeks later in a tearful conversation: "I fucked up. I'm so sorry."

———

Steve was wheeled into the courtroom that afternoon, March 6, 2007. He'd changed out of the suicide suit and back into the black-and-white-striped prison outfit. The courtroom was packed with reporters and cameras, and at the front table sat Kelly, seeing her brother for the first time since his flight. She looked with crushed disbelief at her little brother, who glanced meekly back.

"Given the extreme, extreme seriousness of the charges, the nature of the allegations here, the nature of the alleged flight, the court agrees with the People. I'm going to order you held without bond. Do you understand that?" Judge LeDuc said sternly.

"Yes, Your Honor," Steve said, subdued and barely audible. "Thank you, Your Honor."

The case was making headlines across the nation, and that evening, Sheriff Hackel again took to the airwaves, this time for a return visit to the evening show of CNN host Anderson Cooper.

"Without question, the Baggie we found out in the

fielded area really helped us out, because when there was
human blood there, it was going to give us the opportunity to go back into an area close by a search that we had
done a week prior and check and see what was in that
area," Hackel said about the bag of blood that alert resident Sheila Werner had discovered.

A couple of months later, Sheila would run into Alicia
at one of the many memorials that would be held over the
rest of the year. Alicia thanked her profusely.

"It was because of you the police found my sister," she
told Werner.

But on this evening, before a national audience, it was
the sheriff's office that had found the bag.

Steve's assets were frozen shortly after his arrest, forc-
ing him to file for defense as an indigent. The case would
now be handed to a court-appointed lawyer, and the decision of who that would be fell to Chief Macomb County
Circuit Judge Antonio Viviano, a colorful official and a
Macomb resident for forty years.

Viviano was the Yogi Berra of the courthouse, a fine
orator known for his mixed metaphors, tortured syntax,
and a blue-collar charm that indicated he cared about the
law but never forgot where he came from. A short, bespectacled, Italianesque Archie Bunker minus the rancor, Viviano was a credible man of the people who came to
worldwide media attention in 2001 when he sentenced rap-
per Eminem to two years probation on a concealed-weapons
charge.

Viviano's knowledge of the law was considered impec-
cable, and he had worked his way through the system as a
defense lawyer, an assistant prosecutor, and finally a judge.

Viviano's decision was made difficult by the confession that the sheriff's department had put out, and he is
critical of the department for making it public.

"The confession should never have been released," Viviano says. "I don't know what the circumstances of the confession [were]. But I've got to draw a jury that is going to be impartial and fair to [Grant]. Our duty is to be fair and impartial to the litigants. When you are playing to the media—that's the danger."

On Wednesday, March 7, Viviano handed the chore of defending confessed murderer Stephen Grant to Stephen Rabaut, a buttoned-down gentleman with a reputation as a strong litigator. His appointment rankled with almost everyone, from the sheriff to the local bar association. Hackel protested that Rabaut's wife, Michelle Sanborn, was an administrator at the Macomb County Jail, where Steve was housed. He claimed to be concerned about a public impression of impropriety in that Sanborn might be privy to information about the case. The bar association complained that lawyers on the court-appointed list had been bypassed in favor of Rabaut.

Viviano defends his choice as sound because "the case was spinning out of control, the media was leading with it every day, and it was threatening [Grant's] ability to have a fair trial."

Rabaut had defended every type of criminal in the Detroit area, from two-bit embezzlers to drug kingpins to murderers. Crime was his business, and business was good. Favoring crisply cut suits and sporting a fastidiously trimmed mustache and an expensive haircut, his pristine appearance reflected his meticulous defense of his clients.

The Grant case was hardly the highest-profile one that Rabaut had tried.

Rabaut won an acquittal in 1992 for a seventy-nine-year-old ex-convict accused of being a bagman for a gambling ring, despite witness testimony that had the accused picking up a package of hundred-dollar bills at a New Jersey rest stop.

In 1994, Rabaut defended a teenager accused of statutory rape in the wealthy Detroit suburb of Grosse Pointe Woods. He struck a plea deal that got his client a sixty-to-ninety-day sentence in a case that could have landed him up to fifteen years.

Rabaut also defended government informant Youssef Hmimssa in a 2003 terrorism trial in Detroit. Hmimssa, a self-described scam artist, provided key testimony in a federal terrorism case that eventually fell apart.

One of Rabaut's biggest triumphs was the case of Mark Cleary, a man who was wrongly accused and for whom he won a new trial in 2004 when his daughter recanted the allegations of molestation that had sent Cleary to prison in 1987. Prosecutors dropped the case.

"I selected Steve Rabaut because he was well known to every one of us and he would be sure not to use this as a stepping-stone, as a career move," Viviano says. "Steve Rabaut has been president of the Macomb Bar Association and he was on the appointed attorney list for several years."

Rabaut selected as his cocounsel Gail Pamukov, a former registered nurse who had become a much-in-demand criminal attorney specializing in utilizing DNA evidence in difficult cases. Pamukov was an acclaimed litigator who received the State Bar of Michigan's Champion of Justice Award in 2006 for her work with the Thomas M. Cooley Law School's office of the Innocence Project, the acclaimed national lawyer group devoted to examining possible wrongful convictions.

She had been part of the group almost since its inception in 2001, signing up after seeing cofounder Barry Scheck speak.

In 2003, Pamukov was part of a team that used DNA evidence to prove the innocence of Kenneth Wyniemko, who had been in prison for nearly a decade after a Macomb jury convicted him on rape charges.

Pamukov was not afraid to mix it up it the courtroom and she suffered no fools. The Macomb County Prosecutor's Office was not happy to see her.

Rabaut's humorlessness and disdain for the press was established from the outset. "I will represent Mr. Grant ethically, professionally, and protect his rights," he told a reporter at WDIV on March 8, several hours after learning that Viviano had handed him the case. "Beyond that, I have no statement for the media."

Pamukov, arguably the stronger litigator of the two, said nothing. They immediately pushed for a gag order, which was denied. Not that it mattered. Giddy with the national spotlight, even jailers and secretaries who had little knowledge of the case could not stop talking to the press.

CHAPTER 14

Kelly Utykanski made her first visit to the Macomb County Jail to see Steve on March 8. Sitting across from him, with a sheet of Plexiglas between them, she was overwhelmed by everything that had happened in the past month. She was tough, there was no doubt about it, but this was a traumatic shock. Her little brother, a murderer. It didn't just roll off the tongue.

Before this, she and Steve had been close but not especially tight. They loved each other, but had lived separate lives.

And Kelly had never really understood Steve's attraction to Tara.

"Once they got married, I didn't see Steve so much," she says. "He had to be more subdued around her, we couldn't kid around like we had always done. I felt like he was stifled, so I would see him over at the shop or when Tara was traveling.

"She didn't really like our family, she always seemed

like she was looking down on us. It was not a very comfortable situation, so I just made sure I wasn't around her much."

Kelly was also incredibly capable, willing to do whatever a job demanded, be it take care of kids—she often provided day care for the children of friends—or run her small flower-arrangement business.

Steve had a faithful friend in his sister. She was one of the only people who visited him, along with her husband, Chris, an accountant, and their father, Al Grant, who was having trouble dealing with the situation.

Kelly was at the jail every week during Steve's appointed visiting hours, and in between, the two talked on the phone.

They were aware that all of their conversations were taped, and when they met in person at the jail, the two often relied on hand signals to convey thoughts and ideas and news that they didn't want intercepted by the prosecution.

Much of their talk was of the prickly child-custody situation. After initially saying he wanted Lindsey and Ian to live with Alicia, Steve began to change his mind after learning of Alicia's cold behavior toward Kelly.

Alicia had immediately turned on Steve's family, lawyered up to the hilt in order to get custody of the kids, and refused to converse with Kelly, or even acknowledge her presence during the dozens of court appearances required to sort out the issue.

Steve, who didn't appear to understand the gravity of what he had done, had even initially placed Alicia on his list of approved visitors.

On Thursday, March 8, a local shelter and community center for victims of sexual assault and domestic violence, Turning Point, announced that it was holding a vigil in honor of Tara, asserting that her death was the result of domestic violence.

Turning Point is an influential advocacy group in Macomb County and assists hundreds of residents annually, offering services that range from housing and clothing to counseling and court advocacy. Active since 1980, it is also a quasi-governmental agency, with up to half of its $1.7 million revenue coming from government-agency contracts, tax records show.

Alicia gladly aligned herself with the group, although at no point earlier had she claimed to suspect anything like domestic violence. Still, "What happened to Tara is really the end result of any domestic-violent relationship," she told a reporter.

It was the start of a long courtship between Alicia and the domestic-violence community.

Alicia had engaged a local lawyer, Michael Smith, to handle her request for custody of Lindsey and Ian, and added another, Patrick Simasko, to handle a wrongful-death lawsuit against Steve.

Smith was best known for having handled the divorce case of Kim Mathers from singer Eminem.

Both Smith and Simasko became fixtures in the media, along with Alicia.

That same day, the conversation between Steve and Kelly focused on getting his affairs straight. Sometimes, the discussion got rather spirited.

"Everybody's pissed off at you, you have everybody upset," Kelly told him. "I'm pissed off at you. I love you but I'm pissed off at what you did. I can't ask you anything about it, I can't ask you why, I can't ask you what happened to make you snap, even though I want to. You can tell me later. I'm pissed off that you made a statement without an attorney present."

"That's a whole different story, but yeah," Steve said. "They basically told me that if I didn't sign their statement, if I didn't give them a full statement, they would let my feet fall off."

If this assertion had any truth to it, it was certainly never discussed as part of his defense strategy. Of course Steve was possessed of a freakish penchant for bending, folding, and mutilating the truth.

"Dad's freaking out that you said you did it at the shop," Kelly informed Steve.

"I did."

"Well, he doesn't believe you," Kelly said. "Or if he did, he believes you used your own tools, not his tools, because they didn't take any of his tools when they searched the shop."

"There was nothing to take," Steve said. He didn't have to explain. Officers were still finding the saw blades he had used to cut Tara into pieces out in the park at Stony Creek, along with some of his discarded clothing.

As the conversation wound down, Steve began to cry, as he would do frequently over the course of the summer leading up to his trial. Often it was talk of the kids that elicited his tears; other times it was just the stress of being locked up in the mental ward.

"Kelly, I love you," he said.

"I love you," Kelly responded.

"No, please understand, I'm sorry," Steve said, his voice choking.

"I know."

———

On Wednesday, March 21, Kelly came to the jail for her weekly visit and told Steve of the funeral plans for Tara.

"[It] is going to be next Monday . . . and the visitation is going to be next Sunday," Kelly reported.

"Where?"

"In Escanaba."

"Oh, it's up there," Steve said, a little surprised. "You need to reach out to Alicia, make a phone call real quick . . . Tara didn't want to be buried up in Escanaba."

Actually, both Steve and Tara had previously decided that when they died, they wanted to be cremated and have their ashes strewn, ironically, in Wilderness State Park.

"We decided that when we were getting ready to move to Germany," Steve says. "We realized that we were both on the same plane, and if it went down, the kids would be orphans, so we made our wills. And the cremation was part of that."

Regardless, four days later, on March 25, Al Grant and Kelly Utykanski drove to Escanaba for Tara's visitation and funeral. Detective Kozlowski and Sheriff Hackel also made the 425-mile drive to the Upper Peninsula. Visitation was held at the Crawford Funeral Home, the same place that, thirteen years earlier, Steve had driven to during a service for Tara's grandmother in his bid to win Tara's heart.

Close to 270 people showed up for the funeral, tearfully lamenting Tara's death, with family members and friends giving their personal anecdotes about Tara. They spoke of her tenacity and stubbornness, as well as of her kindness and spirit. Al Grant wept like a baby during the service, and he and Kelly were greeted warmly by most of Tara's side of the family. Lindsey and Ian hugged them.

"Except for Alicia," Kelly says. "She was actually a little upset that her relatives were being so gracious to us.

We were so hurt by everything that had happened, it was so nice of the family to take us in like that."

Tara was buried under a juniper tree in the Gardens of Rest Cemetery in Escanaba on March 26, not far from the family plot where two of her grandparents were buried. Above her grave, hanging on the branches of the tree, now dances a pink heart that reads I LOVE YOU, placed there by Lindsey.

Tara's small gravestone reads, LOVING MOTHER, DAUGHTER, SISTER.

The Wednesday after the funeral, Al Grant came to the jail to see his only son.

"Dad," Steve said sadly.

"I'm so sorry," the father said back, his voice sounding wounded. He was looking at the boy he had taught to fish and hunt, the boy he had raised as well as he could while waging a lifelong battle with alcohol. He had given his son a job when it really mattered, when Steve was trying to help raise a family. And now there was Steve, clad in a black Velcro outfit, the "suicide suit."

The talk was awkward, stilted, and yet still emotional.

"So how are you, Dad?" Steve managed.

"I've been better, but I saw you. We'll get over it."

"I'm gonna get through this," Steve said.

"I know we are."

"No, I have to—"

"I know you do, we all do," Al Grant said.

"You need to understand something, Dad, what is being said is not even close to what happened."

"Stephen, I know, I don't know all of it, no."

"You gotta know that in here, that ain't me," Steve said, pointing to his heart.

"I know it isn't. I know very much it isn't, Stephen, you weren't raised like that."

"I mean shit happened and, well, we can't talk about that."

A day later, Steve called Kelly and the two talked about the funeral.

"At her eulogy, all the stories about her they were telling were like 'yeah, Tara had a horse and she couldn't get it to go, so she started kicking it and kicking it and finally the next week she wears spurs and kicks it.' Then the next story is about her and her steer at 4-H and it won't move and it won't move, so she whales on its nose and it finally moves. I . . . go, 'Can you see a pattern here? Story of her life is like if she can't get something to do what she wants, she just beats it into submission?' What sick stories about her."

"Did anybody mention me at the whole funeral?" Steve asked, as if he was feeling left out.

"No, it was as if you didn't exist," Kelly replied.

"As if I had disappeared."

"Yup, there were no pictures of you—"

"Well, obviously," Steve chimed in, seeming to catch on.

"—no wedding pictures, no nothing."

Steve was incredulous. "Really?" he said.

Kelly continued, "Oh, and they released purple balloons and all wore purple ribbons at her funeral because she was a beaten woman."

She spat out those last words with a tinge of sarcasm.

"What?" Steve exclaimed. It was news to him that Tara was being considered a victim of domestic violence.

"Yeah, that, like, you know, how they have a red AIDS ribbon? Or pink for breast cancer? Well, a purple one is apparently for beaten women."

Now Steve was angry. While in his statement to officers he'd admitted that he had strangled Tara, he was incensed that such an act would be construed as part of a pattern.

"Okay, again, I would really like someone to tell what the evidence is that I beat my wife."

Kelly said she had told her cousin Amy, "I said, 'She was never beaten ever ever ever, she was never even—'"

"Verbally abused," Steve interjected.

"I know that," Kelly said.

"I mean never."

Kelly then related chatter she had heard up north about Stephen controlling where Tara got her hair cut and forbidding her from frequenting a pricey hair salon.

"Oh, that's what they're saying? Is that I told her not to get haircuts there? It wasn't the haircut, I didn't care about her getting an eighty-dollar haircut, I cared about her getting a hundred-and-thirty-dollar dye job."

Steve was worked up, and he let go with a comment that seems to reflect how lightly he was taking this jail thing.

"It's all nonsense from Alicia," he said. "What a stupid little bitch. If I ever get out, Alicia . . ." And with that, he chuckled. Of course he was joking.

The accusations of abuse bothered Steve immensely, and whenever it was mentioned, it got a rise out of him. At one point, he asked his sister about how much this talk of him abusing Tara was going around.

"Yeah, everybody is asking that," Kelly told him.

Again, he went from zero to angry in a second.

Kelly let Steve know that reporters had asked her if she ever saw Steve hit Tara.

"Of course not," she had told them.

"You should have told them it was the other way around, that's what you should have told them," Steve said.

"She was the most emotionally abusive bitch I've ever met, I can't really say that she was the puppet master, I can't really say that right now," Kelly said. "And Alicia's just like her little twin, I can't really say that right now."

But she did.

In early April, Alicia filed a $50 million wrongful-death suit against Steve, which she eventually won, and which gave her the rights to the house on Westridge and Tara's life-insurance money. It was also a means to ensure that Steve could never profit from his misdeed via book deals or any other business agreement.

———

On June 1, a nineteen-year-old girl from Detroit, Jocelyn Berger, was picked up on a probation violation from a previous trespassing charge. She was placed in the mental-health ward on the women's side of Macomb County Jail, where she was assigned to orderly duty, distributing food to the inmates. On the men's side, she would simply shift carts that were then moved around the unit to feed the inmates.

Jennifer Kukla, a woman awaiting trial on charges that she had murdered her two children and the family pets, befriended her almost immediately.

"Kukla was one of my good friends in there this time, and we actually talked all the time," Jocelyn says. But Jennifer had one favor to ask: Would she mind helping her sneak letters to a guy in the men's health ward? It was very easy, just stick them under the Kool-Aid pitchers.

"We would put the notes on the cart at lunch, then he would write and she'd get a letter with dinner when the cart came back around," Jocelyn says. Despite her familiarity with the jail scene, "It was creepy watching two killers communicate like that."

Jennifer Kukla was a thirty-year-old McDonald's worker and single mother who, on February 2, just a week before

Steve killed Tara, grabbed a kitchen knife and slit the throats of her two daughters, eight-year-old Alexandria and five-year-old Ashley. She also stabbed to death the three family dogs in their kennels and sliced up the girls' pet mouse. Investigators said Kukla then sat in the trailer for a few hours until a family member came by to check on her.

She was convicted and sentenced to life in prison in October 2007.

Kukla was heavyset, with a wide nose, mousy-brown hair, and bland features. She was a far cry from the beauty of Tara. Still, Steve couldn't resist.

Once the correspondence began, he was hooked, bragging about himself and even about his crime.

"I saw a little bit about your case, before I came in here, but I am surely not one to judge," Steve wrote. "I'm certain that you have heard about my case, too. I figure that you might like someone you can just talk to. Because of the publicity surrounding both of our cases, it's not like either of us is going to give our letters to the news media . . . at least I hope not." At this he places a smiley face. "A little bit about myself. I'm 37, brown hair, 6'0, 180 lbs. I have two kids, 6 (Lindsey) and 4 (Ian). Like I said, if you want to write, I am here. Steve Grant, #314500."

Steve's notes to Kukla over the next couple of months ranged from conversational to bizarre:

"The reason it's safe for me . . . is the notoriety of my case. I have been told that I am the sheriff's re-election priority. Also, every time that I am in court, the TV cameras are ALL there and if I have a black eye it will be on CNN. (Smiley face.)"

"I'm glad you're not too mad. (Smiley face.) It has been nice writing/talking to you these past couple months.

I still laugh when I remember your one note . . . You asked 'are you scared of me?' (LOL) You are too nice to be scared of. I just wish we could arrange a rendezvous in the closet one of these days. (Smiley face)."

"I hope you know that you will be OK no matter what happens. I'm pretty sure you're stronger than you think you are."

"Before this current situation, I loved being outside . . . running, mountain biking, etc. . . . spending time with my kids also was very important. I really miss them."

"What did you like to do before you ended up here? I was a runner—35 miles per week, plus I ran races almost every weekend. 5K, 10K, half-marathons, etc. I even ran 3 marathons. Besides that, I was Mr. Mom. I spent a ton of my time with my kids. Soccer, swimming, dance, etc."

"I'm sure that you do miss your children. I am truly sorry for your loss. Having lost my children also, although differently, I can understand how much it must hurt. Did you have boys or girls? I have one of each and each night I pray that they know I love them. They were my world before I ended up here. I have to tell you that you are the first person to ask if I miss Tara and the answer is yes. She, for the last 13 years, has been the one I went to with my problems and now I don't have that person to ask for advice."

Steve felt free to continue misrepresenting his academic accomplishments. "What is your favorite movie?

Mine is *Last of the Mohicans*. James Fennimore [sic] Cooper is one of my favorite authors also. I have to explain, I graduated from MSU with degrees in history and political science so I tend to like historical novels."

On September 6, during Kukla's trial, Steve wrote, "Good luck tomorrow. I hope the jury sees you for the nice person who has had these nice 'conversations' with me."

Steve also befriended Crystal Conklin, a twenty-seven-year-old inmate charged with child abuse and murder in the death of her two-year-old son, Sean. Conklin was accused of causing a massive head trauma that killed the boy. A doctor who cared for the child when he was brought into the hospital said he was in a coma and had more than three dozen bruises on his body, as well as eye injuries.

"How old are your kids?" Steve asks in one missive. "Mine turn seven and five in November. I know exactly what you mean about being without them and missing them . . . We are in the same boat in regards to our jail experience. This is my first time also. My lawyer joked that when I do something, I must have a motto of 'go big or go home.' (Smiley face) I also have never had any history of mental probs . . ."

Such communiqués are common in jailhouses everywhere, and are not so diligently policed unless there might be an exchange of information that could help the state's case.

Steve explains that the letters—despite the seeming cluelessness about the gravity of the crimes committed by his pen pals—were a product of boredom. You stick someone among thieves, and sooner or later, they begin thinking like a thief, he claims. It was a *One Flew over the Cuckoo's Nest* kind of acclimating.

"Passing letters was something everyone in there did," Steve says. "It was a bad situation, and if I didn't find some way to join the craziness, I would go crazy. I just saw an opportunity to do something, anything, to communicate with someone inside who wouldn't hurt me."

In November, Jocelyn Berger went on a local radio station and talked about being a conduit for notes between Grant and Kukla. An alert assistant in the Macomb County Prosecutor's Office, Sara Fillmore, heard the tail end of the interview and passed along the news to a sheriff's deputy, who called the station and tracked down Berger.

In an ensuing report, investigators note that Jocelyn said, "Mrs. Kukla told her that Mr. Grant would hide notes under the cool-aid [sic] container on the food cart and Mrs. Kukla would retrieve them when the food cart came around. Jocelyn told me that Mrs. Kukla kept the notes and allowed her to read them. She said the notes from Stephen would say 'how he killed his wife and that he thinks he's cool that he is a celebrity now because he is on TV.'"

Jocelyn says that Steve was very proud that the guards called him "celebrity" because of the notoriety of his case.

"He will be very popular when he goes to prison," she says. "Everybody will know what he did and why he is there. But it will definitely be a negative for him, because even in prison, people don't like what he did. You don't marry somebody and chop her up a few years later just because you are tired of her."

Jocelyn was assuming that Steve was going to prison, just as everyone was. Despite his confession, however, he entered a plea of not guilty, emboldened by a defense team that encouraged him to stay positive. By the end of November, the trial was ready to start. The first obstacle was to find a jury that could avoid bias. Everyone had heard of the case, of course. Now, just who would sit on this panel?

CHAPTER 15

"He killed his wife, cut her into pieces, and ran," the twentysomething man said blandly, when asked by assistant prosecutor Therese Tobin what he knew about Stephen Grant. The thin, scraggly gentleman was part of the jury pool for Stephen Grant's trial.

And he was not going to make the cut.

His was among the tamer responses. Some prospective jurors took the opportunity to air serious and pent-up feelings; but opinions were free, and for some, the more inflammatory the better. They gathered in a room to pore over the legal document they were asked to complete, a twenty-five-page survey with 130 questions.

The questionnaire was mostly standard, quizzing the possible jurors on their education, marital status, occupations, criminal history, and politics. Closer to the point, they also inquired as to experience with domestic violence, and finally, just how much they had been able to avoid the maelstrom of publicity that Grant's alleged misdeed had induced.

Five hundred Macomb County residents—several hundred more than normal for a trial—had answered a jury summons to go to the fifth floor of the Macomb County courthouse on Main Street, a gray-stone monolith that was built in 1977. The building punched through the tiny downtown skyline, one of only a handful of tall structures in the county seat of Mt. Clemens, a town that struggled as progress moved miles away on the M-59 corridor.

Most who turned out on the gray and frigid morning of Tuesday, November 27, feared being selected, and their expressions showed the strain as they lined up to go through the courthouse's metal detectors at just after 8 A.M. under nearly dark skies.

The defense and the state needed sixteen jurors—twelve members of the panel and four alternates—who came to the Grant case with little prejudice.

Fat chance of that happening though. In a county of nearly nine hundred thousand residents, few had escaped noticing the publicity of the Grant case. It was a juicy story that ran via news crawls on the major news networks, stuck in the headlines of local newspapers for several weeks, was featured on Web sites around the United States for months, and was the subject of a three-page spread in *People* magazine. The case had continued to compel throughout the year as the media captured every movement of the players.

In July, the defense had filed for a change of venue, noting that the public had been "inundated and bombarded" with inferences of Grant's guilt over the past months. Defense lawyer Gail Pamukov told the judge that "we have blanket [media] coverage, we have unabated coverage. The most prudent course of action is change of venue."

The case would be heard in the courtroom of Judge Diane Druzinski, who had declined to rule on the change-of-venue motion, hoping that indeed, by being careful, the two sides could seat a panel that was impartial. The case most certainly had political ramifications. If the county handled this high-profile and costly case with finesse, it would bode well for the cast of elected officials, including Prosecutor Eric Smith and Sheriff Hackel, both of whose legal skills were under the national—and local-taxpayer—microscope. Many residents and more than a few critics, however, were not so sure that the case could be safe from a successful appeal if heard in Macomb County. Some were shocked that Grant would be tried in the very county where he'd grown up—and where the murder had occurred. Already Grant's attorneys had argued that all the media attention would make it hard to empanel a jury that had not already formed an opinion. But Druzinski was unmoved.

Druzinski was a former civil attorney who'd been elected to the Macomb County Circuit Court in 2002. She completed her undergraduate studies at Oakland University and had received her law degree from the University of Detroit–Mercy School of Law, graduating magna cum laude. Druzinski was handpicked by Chief Judge Antonio Viviano to handle the Grant case. While she had presided over murder cases before, this one would be by far her biggest.

Despite her petite frame, her highlighted hair, and tight smile, her presence loomed large as the trial was set to begin, with several television stations filing motions to cover the case live, even after Druzinski had steadfastly ruled against it.

"She fears a Judge Ito situation," said Fred Rothenberg, a *Dateline NBC* producer, who put together an episode on the trial despite the ban on cameras. "We tried a number of ideas and none seemed to appease her. It was her way, the only way."

In a strident ruling denying cameras in the court, Druzinski wrote that the case had already drawn a "media feeding frenzy" and that during the November sweeps month, "competing television stations apparently engaged in a game of ratings one-upmanship in an effort to manufacture an audience."

————

At 1:30 P.M. on November 27, the defendant Stephen Grant was ushered in, looking neat in a black suit and white shirt and with a fresh haircut. Gone were the hand shackles of his previous hearings, leaving only his feet bound loosely by ankle bracelets. Wide-eyed and pale from living several months in the Macomb County Jail, Grant took quick, uneasy glances around the room before sitting down at the defense table with Pamukov and lead defense counsel Stephen Rabaut. The three had met weekly over the past several months, and there was an air of calm around them.

The prosecution team, seated on the right side of the counsel table, included Detective Sergeant Brian Kozlowski, now with a shaved head, who swiveled his chair and glared at the media members who gathered in the courtroom every day ahead of the public.

To Kozlowski's right was Assistant Prosecutor Therese Tobin, the county's chief trial lawyer, a tall, well-spoken, and likable woman. A former member of the St. John Fisher College women's basketball team, she had led her squad to the NCAA Division III title game during her senior year in 1988. Born in a family of thirteen children—she was eleventh—Tobin, who graduated from Detroit College of Law, served on the Grant case as the workhorse litigator, manning the questioning of witnesses with graceful manners and a snappy pace, designed to keep them focused on answering the question at hand rather than speculating.

"We can't let these people down" was her credo, having worked for the county's sex crimes unit and won five murder convictions over the course of about five years. She was a determined advocate who devoted much of her life to her work. Next to Tobin was the youthful county prosecutor Eric Smith, a local boy in his early forties whose high energy and wide smile clearly charmed prospective jurors. In Macomb County, Smith was a shining star who'd risen to prominence after toiling for eleven years as an assistant prosecutor. A law school classmate of Tobin's, Smith also had strong ties to the county, having graduated from Detroit College of Law and Central Michigan University. When he ran for prosecutor as a Democrat, the handsome attorney had tried more than one hundred cases, and he used his experience and magnetic appeal to win a close election.

The Grant case was the first, however, that he'd tried after two and a half years as prosecutor. He'd spent the first couple of years reorganizing the office, but this time he would not miss the chance—or the highly political publicity the year before he ran for reelection—to lead the prosecution of a guy who had become the scourge of the entire county.

Smith said the Stephen Grant case was one he took personally, having spent the months since Grant's capture meeting with Tara's family and friends and touring her home as he planned his strategy for the prosecution. He was close to Steve's age, and with a small child at home and another on the way, had been deeply affected by the plight of the Grant children. Steve Grant had ruined his family with his jealousy and selfishness, all in an attempt to replace his wife with the teen nanny, Smith postulated. Grant had seen an opportunity for a new life with a new wife, and with insurance and Tara's 401(k), the path would be clear for him to chart a new relationship with Verena, who had already earned his children's trust and love. A new and readymade family were there for him in the wings, Smith would argue. The only obstacle: his wife.

This was the prosecution's argument and one they hoped to prove as they settled in to question the prospective jurors, who stepped up one by one, entering the courtroom through a door right beside Steve.

While Tobin and Smith were to be the most visible in the case, the mechanics and much of the strategy for the prosecution came from William Cataldo, a criminal attorney for twenty-one years before joining the Macomb County Prosecutor's Office as chief of homicide in 2006. Small-boned, mustachioed and rapid talking, Cataldo's signature was his full head of flowing gray locks, which prompted his colleagues to nickname him "Shaggy." Cataldo claimed he grew the hair because of his part-time avocation, playing rhythm guitar in a local rock cover band called Hung Jury. Cataldo was Detroit born and bred, the son of a stern Sicilian father. His law career was not his first. He'd leaned toward radio as a vocation in his years at Western Michigan University in Kalamazoo, where he worked in news and sports at the college station, WIDR. Cataldo picked up some part-time radio gigs in the Detroit area after graduation, but drifted into the film industry as a tape operator before law came calling. By 1995, he had both a law license and was cohosting a call-in legal show, *Ask Your Attorney*, living the best of both worlds.

As the best organizer among the state's legal team,

Cataldo was charged with coordinating the exhibits and making sure the case moved swiftly and smoothly. If Eric was the lead actor and Therese was the costar, Cataldo functioned as the executive producer and the team's technical guru, whose manic energy served him well in a case that would take weeks to try.

The trio arrived before daylight to their offices on the fourth floor of the county administration building, then stayed well into the night as they rehearsed the case, prepped witnesses, and pored over mounds of documents to plan their presentation.

"We were getting in at five-thirty every morning," Smith says. "We would stay until nine-thirty, ten at night. Normally when you try a case, you have court in the afternoons, so you have the morning to get your witnesses together. But this was different. First, we were there all day in court, and second, there was so much going on. [We] didn't know whether we had to be ready for closing this day or closing next week. The whole state—the nation, actually—was watching, so we had to make sure we were on our game."

In being pitted against Rabaut and Pamukov, the state's team was up against two of the strongest, most experienced defense attorneys in the area; it was A-game or no game in terms of efficacy.

When the trial finally began, there was no sign of weariness among the three state's attorneys, only adrenaline and anticipation. Nearly nine months had passed since Steve had been captured and charged with murder. It was time, they reasoned, for him to get his due.

Into this spotlight walked juror number one, a short, stout Asian woman in her forties who worked for Blue Cross/Blue Shield, whose work Smith dubbed "a fairly sophisticated job."

"In your questionnaire, it says you didn't pay much attention to this case," Smith began, hesitant, a little dubious.

"No, I just don't watch much TV or anything," she said.

She was in.

The next juror, a tall, white, blue-collar man in his fifties, said the same: "I deliberately avoid the local news," he said. "I'm sick and tired of hearing about dead babies ending up in Dumpsters."

He also said he was medicated for ADHD and had an "upper-spine problem" that bothered him when he sat for a long time.

"But if I were to sit at the back of the juror box, where I could put my head against the wall, I'd be all right."

He was in.

Other prospective jurors came full of hatred for the timid-looking Grant sitting at the defense table, who, despite his athletic frame, seemed very much like a little boy in his suit. Just looking at him, it was hard to picture him so enraged he could strangle—let alone chop up—his petite wife.

One woman wrote on her questionnaire that "what happened to Tara Grant should happen to Stephen Grant," noted Rabaut as he questioned her.

"Do you really mean that?" he queried, with some surprise.

"I believe in an eye for an eye," said the straight-shooting blonde. "I am my own person," she added when pushed. "I listen and make judgments based on what I think," she said, noting that she thought the media was pretty much correct in what it reported.

Dismissed.

Then there was a self-proclaimed "news addict," who

said "from the information I've seen, it's overwhelming that he's guilty. I'd have a tough time getting over that opinion."

Dismissed.

———

For over a week, the procession of jurors entered the second-floor courtroom to take their turns in the exhausting selection process. It was a rotating door of complex opinions that ranged from angry to disinterested.

One woman declared the entire selection process "annoying," then began to cry as she was questioned about her fitness to serve. Others, it seemed, tried their hardest to remain on the panel, eagerly telling the attorneys that Grant was "innocent until proven guilty," and expressing that they'd heard little about the case. It was a hodgepodge of personalities—some stiff, some fearful, some jittery as they faced up to a gallery of a dozen reporters who were taking notes and scrutinizing their every word as they answered questions designed to probe their opinions and moral styles.

"What have you heard or seen from any source including radio, television, newspapers, Internet, friends, family, coworkers, etc., regarding a case where Stephen Grant is accused of killing his wife," one question read.

"Guilty," wrote one juror. He was dismissed quickly, with extreme prejudice. The days of selection passed and more oddballs popped up. One man made it through to the finals despite his notion that Grant had "evil eyes" in TV clips.

"He made those evil eyes and [I] knew he did it," he wrote.

A man in his thirties wrote in his questionnaire that he believed Grant has "mental problems" and is "sick" but said he could remain objective as a juror. However, he sealed his dismissal when he told Smith, "[Grant] told my friend in jail that he was guilty."

Another woman simply wept when challenged about her views on the case. Sometimes, it appeared the two teams involved in the process might do the same.

By Wednesday, December 5, it was clear that the process was wearing on the legal teams. And it was also getting to Grant. He also wept as one potential juror took the stand; it was the mother of Deena Hardy, his old girl-friend. "I looked at the list and couldn't believe it; of all the people. I knew ahead of time and it still hit me very hard. This was a woman who was almost my adopted mother over the years," Steve says.

Deena's mother had called Steve to check in on him long after Deena and he had broken up. And now here she was, called as a juror in his murder trial. She was dismissed.

Aside from the appearance of Deena Hardy's mother, Grant was mostly stoic during the questioning. It became clear, though, that hearing what the world thought of his acts that night at the house on Westridge was taking its toll on his emotional health. He knew he deserved the epithets, but he struggled, it seemed, to hear himself dubbed a monster, a madman, a psychopath.

On Friday, December 7, the pool of jurors had been whittled down to a manageable sixty or so, who packed into Judge Druzinski's courtroom for a second round of questioning. The room was jammed, with the potential jurors seated all around the room, and the media members in the middle gallery benches.

The day started out with the judge addressing the anx-ieties of a number of those called for jury duty. Most feared the trial would run into their holiday.

"We are cautiously optimistic that this trial will conclude before the holidays," the judge told the courtroom. Defense attorney Rabaut quizzed a few more jurors; he was becoming more intense and intimidating, causing some in the media to reflect that indeed, this was a contender, a pitbull in a dapper package. The panelists were questioned swiftly, and if they met with any disapproval from either side, they were politely thanked and dismissed.

By 9:20 A.M., sixteen jurors who had met the approval of both the prosecution and the defense sat in the box, all having passed the same rigorous test, while the excused jurors filed out of the courtroom, pulling off their red badges that read JUROR.

The jurors stared out into the audience of press members, at the pens dancing over pads of paper, some appearing amused, others stoic. They ranged in age between their twenties and sixties; some had frosted hair or goatees; they wore flannel shirts, Wal-Mart blouses, polo shirts, and business suits. Among their ranks were two registered nurses, a paramedic, a tool salesman, a private contractor, and a grandmother. Most were aware of the case, and several had already stated that they believed Grant was guilty. There were six men and six women.

After a week and a half, most were ready for the actual proceedings to get going.

For the defense, getting Grant's murder charge knocked down to second-degree or manslaughter would mean a shot at parole. Eric Smith feared that if he didn't get a first-degree-murder conviction, he might have a hard time gaining that second term he so dearly wanted.

The judge swore the jurors in. The rumble was on.

CHAPTER 16

Just a little over an hour after the jury was seated, Judge Druzinski ordered testimony to begin. Tara Grant's family—her mother, Mary Destrampe; her sister, Alicia and brother-in-law, Erik Standerfer; as well as family friends Jennifer and Melissa Elliott—walked in as photographers scrambled to grab a shot. Kelly's husband, Chris Utykanski, also arrived for the opening of the proceedings, sitting on the left side of the counsel table behind the defendant. The media and onlookers followed, filling up the last four rows of the gallery's wooden benches.

It was the beginning of the end of those months of speculation by the self-proclaimed pundits, of the bickering that characterized the custody battle for the Grant children, and, for Steve, it was the final say on his deed.

The biggest issue from the outset was the prosecution's determined effort to charge Grant with first-degree premeditated murder rather than second degree, which would mean that the act was not premeditated.

"It was open murder to begin with," says Eric Smith.

"There are all possible murder charges under that, so we move on and determine where the crime fits. Once we found out that it was strangulation . . . it was an easy choice."

Michigan law already had numerous precedents regarding strangulation as a reason for conviction of first-degree murder, particularly the notion of "second look."

In the case of Daniel Jesse Gonzalez, a man who was convicted of first-degree murder in the 1998 rape and strangulation murder of a woman in Saginaw, an appellate court in 2003 overruled a challenge to the first-degree conviction, writing that "strangulation can be used as evidence that a defendant had an opportunity to take a 'second look.'" Gonzalez was also accused of setting fire to the deceased's apartment in an effort to cover up his crime, not unlike the dismemberment and dispersal of Tara's body. To that act, the appellate court wrote, "A defendant's attempt to conceal the killing can be used as evidence of premeditation."

———

Stephen Grant was brought in wearing a brown suit, white shirt, brown tie, and a worried look, although he held his head up, looking at the defense table where he was to sit. Alicia and Erik scowled, staring hard at their brother-in-law and avowed foe, who they claimed had ruined many family gatherings with his brusque, know-it-all tone and argumentative behavior.

Grant looked back at the gallery but did not make eye contact with anyone as he joined defense attorneys Stephen Rabaut and Gail Pamukov at the table, greeting them anxiously and chatting quietly about the case. On the other side of the table were Detective Sergeant Brian

Kozlowski, chief trial attorney Therese Tobin, and Prosecutor Eric Smith. Assistant Prosecutor Bill Cataldo sat behind the state's table.

Before the jurors were brought in, Judge Druzinski addressed the court. Formalities, really, nothing big, and a time for the jury to go over some of its duties in a back room while the lawyers ran over some mundane issues in the courtroom. The jury would be brought in when opening statements were made. No one expected anything.

But then Grant rose, along with his attorneys, and Rabaut addressed the judge: "Your Honor, we would like to plead guilty to the second charge, dismemberment of a corpse," Rabaut said. Druzinski paused and gave a long look at Grant and Rabaut, who stood shoulder to shoulder at the defense table. Grant had a good six inches of height on the slighter Rabaut, which gave the men a Mutt-and-Jeff vibe.

The judge summoned the two to the bench. She had been through pleas before, and immediately launched into the legal requirements, asking Grant his age and state of mind.

"You understand that this plea is by no means granting you a promise of leniency and that there is no agreement, is that right?"

"Yes, Your Honor."

"Do you understand what you did?"

"I mutilated a dead body."

Grant had just nailed down a ten-year sentence with the admission.

————

When the jurors came in minutes later, the judge instructed them to no longer consider count two. One of the arrows had been taken from the state's quiver, but Smith moved on. It was his time to shine, and he did in his opening statement.

"Have you ever wondered what goes through the mind of someone who just killed his wife?" he asked the jury.

"Sex," he hissed, capturing the attention of everyone in the room.

Smith continued with his opening, captivating the crowd with a tale that was salacious enough for the tabloids.

"He's naked. He texts the woman he's fallen in love with that she owes him a kiss. Then he left a note on her pillow saying the same thing, in case she didn't get the text. To do this, he had to walk past Tara's still warm and lifeless body while her children slept a few feet away."

Smith had taken his information directly from Grant's confession, driving home the four minutes the county medical examiner said it took Tara to die.

Snapping his fingers and exclaiming "like that," Smith said that Grant was fully organized as to what to do after his wife was dead. "He already had his lies in place."

He outlined the calls placed to Tara's cell phone, commanding her to "at least call home and talk to your kids."

It was all part of a scheme, Smith said, to start a new life with the au pair.

"She is the perfect person to take Tara's place," Smith said. "She's good with the kids, she's young, she's impressionable. The defendant had fallen in love with Verena. When he slept with the au pair, it marked the end of Tara's life."

Smith spat out his words with a snarl of contempt that he hoped would be shared by the jurors.

He then inadvertently noted something that would

loom large later. Casting Tara as an angelic presence who had it all as a mother and professional businesswoman, Smith praised the ambition that had placed her in a program at Washington Group International for select young executives on the rise. Then he changed his tone.

"But her most important job was as mother to Lindsey and Ian," Smith said, adding warmth to the victim's personal life as the jurors listened with rapt attention.

"Defendant Stephen Grant was living a life separate from his wife," he continued, setting the defendant up as a conniver who planned a future without his wife.

Driving back to the charge of first-degree murder, he laid out his case. He said that Grant had an opportunity to weigh the pros and cons of killing Tara and to think before taking action. Furthermore, the killing did not occur under mitigating circumstances that would allow reducing it to a lesser crime.

His opening was powerful and Smith hoped that it established the motive for why a soccer dad who until that time had only speeding tickets on his record would strangle his wife and then chop her to bits.

———

Defense attorney Gail Pamukov, tall, poised, and clad immaculately in a gray tailored pantsuit, delivered a technical thirty-minute opening statement, pushing jurors to consider, in the most concentrated manner, the idea of a preconceived murder, how wrong that notion was, and Grant's actions on that February night. Compared with Smith's drama, her opening remarks seemed less powerful but also thoughtful, taking the edge off the hype he'd created.

Tara's travel schedule had long been a point of contention between the two, but murder never crossed Steve's mind until the night in question, Pamukov told the jury. And as for the cutting up of the body?

"These were the actions of a man who was panicked," she said. "I'm asking you to keep an open mind. This is a terrible, tragic story. There are no winners, and at the end of this trial, there will be no winners."

Pamukov promised that her team would prove that Grant had reacted to "demeaning statements" made by his wife. Were these to include events before the murder? She didn't say, but allowed that "the events of February ninth were the results of a pot that had simmered for a long time before it finally boiled out of control.

"At best, his thinking was chaotic, his actions impulsive," she defended, setting the stage for doubt that his actions were premeditated. "Things were done in excitement, fueled by jealousy, anger, fueled by remarks made, angry, mean-spirited words, meant to wound, were exchanged between the two. His thinking that day was out of control, not measured, not considered, and certainly not planned."

She had planted the best seed she could. This was a marriage on the rocks between a wife who was accomplished and driven and a husband who felt neglected and demeaned. Steve reacted in the heat of the moment, then ran scared and bumbled as he tried to cover his tracks. He was no cold-blooded psychopath but an enraged, dismissed husband who snapped.

On Tuesday, December 11, the first of the state's witnesses was called, and Tara's sister, Alicia, took the stand clad in a modest brown sweater, white blouse, and gray skirt.

In the gallery, Steve's lone supporter was his brother-in-law, Chris Utykanski. Kelly was not allowed into the courtroom because she was a potential witness, and

Al Grant was not emotionally able to handle the stress of seeing his beloved son on trial for his life.

"I need to be here to listen to what Alicia has to say," Chris said, well aware that Alicia's statements could eventually trickle into the acrimonious custody fight that was going on concurrently.

———

Alicia described Tara as hardworking and family-oriented, despite her ambitions. She had come to believe her sister had been emotionally battered, the victim of a cycle of power and control that she would later claim had consumed the family household, with Steve belittling the children and raising his voice in a show of force against his family.

As the state's witness, the prosecution had worked with Alicia over the previous several months, backing her efforts to gain custody of the Grant children, and Eric Smith and she enjoyed a warm familiarity as the questioning went on.

Alicia and Tara were the closest of friends, Alicia said, speaking every two weeks, seeing each other four times a year, the last being Thanksgiving.

Her sister's travel and job was all-consuming, although "Tara always found time to call the kids at least once a day."

On the last call between the sisters, they spoke of Tara's upcoming trips, Tara's return to Puerto Rico the following week, the kids, "and just girl stuff, sister stuff."

———

Pamukov stepped to the podium for cross-examination.

"Is it okay if I call you Alicia?" she asked.

"Please do," Alicia answered with a broad smile.

Gail brought out that the two sisters, despite Alicia's

assertion that they were close, did not visit much, given the physical distance and Tara's busy travel schedule.

"So your ability to see how well Tara acted with the children was limited," noted Pamukov. "Did you argue?"

"Yes, all siblings argue, neither of us were shy about voicing our opinions." On Thanksgiving, the last time the two were together, they had a heated dispute over "family issues," Alicia said.

Moving on . . . "Tara was a dedicated employee of the Washington Group?" Pamukov asked.

"That's right."

"She would do whatever is necessary to do her job, is that right?"

"Yes."

Pamukov's questioning also revealed that Tara and Steve had gone through "numerous" au pairs, some for weeks, some for months, some for years. It was cheaper for both of them when they were working than day care. It was a financial decision, Alicia said.

"When Tara was on the road, Stephen was the primary caregiver?"

The au pair was, Alicia said, although Steve was the caregiver at night. And Steve took the kids to school events, medical appointments, and so on.

On February 9, the day she went missing, Tara was "in good spirits"—she planned to return to Puerto Rico on Monday. Then Pamukov pointed out a discrepancy in Alicia's testimony, showing her a copy of the interview Alicia had given to the *Detroit Free Press* on February 20, in which she said Tara was going to return earlier. Alicia studied it, then looked up sheepishly. In the interview, Alicia had said that Tara was planning to return Sunday, not Monday.

"At that time, I can't recall what I said," Alicia said.

Then she claimed it was Steve who had told her that Tara had decided to return a day earlier than planned.

"It may be what I said, but not what I remember."

Then Gail asked about the tension that the incessant travel had caused in the marriage.

"She didn't speak about the marriage, but about herself and the travel and how it tired her out sometimes," Alicia said.

Alicia also said that she rarely spoke with Steve much anymore, but "early on, when Tara would travel, he would call me and say he was lonely. He'd call just to talk." But as far as troubles in the marriage, Alicia said, "Tara was a very private person, she would not have told me if there were any troubles, she would talk about work."

Were they close friends or were they simply sisters? The statement posed more questions than it answered.

"Did she ever say she wanted to stop being so controlling and domineering in the marriage?" Pamukov asked. The attorney had read Tara's journals, in which she said one of her goals for 2007 was to "stop yelling." Pamukov was referring—although the information was disallowed by the judge—to the letter Tara had written to Steve after her Landmark Forum experience, in which she'd said that she wanted to stop "dominating you to avoid being dominated."

This bombshell was the crux of what many expected was to be the defense's strategy in the case: portraying Steve as a beleaguered husband at the end of his rope, driven to murder by one final, vindictive diatribe from his spouse. That would frame second-degree, or even voluntary manslaughter, and give Grant a shot at freedom someday. With first, he would be put away forever.

Alicia took the bait and responded with what seemed like a muted display of anger: "She wasn't the dominating person in that marriage. She was the breadwinner in the marriage, but she was by no means the dominant one."

There was unease in the courtroom after her comments. Judge Druzinski knitted her brow, a gesture that acknowledged that the victim's character had been attacked.

But Pamukov continued to look down at her notes and kept moving.

"She was very proud of her finances," Alicia told the jury.

"Did she ever speak of reconnecting with her husband?" Pamukov asked. Again, the lawyer was referring to the journals found in the truck in which Tara expressed a wish to restate their marriage vows.

"No, we spoke about work, the kids," Alicia repeated.

She testified that Steve had also told Tara that she should stay longer in Puerto Rico and that if Tara could come home on a Wednesday and be with the family, it would be less disruptive.

It was impressive cross-examining. Pamukov had done her job.

Still, the defense was in an unenviable spot, that of both making Tara look less than perfect while defending a man whose actions over the course of three weeks had been absolutely evil. The predictable advocacy crowd took shots at the defense—Pamukov in particular—over the next couple of weeks for daring to suggest that Tara's professional ambitions were anything but admirable.

———

One local columnist, Laura Berman, in a piece titled "Tara Gets Bad Rap by Grant Lawyers," took Pamukov to task without even knowing the context of her questioning.

"So Tara Grant, the family breadwinner, gets suggested

demerits for being 'controlling' and 'domineering' in prods from defense counsel Gail Pamukov," Berman wrote. "These are the primal key words, the ones that carry psychic weight."

However uninformed the local observers were, though, the defense did some heavy lifting in its work.

Lou Troendle, Tara's boss at Washington Group, also took the stand on the first day of the trial.

A large man, six-foot-three, broad, kindly, with a mustache and glasses, Troendle looked like everyone's good-natured Midwestern uncle.

He told the court that Tara had come to the Washington Group in 1994 and had quickly worked her way up in the company and ended up as Lou's operations manager.

"She was one of our highest potential employees. We were friends outside of work, my wife and I and her and her family did things together, parties for the kids," he remembered. "It was not just a work relationship."

Tara was not married when she interviewed, but spoke of Steve at the time, he recalled. Troendle had also seen Steve in Puerto Rico in mid-January when he'd come down for a long weekend. Prior to that, they had all gotten together to celebrate Christmas in mid-December 2006. Tara never talked about the travel creating stress or conflict, he said.

Tara called home "several times a day," said Lou, who noted she would often excuse herself to speak with her family. He told the jury that she was very up-front when she needed to take off for family time, including "things with the children or take a trip."

When Pamukov took to the podium for cross-examination, she set Tara up as a driven businesswoman.

"Sounds like Tara was an apt student . . . She was on a

leadership track with the Washington Group, which could take you anywhere in the world," she said to Troendle.

She ticked off a list of corporate attributes: "Intelligent, quick on her feet, decisive, can hold her ground, able to take circumstances into account and react to them quickly"—all attributes Lou agreed that Tara had. He noted that the Puerto Rico office that Tara was leading was downsizing and that Tara was part of deciding who would go.

"Who would go and who would stay—this was no shrinking violet, is that right?" asked Pamukov.

Troendle told the court that as Tara moved through the company, international travel was common, and sometimes she worked weekends.

"She did not share the nuts and bolts of the family?" wondered Pamukov.

"Kids were a big part of what she talked about," Troendle defended as Pamukov kept the focus on Tara, not Steve.

"When she was working and her phone rang, her cell, would she take these calls from Steve?" asked Pamukov.

"For the most part, yes," said Troendle.

He offered nothing shocking about Tara or damning about Steve. Troendle had simply established that Tara was committed to her career.

Detective Sergeant Pam McLean took the stand, and after some standard examination from Eric Smith, Rabaut took a crack at the confession. Why, he asked, was it not videotaped?

It certainly would have gone a long way to show Steve's state of mind. "There was the state police right there," he pointed out, noting that a camera must have certainly been available, but somehow, the detectives had decided that having a videotape of the confession was not terribly important. If nothing, Rabaut suggested, it was selective evidence gathering that benefited the cops.

———

During the noon break, nine of the jurors went to Gus' Coney Island for lunch across the street—over plates of fries, gyros, and hot dogs, they talked about anything but the trial, per Judge Druzinski's instructions—although one fellow, between bites of patty melt, mused: "I don't know if this is talking about the case, but if I had someone missing, I sure would call someone before four days."

The response was a responsible silence. The jurors, it seemed, were trying their darnedest to be good. They had heeded the judge's instructions. They wanted out for Christmas.

———

Deena Hardy, Steve's former live-in girlfriend from Lansing, took the stand after the break, clearly embarrassed to be there and wanting to distance herself from this unseemly episode in her life.

Hardy would occasionally giggle nervously during questioning—and when asked about the most recent exchange in January with Steve, allowed that "this time it was more flirtatious."

She said that while they had spoken on the phone, they had never e-mailed before January 2007. But this time was different, and they exchanged addresses.

She told the court that she and Steve made plans to meet tentatively for dinner January 30 or 31, with no place in particular selected for that rendezvous.

Pamukov cross-examined Hardy, and in contrast to her cross of Alicia, was stern and intimidating.

She outlined Hardy's personal history with Steve and then questioned the nature of their friendship.

"You knew about his marriage and when children came along?" Pamukov asked her.

Deena, eager to please, nodded, and said yes, smiling.

"To get contacted in January 2007 was not out of the ordinary, right?" Pamukov pressed on.

"No."

Pamukov probed deeper.

The last time she and Grant had had sex was in 1993, Hardy said.

"You agreed to get together in January but there was no sex, nobody acted on anything, did they? Mr. Grant canceled the meeting for dinner," Pamukov said.

"Yes."

"And those e-mails were sent on days that were pretty boring, slow days at work?"

"Yes, that's fair."

Pamukov, appearing disgusted, walked away quickly from the podium, and Hardy was excused.

————

There was a nearly audible gasp among the media as Verena Dierkes was called to the witness stand. Many had speculated over whether the au pair would return from Germany to discuss her relationship with Steve, and here she was, gingerly stepping into the courtroom, her once-blond hair now cut in layers and colored a chocolate brown. Thin, waifish, and naturally beautiful, she wore a gray sweater, white blouse, and black pants, a modest ensemble that chipped away at any theory that she was a seductress who had ruined the happy Grant marriage.

She appeared timid and nervous but not without resolute anger as she was sworn in and kept her eyes focused on the prosecution team.

It was Bill Cataldo who had worked for months to convince Verena to make a star appearance at the Grant trial. He was honest with her, explaining how much her testimony meant and how she could help put away a man, this predator who, he said, had lied to her, seduced her, and broken the trust of a naive teenager. Coming back to Michigan to testify was the right thing to do, Cataldo told her, and Verena, with a sense of justice, had come forward to explain once and for all what had transpired in the Grant home.

Verena had come back once before, in the summer, to talk with Cataldo and Smith, and to discuss just what would be expected of her. The team elicited a promise from her to return.

She was smart. That was readily apparent. Her command of English was excellent, and as a witness, she was a star.

She looked over at Steve nervously as Therese Tobin did the questioning. She described coming to the United States and meeting with the Grant family, and how much she had enjoyed working for them.

When she first started working at the Grant home, Tara didn't travel every week, Verena said. Her travel grew longer later on. She never witnessed arguments between the couple, later acknowledging that their life was normal, with the normal squabbles and spats. Not angry or violent in her presence. Steve, she said, had not complained to her about Tara or her work.

Verena outlined the affair she and Steve engaged in, the nights of talking, the sexual tension, the police, and finally, the story Steve told her about how Tara walked out.

She told how Steve had asked that she keep their relationship quiet, and that he'd said if anyone were to find out, the police would believe that he had something to do with Tara's disappearance. And Steve swore he did not.

"I believed everything he said," Verena blurted out, finally starting to cry. Steve had listened and watched his former lover, but at this, he bit his lip and cringed.

Intermittently, her anger growing, Verena shot cold looks at Grant. Yes, she told the court, Steve had told her he was falling in love with her. And yes, she added, she felt the same way, or at least she had thought so. Her feelings were intense, overwhelming, disturbing, and complicated.

After she flew back to Germany on the twenty-first of February, she and Steve continued to talk and email each other, she said. The two created new email addresses because Steve feared that the police had his others and he worried that they were monitoring them.

Verena finally said that on March 2, as his house was being searched, Steve had called her.

"He said this was a 'good night,' not a 'good-bye,'" Verena said. Steve told her that Tara's nosebleeds—which Tara was prone to, Verena said—would have caused blood to be left in some parts of the house. The next night, March 3, Verena said she got another call from Steve at 8 A.M. her time—2 A.M. in Michigan—and he confessed to her.

"He called to say good-bye and that he was going to prison for the rest of his life," she said. "He said it was an accident, that she hit him first, but she fell and hit her head. He said he could have walked away but he didn't."

Two hours later, she received another call from Steve.

"He asked me to call the kids and tell them that he loves them. He wanted me to say that I love him."

"Did you love him?" Tobin asked.

"Yes, I think I did," Verena said, choking up once again. But not enough to keep her from calling Kozlowski, the detective who had spoken to her several times since her return to Germany. She told him of the call from Steve and that he had told her he killed Tara.

"Were you calm during that call to Sergeant Kozlowski?" Tobin asked.

"No, I was crying," Verena said.

"Why?" Tobin asked, very gently.

"Because I realized that Tara's dead," Verena said, bursting into tears.

The prosecution was satisfied that the intense, emotional testimony cast Steve as a deceitful, murderous cad who'd taken advantage of a young woman nearly half his age. The courtroom gallery emptied quickly after Verena was done, but anyone who tarried saw a heart-wrenching sight: Verena was led to the prosecution's table by a paternal Cataldo, where she wept openly, standing, looking around the room, as most people looked away. Cataldo put his arm around her shoulder to comfort her.

Eight feet away, as she wailed, Steve shuffled back to his holding cell behind the courtroom. He never looked her way.

———

On day three of the trial, Mike Zanlungo, the friend who had loaned his truck to Steve on March 2, walked the jury through the friendship he and his wife, Leanne, had formed with the Grants. The Grants' was a relationship that they had envied, and they believed in Steve's innocence to the end. So steadfast was their belief that Mike had granted an interview with a local television station at his request, stating his support. That backing "was the worst decision of my life, but I believed it," he said.

He said that Steve was upset at police for badgering him and that while Tara was missing, Mike and his wife had cooked dinner for the kids to help ease the stress on Steve.

"Why were you helping him out?" Smith asked.

"We were friends. Not just him but Tara. I never believed that what took place could have happened."

———

Detective Sergeant Kozlowski was no doubt the man who solved the case, and eventually took the confession from Steve. But he was also the man who helped turn the trial around for the defense. The prosecution was content to allow the detective to retell the story of his relationship with Steve, but for the defense, Rabaut was clearly ready to cast doubt on the notion of a planned murder.

Rabaut established that there was a degree of thoroughness to the investigation, with the phone and credit-card records carefully scrutinized and the laptops and thumb drives analyzed.

"You obtained various results in your investigation," Rabaut said.

"We knew there was a homicide, we knew Grant killed his wife, we knew that there was an altercation between the two," the detective replied.

Both parties were injured, Rabaut said; Tara died and Steve was noticeably scratched, and much of the evidence the state presented came from Kozlowski.

"Based on this thorough investigation you conducted, would you agree that there is no evidence of advance planning that you have found?"

"I'm certain he planned it," Kozlowski shot back. Still, though he had played the audiotape of the confession, and also some of the voice messages Steve had left for

Tara, there was nothing in his presentation that spoke to premeditation.

"Can you give me specific evidence?" Rabaut countered.

"Yes, I believe I have," Kozlowski asserted.

"Are you going to suggest to this jury that you found evidence on the planning of cutting up and disposing of the body?" Rabaut asked.

"No."

Rabaut asked if there were any purchases that might speak to advance planning, anything to show.

"No, I couldn't do that," Kozlowski said.

"Did you check the stores to find if anything had been purchased in advance?"

"No."

Rabaut was clearly sailing and the overwhelmed detective was shifting uncomfortably in his seat. Rabaut stood in the center of the courtroom, his hands in his side pants pockets. He looked smooth.

He was establishing that almost all of the information about the crime had come from the defendant, implying that if Grant's words were being used to convict him, those words could not be cherry-picked to fit a specific story. Rabaut talked about the argument between Steve and Tara.

"All the information I have about arguments came from Mr. Grant," Kozlowski said.

Bingo.

Now Rabaut read directly from the confession, about how Grant said he "lost it" and the wrist grabbing, about how Tara slapped him and spewed "venomous words," all the while confirming with Kozlowski, who came back with "all this information came from Mr. Grant."

Rabaut pushed on, told of Tara saying, according to Grant, "I could ruin your life."

"And that's where he put his hands about her neck—" Rabaut said, but the officer cut him off.

"He said hand." Kozlowski showed a flash of anger. He was getting testy. Rabaut smelled blood and pressed on, noting that Kozlowski never asked Steve how long the physical confrontation had lasted. Once it had ended, Rabaut said, Steve's assessment was, according to the confession that the state's case hinged on, that "I knew I had killed her. I didn't know what to do."

The statement, in context, indicated second-degree murder, a panicked, unplanned occurrence committed in a rage rather than a premeditated act.

By now, the blustery, steely officer lost his nerve. His tone became softer, his voice more tentative. Smith and his colleagues looked on as the detective who had carried the case was himself carried away on the witness stand, metaphorically speaking.

Rabaut then tied it all together.

"Where Mr. Grant said he threw the parts is where they were found, correct?" Rabaut asked.

"Correct."

The call to Bryan Rellinger, the note to the children, the panic, all of it played to Steve's story, which, Rabaut said, was true.

Before he sat down, though, Rabaut made a stab at introducing the unsent notes found in Tara's notebooks, which were discovered in her car. These were the letters she had written to her parents, sister, and Steve after her session with the Landmark Forum in 2005. The same letters, in fact, that Pamukov had used to inform her cross-examination of Alicia several days before.

Smith objected. Hearsay, undated. Rabaut contended they spoke to the condition of the marriage, which was undoubtedly true. Tara, in her letter to Steve, admitted that she had been emotionally absent for most of their marriage.

Judge Druzinski disallowed the letters. But Rabaut had scored some convincing points, introducing doubt and clearly positioning the murder as second degree. It turned the case around.

Macomb County medical examiner Daniel Spitz told the court that it took Tara about four minutes to die, but that gave the defense another opening. Pamukov, who was quite familiar with medical testimony because of her former occupation as a nurse, immediately challenged Spitz's assertion.

"You testified there was an altercation," Pamukov said. "During an altercation, doesn't the brain demand more energy?"

Spitz said it did.

"The fact that Mrs. Grant's brain needed oxygen could have shortened the time it took for her to die, wouldn't you agree?" Pamukov asked. Spitz nodded.

"You don't know how long it took Tara to die, do you?" Pamukov countered.

Spitz pushed back. Maybe three and a half minutes, which is the general rule.

"But you don't know, do you?"

"I wasn't in the room witnessing the strangulation. I can't say if it was four and a half minutes or three and a half minutes," Spitz managed.

"You just don't know in this case, do you?" she forcefully asserted with a touch of anger.

During the nine days of testimony, the prosecution put on twenty-eight witnesses and a bevy of physical evidence, including the Grant kids' red sled on which Steve had stacked Tara's dismembered body. A tape of the confession was played, as well as eight voice mails Steve had left on Tara's phone after the February 9, outraged, expletive-filled calls ordering her to call him back and tell him where she was.

The court also watched a collection of TV interviews, some in which Steve cried, begging for someone to help find his wife. It heard that Tara's sternum was fractured, that her head was found by a log, that her hands and feet and chunks of flesh were tossed out like garbage.

The defense put on one witness, Bader Cassin, the chief medical examiner from Washtenaw County in southeast Michigan, who had performed an independent autopsy on Tara. He argued with Tobin like a man unaccustomed to having his work challenged.

At one point, he said he gained information on the case before he examined Tara's remains from a number of sources, including the news.

When Tobin hinted that perhaps there are more solid sources than the news, Cassin lost it.

"Oh, thanks a lot!" he said, adding that he takes many versions of events into consideration and not all of them ultimately prove reliable. "I also get my information from investigators who don't always give accurate information."

When Tobin asked facetiously if he was sure the body was in pieces, Cassin said with disgust, "No, I'm pretty certain about that."

It was all the defense had. The idea of putting Steve up there had barely been considered, although he'd wanted to testify and had fully intended to push the issue.

"I was pretty insistent that I be allowed to get on the stand," Steve says. "When we got to the end of testimony, we all kind of looked at each other and then asked to take a break."

Steve was taken back to the holding cell, the jury was

led out, and the lawyers gathered at the front of the bench, speaking to the judge.

"The day ended and I went back to the jail, and Steve [Rabaut] and Gail [Pamukov] came over that night and we talked for two hours," Steve says. "They talked me out of it by letting me know that if, under cross-examination, I missed even one date or got something out of order, the prosecution would score big points. I saw their point and dropped it."

———

On Tuesday, December 18, Eric Smith delivered his closing argument. It was his last shot to convince the jury that the murder of Tara was planned, premeditated, and that murder in the first degree was the only way to go.

"On February ninth of this year, Tara Grant had no idea what she was walking into," Smith began. "He was lying in wait for her, naked, like a coiled snake."

He said Tara had no idea that anything was wrong while Steve was planning a new life.

"His whole world had changed," Smith said. "He wanted a new family—a new wife. The only thing that was in his way was Tara. With no conscience or speed limits, he executed his plan."

Smith hit on the voice messages left on Tara's cell phone from Steve, calls whose objective had been subterfuge.

"Did you like the calls on the cell phone? And did you like the tears? Nice touch, huh? That was pretty good. He's giving the performance of a lifetime. In his twisted mind, he's winning an Emmy. He was having too much fun. This isn't panic—this is mission accomplished," Smith stated.

"He's not getting out of town, he's staying. Have you

ever seen someone who loves the camera more than him?" he added.

"You heard from everyone who knew Tara Grant— those kids were her life," Smith said. "Tara had a demanding job, but she made incredible sacrifices for her family. She flew home every weekend. She called her kids constantly. She had to sacrifice and provide because [Stephen Grant] certainly wasn't going to do it. Now she's being attacked for succeeding in a man's world," Smith said. "If Tara Grant was a man, you'd never have heard these arguments: that being a loving mom and a hard worker somehow excuses her murder. She's working hard thousands of miles away, and what is the defendant doing? He's sleeping with the nanny.

"He hated her. He must have hated her living guts. The question is why?"

Smith noted that Grant told authorities that during his final argument with Tara, he accused her of having an affair with a coworker, and she slapped him. Then Grant had said, "I realized I was going to prison for hitting her. I've got to not make her tell."

Smith argued that that amounted to premeditation. "How does he make her not tell? We all know the answer to that question: He murders her. He makes up his mind: 'If I don't kill her, I'm going to prison.' So he did. That's a conscious choice.

"You heard about alleged affairs. Was Tara Grant having an affair? I don't know and I don't care."

To end his impassioned statement, Smith brought out a stopwatch. He stood at the podium facing the jurors, the watch in his right hand. After fifteen seconds, he clicked the watch and said, "Tara Grant is now unconscious." Smith stood for another three minutes and forty-five seconds staring at the watch, looking up just once at the jury, which sat calmly watching him.

Finally, *click*.

"Tara Grant is now dead. Stephen Grant had a choice of life or death at that time. Now make him pay."

The fifty-five-minute close was strong and emotional— but was it enough to shake the stone-faced jury?

In between closings, Smith and Rabaut found themselves in the courtroom with few others around—Smith approached Rabaut and held his thumb and forefinger two inches apart. "This close to done," he said to Rabaut. "I'll bet the hardest part of today was getting up."

———

Rabaut's closing was every bit as strong as Smith's, if less dramatic.

"Who is Stephen Grant? We know he was a husband. He, too, was a father. We've heard descriptions of him as a homemaker. He was involved heavily in the kids' day-to-day activities, he did laundry, made meals, took the kids to their doctors' appointments. He had a limited personal life. He had a very mundane lifestyle. He wasn't out with friends. He was a very lonely person. We know this because [Alicia] testified that sometimes Stephen Grant would call her when Tara was gone, because, in her own words, he was lonely.

"One thing Stephen Grant was: He was a good father. No one who testified in this case has ever suggested otherwise. This was a relationship where you had Tara, who was becoming more and more successful, and Stephen, who dealt with the day-to-day running of the household. He felt he was in a menial role. He was probably jealous because of her successful employment. He becomes frustrated and angry, and it all builds up over a period of time. Up until February ninth, 2007.

"We know that on the night before, Steve and Tara had a discussion about Tara's travel schedule.

"Stephen Grant said when his wife came home on February ninth, he called to her, but she didn't answer him because she was listening to music on her headphones. He feels he was being disrespected because Tara hadn't been home for a week, and he calls out to her but she's listening to her iPod. Then he asks about her travel, but Tara responds, 'It's none of your business,' and tries to walk away. Then he pulls her and says, 'No, we have to talk about this.' "

He described the punch that Grant confessed to, knocking Tara to the floor.

"Then Stephen Grant says she starts spewing words of venom to him. She said, 'Screw you. You'll never see your kids again.' He said, 'All I wanted to do was stop her from talking.'

"Ladies and gentleman, this is an individual who is acting out of anger, out of built-up frustration," Rabaut said. "He was not in control. Mr. Smith gets up here with a stopwatch to show you how long four minutes is. But is that what occurred here? We're not talking about four minutes of looking at a stopwatch. We're talking about four minutes of passion, of anger and frustration. There was a struggle."

Rabaut touched on storing the body in the car. Did that suggest premeditation?

"I'd suggest no," he said, painting Steve as a bumbling, inept criminal, prone to massive screwups. For an escape vehicle, he chooses a canary-yellow pickup truck. He can't find a gun at his sister's house as he flees.

"He is living a chaotic paragraph in his life . . . There is no plan here, this is a pathetic individual."

As he wrapped it up, Rabaut asked, "Who strangles someone in premeditation?" If the confession is taken as gospel, as it had been treated by the prosecution, he said, then in it, Steve comes off as ill-equipped to deal with his own actions.

"Impulse, that's what I'd suggest to you that it was," and with that Rabaut asked them to find Steve guilty of voluntary manslaughter—a felony with a maximum sentence of fifteen years.

The cases made, the jury left, as inscrutable as when it arrived.

CHAPTER 17

The verdict came in around 2:50 P.M. on Friday, December 21, after jurors deliberated for sixteen hours. The panel had weighed voluntary manslaughter, which would consider whether Grant's conduct had been pushed to an extreme by passion and excitement rather than good judgment. It had considered first-degree murder, for which Prosecutor Eric Smith had contended vehemently. As they deliberated, the jury had asked to see autopsy photos and the autopsy report, a transcript of the testimony from Chief Medical Examiner Spitz, the missing-persons report that Steve had filed February 14, floor plans for the house on Westridge, Grant's written statement of confession, and the five photos of his injuries taken by a deputy at the Macomb County Sheriff's Office. The panel also asked to hear the three-hour tape of Grant's confession, and see the phone records for Tara and Steve, showing the calls between the couple on February 9, the day Steve killed her.

The jurors walked in with the same blank expressions they had collectively carried throughout the proceedings.

Then the jury foreman rose from his seat and told the packed courtroom that Stephen Grant was guilty—of second-degree murder.

It meant a chance at parole, somehow, someday.

Steve's expression never changed, but he looked to his right and whispered in Gail Pamukov's ear: "Thank you."

Kelly and Chris Utykanski sat with their eyes straight ahead, saying nothing.

Alicia Standerfer sat with her arms crossed and held the same distressed, angry look she had maintained for the entire trial, but leaned into her husband Erik, who whispered into her ear, as her mom, Mary Destrampe, reached around and squeezed her arm.

Prosecutor Eric Smith was visibly shaken. He had staked everything on a first-degree conviction, and he had failed.

Judge Diane Druzinski graciously thanked the jurors and dismissed them. The panel filed back into the jury room.

Smith followed them.

"I don't want to say anything because I'm afraid I'll say the wrong thing," the prosecutor told them. He had lost cases before—though not many—but nothing had ever hurt like this. Besides, he had actually gotten the conviction.

"I don't think you proved your case," one of the braver jurors said.

"What part of this case did I not prove?" Smith asked, trying hard not to be challenging.

The reality was that he *had* proved his first-degree case to eight of the jury panel members. One female juror had vacillated between the two murder charges, and three males had been strident that this was second-degree.

Among their concerns:

- Why would Grant plan to kill his wife knowing that he would probably lose everything?
- Grant was a "wimpy person" and not the man of the house. His wife made the decisions.
- If Grant had killed his wife, carried her down the stairs, and placed her body into the cargo hold of the truck, then run upstairs and dressed as Verena came home, why wasn't he sweaty, out of breath, or at least somewhat flustered?

There were heated arguments during the deliberations. One juror got upset enough to begin hyperventilating and another had to walk away from the table to cool off. One female juror declined to look at the autopsy photo of Tara's head.

James Vangorder was one of the jurors who'd been set on first-degree. During the trial he was simply juror 126, but in real life, he was a forty-two-year-old father of three who worked as a materials coordinator at a local automotive supplier.

"The three that held out for second were swayed by the fit-of-rage defense," Vangorder says. He felt they had been swayed by pretrial publicity, especially the fact that the confession was out there before the trial and it had sounded like a passion killing to them all along.

"One of them said, 'I can't come back with first-degree, what would I tell my friends?' " Vangorder says.

The jurors discussed the difference in penalties between first- and second-degree murder, and the fact that a conviction for first would likely send Grant away for life with no chance of parole.

"The first day we made a list of qualifications for murder one," he says. "We went down the list and we checked what was met, and what wasn't. Four of the six were met for murder one. And once you cannot agree on that, you go to the crime that you can all agree on, so we went to murder two, and we all agreed on that. Then by the second day, we were up to trying to look at murder one again." But it never happened.

Smith and his team were devastated.

"I don't think that there's one thing we would have done differently, not one thing," Smith said immediately after the decision was handed down. "I thought since day one, this was a first-degree-murder case."

He vowed to ask the judge to exceed sentencing guidelines as she considered the twenty offense variables for a second-degree conviction. She would do so, aware, no doubt, that appellate courts dig deeper into sentences that surpass existing standards. Grant was eligible for a sentence of as few as nineteen years and as many as forty. His ten-year sentence for dismemberment would run concurrent with whatever penalty was meted out.

The prosecution team retreated to Smith's office and watched the TV reporters interviewing jurors. One female juror tearfully lamented the verdict and the three prosecutors were beside themselves.

"We got a kick out of one of the jurors crying," Smith says. "[The interviewers] said, 'What would you say to Tara's family?' 'I'm sorry. Tell her I'm sorry.' I'm like, they know what they did was wrong."

So he headed home, as did Cataldo and Tobin. But they couldn't wash the decision away. They texted one another the rest of the evening as they watched still more of the TV reports.

Tobin took some time also to get some Christmas shopping done with one of her sisters at Macy's.

"I hadn't done any Christmas shopping, and after this case and the verdict and all, I was like the walking dead,"

Tobin says. "And we were at the cosmetic counter talking about it and waiting and this clerk says, 'Oh, you're talking about the Grant case. He was too stupid to plan it.' I was ready to jump the counter."

Such was the watercooler factor of the case. But there was still more. Sentencing was set for February 21.

CHAPTER 18

Wild speculation of a sentence from Judge Diane Druzinski exceeding the state's guidelines floated about in the days leading up to the February 21, 2008, pronouncement. The tapes of Steve's jailhouse chats with his sister Kelly and the letters to his fellow female inmates were publicly introduced, via the media, as supposed statements of his character. Both were aimed at hurting Grant in the days leading up to the sentencing, with the prosecution hoping that his seeming lack of remorse in the tapes and in the letters would give the judge some guidance.

But there had to be more. There had been rumbling that part of the dispute during the custody hearings had been that at least one of the children had seen the murder. Something was in the works.

Finally, a week before the sentencing date, Detroit newspapers fell all over themselves asserting on the say-so of Alicia and her lawyers that the kids had witnessed the killing, and the prosecution asserted as much in a forty-page sentencing memorandum given to the judge.

GRANT KIDS SAW MOM'S MURDER, blared the *Detroit News*, unquestioningly. The *Detroit Free Press* followed suit, as did local television stations. It was never disputed in the press: The kids saw it.

The only trouble was the source of the story—Alicia—who claimed that her niece Lindsey had pulled Erik and her aside on Christmas evening and told them that she and her brother had seen the murder.

"She just started telling us," Alicia told a reporter at the *Macomb Daily*. "She free-flowed with information. We just let her go. She needed to get it out. She now is able to share her burden. She doesn't have to hide . . . anymore."

In an interview with the *Free Press*, Alicia asserted that Lindsey had been afraid to tell anyone before the trial because she knew she would have to testify against her father.

"She kept it in for a reason," Alicia told the paper. "And that reason was fear."

But Alicia's contention also contradicted Sheriff Mark Hackel's, who told the *Detroit Free Press* in March that the kids did not see the murder.

And there were some elements from Lindsey's account, as related by Alicia, that disputed the very confession the prosecution had relied upon to convict Grant. Lindsey told her aunt that the murder had occurred in the family room, while Grant asserted it happened in the bedroom.

Nevertheless, Prosecutor Eric Smith's filing was vehement. He told the judge that the children's lives "have been turned inside out and upside down irrevocably . . . There can be no doubt this is one of the most brutal murders in Macomb County history," the memo said. "Medical testimony in this case clearly showed Tara Grant suffered greatly at the hands of the defendant prior to her death. To Stephen Grant, the case was a circus and he was the ringmaster. He mocked all of us with fake tears and disingenuous sadness during countless press interviews.

"Stephen Grant's two small children witnessed a life-changing event, the murder of their mother, and their future psychological harm has been established."

The memo also noted that after Grant was convicted of second-degree murder, which gave him a chance for parole, he protested being put in an observation cell to prevent a possible suicide.

"Why would I kill myself, since I just hit the lottery at court today!" Smith quoted Grant as saying.

Smith begged the judge to hand down the "strongest possible sentence," fifty to eighty years in prison.

Druzinski approached the bench at 8:55 A.M. on a sunny, five-degree day, with three recommendations for sentencing: fifteen to twenty-five years from Grant's defense lawyers, forty to sixty years from the probation office, and the fifty to eighty years from the prosecution.

The courtroom was more packed with onlookers, media, and family from both sides than it had been on any day of the two-week trial in December.

Kelly and Chris Utykanski sat at the side of the room, where Kelly took an occasional note in a small spiral notepad.

Steve entered the courtroom clad now in his jailhouse blues, shuffling the fifteen feet from the door to the courtroom to his seat at the defense table unassisted for the first time in the proceedings, hobbled by leg chains. In just two months, his hair had almost gone to gray, and his face was puffy and red. He now looked like a seasoned inmate who rarely saw daylight and dined on cheap, institutional food.

————

Impact statements generally have two aims. One is to pay tribute to the victim, and in doing so, demonize the convicted perpetrator, and the other is to tell the court how the crime has changed the lives of the survivors of the crime. These statements are often grave, strident, etched in pain, yet cathartic and part of the closure needed by surviving friends and family members at the same time.

Alicia's husband, Erik Standerfer, strode to the middle of the courtroom with a burning hatred, which contrasted oddly with his otherwise gentle appearance.

With his voice cracking just ten seconds into his delivery, he told the judge that "Alicia and I were thrust into a life-changing circumstance" when his brother-in-law murdered Tara.

As he urged the judge to go beyond guidelines and hand down the harshest punishment on Grant, Erik stressed that Stephen "is living proof that the devil lives and works among us."

The night before, Alicia had, as usual, done plenty of interviews. In one segment called "Facing the Music" on the local Fox affiliate, she portrayed herself not only as a victim but also as potential prey, referring to a comment from Stephen in the jailhouse tapes in which he derided her continued courting of the press, and threatened, "If I ever get out, Alicia . . ."

"He has made threats against me, so I do have some fear that if he gets out, I would be target number one."

But Alicia also added that she would miss the limelight: "I'm nervous for the cameras to go away . . . it's been therapy."

————

Twelve hours later, she strode to the podium and faced the judge.

"On Christmas Day, we found that Lindsey, Tara's daughter, not only saw her father choke her mother with his own hands, but also heard her take her last breath," Alicia said, her voice cracking.

"Stephen took pride in causing pain," she went on to say. "He's not a kind man; he's a master manipulator and a psychopath. He has such a need for control, killing [Tara] wasn't enough—he had to cut her body into fourteen pieces.

"Stephen Grant drove a wedge between me and Tara, and Tara and my family."

Alicia's ten-minute statement included allegations that Grant was an unfit father, "teaching by example that lying was okay."

Lindsey and Ian suffered years of mental abuse from Stephen, she said, who "ripped the innocence from them."

She explained that Tara had been mentally abused by her husband, who was jealous of her success. "He could no longer control her. He's not worthy of being called human. And I'm going to take it one step further: Stephen Grant is Satan in the flesh."

By the time her vitriol was spent, the courtroom was shrouded in silence. But before she was finished, there was one more thing: a video that featured Tara as the star, with Alicia as her costar. With the Carrie Underwood tune "Don't Forget Me" playing behind it, the four-minute video featured forty-five seconds of Alicia in shots at press conferences, as well as several pictures of the two sisters together. There was one shot in which Tara was holding Lindsey as a baby, others from her youth, one shot of her father, three of her mother.

The presentation touched some of the audience, with several in the gallery crying quietly. But perhaps the most notable effect was on Stephen Grant. He teared up in the first ninety seconds, and then dipped his head as the pictures of Tara, some of which he'd taken, smiled back from the television monitor at him.

———

If Steve was ever going to speak out on his own behalf, now was the time. But he and Stephen Rabaut, his defense lawyer, quickly determined that this was not the moment for an apology, no matter how quick-tongued and convincing Grant may have been in his past. His reserves of charm and manipulative acumen had hit a wall.

"On the advice of counsel, Mr. Grant declines to address the court," Rabaut said.

While judges follow a sentencing point system that uses variables in which to determine a convict's suitability for lesser or larger sentences, Judge Druzinski had the ability to take other factors into account. With Grant standing ten feet away, looking up at her stern, matronly visage, she said that she would do just that, noting that those guidelines do not calculate "the overall psychological damage that was done to his two children and the rest of the family.

"It is only in exceptional cases [that we] go beyond guidelines," the judge said, then added that there are numerous reasons that are, legally speaking, "objective and verifiable" that enabled her to go beyond the recommended sentence.

Among those reasons, she cited the effect of the murder on Tara's family, especially their children, who lost the "nurturing" from their parents and who would be hearing about the case for years to come. She said that Grant's deception was deplorable.

Druzinski said she also considered in her sentencing decision Grant's affair with the family's au pair, Verena Dierkes, and Grant's taped jailhouse conversations with his sister, in which the two joked about aspects of the case.

"The defendant lied about his affair with the nanny, and then tried to get her to help cover up the crime," Druzinski said. "The court is satisfied that the upward departure in sentencing is warranted because of the demonic, manipulative, and barbaric actions in this case."

On count one, second-degree murder, the judge handed down a sentence of fifty to eighty years, with credit for 354 days. Steve would be eighty-eight before he could apply for parole. On count two, mutilation of a corpse, he received six to ten years, with 354 days credit. The sentences, per Michigan law, would run concurrently. Druzinski also assessed Grant charges of $41,000 to cover the cost of his legal team.

"Do you have any comment on the attorney fees?" she asked Steve.

"No, your honor, I don't know how that works," he said. As his rights quickly diminished, appeal papers were placed on the wooden desk in front of him.

And with that, court was dismissed.

––––––

In the post-event press conferences, prosecutors Eric Smith, Bill Cataldo, and Therese Tobin were all smiles. While they had not gotten the verdict that they wanted, they had definitely hit a home run with the sentence. In fact, Druzinski had used several of the passages from the prosecution's brief verbatim in her reasoning for handing down the extended sentence.

Smith was loose and at his best, sharp-dressed and

sporting a new goatee. The conference went smoothly, and when asked if he would have wanted more than fifty years on the low end of the sentence, he was prepared.

"More than fifty years?" he said. "We would like life in prison without parole. But having said that, fifty to eighty years is essentially the rest of his life behind bars. He's thirty-eight right now. That means he would be eighty-eight when he's up for parole, not when he's released—that's up for parole. And I'll be ninety-one at that time. So someone will wheel me in and I'll object to that parole. So we're very pleased with the sentence of the judge and very pleased with the record she made. I don't think this case is ever coming back."

Alicia took the front of the makeshift media room, flanked by her mother and her husband, and declared herself pleased.

"Lindsey and Ian will never have to see their father," she said. "They will never have to experience his abusive ways, his hurtful ways, anymore. That definitely sits well with us."

A reporter noted, "Alicia, you indicated in court that he drove a wedge between you and your sister and there was almost a nuance that you felt you could have been closer to her had it not been for him."

"Absolutely drove a wedge and I can pinpoint that in the month and the year and the date when it happened," she said, though when pressed, she declined to name that date. "But I can tell you a wedge was driven. [Tara] didn't talk about her personal life, you know, from that moment forward our conversations stemmed around her job, her kids. Never once did she delve into the personal aspects of her and Steve's relationship."

She also declined to explain how she knew that Grant had abused Tara and their kids for years.

"I have to tell you so many stories, so many stories," she said. But she would not tell any of them.

———

Three hundred and seventy-seven days after killing his wife, Stephen Grant was led from the courthouse into a van that took him down I-94 to the Charles Egeler Reception and Guidance Center in Jackson, Michigan, where he arrived at 2 P.M. His exit from the courtroom was swift, too quick for it to be captured by the media. Meanwhile, Sheriff Hackel was shopping for a press conference after the sentencing, but he had few takers. He spoke to a local news crew to whom he explained how Grant was taken out, talked about the money that had been spent on the Grant case, and noted that three vans were used to get Grant out, one holding the prisoner and two with decoys.

He went on the radio and spoke of how glad he was that the taxpayers would no longer foot the bill for Grant's stay in Macomb County. It mostly fell on deaf ears. The case was over, and reporters were already onto the next big story, whatever they deemed it to be.

———

"What's going to happen to me now?" Grant asked deputies escorting him through the bowels of the courthouse. As they neared the white Macomb County van, he began to cry softly. He was taken back to the cell that had been his home since March, but it became clear that he was leaving town and never returning. He was given an hour to gather his things, which were shoved into a box. Steve was then taken back to the transport van and handed a brown bag containing his lunch: a bologna sandwich, a juice box, and an apple. And with that, he was whisked to a processing center in Jackson, fifty miles to the west.

On arrival, the van pulled behind the barbed-wire Cyclone fence and dropped him off for the start of his new life. At Jackson, his picture was taken and he was given a number, 674421. A few weeks later, he was moved to his permanent home, Bellamy Creek Correctional Center in Ionia, Michigan, a farming community 140 miles from Sterling Heights. The 1,500-bed prison is set on a series of rolling hills and farmland. The facility is set in two parts on each side of a two-lane highway, with the most dangerous offenders, including Steve, living in a compound rimmed by two fences topped with razor wire and overseen by twin gun towers.

Grant is in a single cell, about seven by ten feet, in the protective custody wing of the prison, used to house high-profile inmates, including snitches and bad cops. He will not be eligible for a parole hearing until 2058, the year he turns eighty-eight. He applied for a job in the jail and can receive visitors five times a month. Usually those visits come from his devoted sister, who sits with him for hours, talking about everything from family to sports. They look directly in each other's eyes, and her love for her little brother is clear.

But there was one more twist in this dark tale. On the afternoon of June 13, 2008, sixty-six-year-old William "Al" Grant called the St. Clair County Sheriff's Office from his home in Emmet Township, north of Macomb County, to report a suicide. When the dispatcher asked who had committed the act, Al Grant replied "me."

A deputy dispatched to the scene arrived in time to hear a single gunshot coming from the garage of Grant's home. Al Grant died three hours later at a local hospital. It was the day before his daughter's birthday, and there had been tentative plans for Kelly and Al to visit Steve on that day. The two were supposed to have made the 135-mile trip together in May, but it hadn't worked out. Al Grant had never made it to any of his son's hearings and made few visits to the Macomb jail. When custody of Steve and Tara's kids was awarded to Alicia and Erik Standerfer, it was understood that visits from the Grant grandparents would still be allowed, but they never happened.

"Those visits were never given, and it really hurt my dad," Kelly says.

It was widely assumed that the stress of coping with fallout from his son's crimes had finally pushed Al over the edge.

When Steve was being admitted to Bellamy Creek, he says he was listed as eligible for treatment of a number of maladies, including alcoholism.

"I was an alcoholic at the time I was arrested. I didn't realize it at the time . . . Two, three, sometimes even five days a week . . . I would [go out to lunch and] drink for two hours, then go back to work for a while, then stop and run on the way home, then start drinking again. I would have a glass of wine with dinner, then kill the bottle, then have something else. I liked those twelve percent alcohol beers, those specialty beers. I would drink a six-pack of those . . . I was drinking to fall asleep and then taking an Adderall to wake up in the morning. I was prescribed Adderall for my attention deficit disorder, so I had all I wanted."

Steve is soft-spoken and has been clearly humbled by the consequences of his heinous act. Yet his hands, large and strong, remain the hands that murdered and dismembered the woman he had sworn to love and protect, the ultimate betrayal.

"I miss Tara, and I know that sounds so bad," he says. He still can't explain what happened that night, and is aware that he is locked up both for that action and for the possibility that he might pose a danger to others if he were to be released.

"I pray for forgiveness every day, I pray to Tara, I talk to Tara. When I first entered the jail in Macomb, I was really having a lot of trouble dealing with this, with Tara being gone, and one of the psychiatrists suggested that I write her letters. So I did, and I still do. I hope I see her again . . . I miss Tara, which I know people don't understand. She was part of my life for thirteen years. I really did love her."

ACKNOWLEDGMENTS

The authors thank their Detroit-based agent, Christian Fuller, Esq, for his unwavering guidance; editor Shannon Jamieson Vazquez; the men and women of the Detroit press corps, including Hank Winchester and Charlie Langton; NBC *Dateline* producer Fred Rothenberg; *Detroit News* photo editor Bob Houlihan; and the diligent legal team at the Macomb County Prosecutor's Office, in particular chief of homicide William Cataldo. Thanks are also extended to Detroit lawyer David Griem, as well as to Boyd and Julie Miller, William McKeen, Holly Gleason, Courtenay Carr Russo, Janelle Ray, Jeri Alley, Ron Boyko, and Dave Boyer.

Don't miss the page-turning
suspense, intriguing characters,
and unstoppable action that keep
readers coming back for more from
these bestselling authors...

Tom Clancy

Robin Cook

Patricia Cornwell

Clive Cussler

Dean Koontz

J.D. Robb

John Sandford

Your favorite thrillers
and suspense novels
come from Berkley.

penguin.com

M14G0907